The Beckett Critical Reader

Archives, Theories and Translations

Edited by S. E. Gontarski

EDINBURGH
University Press

For Marsha,
Come sempre

Edinburgh University Press Ltd
13 Infirmary Street, Edinburgh, EH1 1LT

www.euppublishing.com

First published in hardback by Edinburgh University Press 2012

Typeset in 10.5/13 Adobe Sabon
by Servis Filmsetting Ltd, Stockport, Cheshire, and
printed and bound in Great Britain by
CPI Group (UK) Ltd, Croydon CR0 4YY

A CIP record for this book is available from the British Library

ISBN 978 0 7486 6570 9 (hardback)
ISBN 978 1 3995 6753 4 (paperback)
ISBN 978 0 7486 6571 6 (webready PDF)
ISBN 978 0 7486 6572 3 (epub)
ISBN 978 0 7486 6573 0 (Amazon ebook)

MIX
Paper | Supporting responsible forestry
FSC® C013604

Contents

Acknowledgements

Any research project relies on a complex network of support to bring it to fruition, and the current collection of essays is the fruit of nearly twenty years of such collaboration. Chief among the partners is my home institution, Florida State University, which through that period, 1990–2008, and through a variety of Deans of the College of Arts and Sciences and a series of Chairs of the Department of English, most of whom threw their support behind the publication, was the chief financial support of the *Journal of Beckett Studies*. As any editor knows, subscription income represents only a fraction of the funding necessary to run an international journal, even a semi-annual as the *Journal of Beckett Studies* has been and remains today. As important are the contributors whose work forms the core of a successful publication and on whose work the reputation of a journal rests. Behind those contributors lies a network of assessors, reviewers and student assistants who volunteered their time and energy for nothing less (or more) than the greater scholarly good. The only paid employees involved in running the *Journal* over that nearly twenty-year period were the two managing editors whom we shared with other publications, Roxane Fletcher and her successor Jack Clifford, both of whom donated many hours of personal time to the *Journal* above their allotted paid hours. A series of graduate students developed from student assistants to Assistant Editors and then Associate Editor; chief among them were Sean O'Hare, Graley Herren (both of whom went on to edit journals of their own), Paul Shields and Dustin Anderson. Many others volunteered or were part of editing practica and internships. Most recently Jennifer Doyle-Corn has overseen a team of graduate students in an editing practicum to regularise the formats of the essays in this volume. That team included Eric Bledsoe, Julie Dow, Adam McKee and Sarah Morrow. My thanks to them all.

The essays collected here have all appeared in the *Journal of*

Beckett Studies as follows, published currently with some revisions and corrections:

Francis Doherty, 'Mahaffy's *Whoroscope*', 2.1 (autumn 1992), pp. 27–46.
C. J. Ackerley, 'Beckett's "Malacoda": or, Dante's Devil Plays Beethoven', 3.1 (autumn 1993), pp. 59–64.
Bruno Clément, 'A Rhetoric of Ill-Saying' (trans. Thomas Cousineau), 4.1 (autumn 1994), pp. 35–54.
Alain Badiou, 'Beckett's Generic Writing' (trans. Alban Urbanas), 4.1 (autumn 1994), pp. 13–21.
David Wheatley, 'Beckett's *Mirlitonnades*: A Manuscript Study', 4.2 (spring 1995), pp. 47–75.
S. E. Gontarski, 'Refiguring, Revising and Reprinting *The Lost Ones*', 4.2 (spring 1995), pp. 99–101.
Phil Baker, 'The Stamp of the Father in *Molloy*', 5.1 & 2 (autumn 1995/ spring 1996), pp. 143–55.
Daniela Caselli, 'Beckett's Intertextual Modalities of Appropriation: The Case of Leopardi', 6.1 (autumn 1996), pp. 1–24.
Mary Bryden, '*Pour finir encore*: A Manuscript Study', 8.1 (autumn 1998), pp. 1–14.
J. D. O'Hara, '"Assumption"'s Launching Pad', 8.2 (spring 1999), pp. 29–44.
Justin Beplate, 'This Little Sound Now in Beckett's *From an Abandoned Work*', 11.2 (spring 2002), pp. 57–61.
Paul Lawley, '*Endgame* in the Subjunctive', 13.1 (autumn 2003), pp. 1–11.
John Pilling, 'Dates and Difficulties in Beckett's *Whoroscope* Notebook', 13.2 (winter 2004), pp. 39–48.
Norma Bouchard, 'Recovering Beckett's Italian Translations', 15.1 & 2 (autumn 2005/winter 2006), pp. 145–59.
James Knowlson, 'A Note on Benozzo Gozzoli', 15.1 & 2 (autumn 2005/winter 2006), pp. 118–23.
Mark Nixon '"the remains of trace": Intra- and Intertextual Transferences in Beckett's *Mirlitonnades* Manuscripts', 16.1 & 2 (autumn 2006/ winter 2007), pp. 110–22.
Shane Weller, '"All the Dead Voices": Beckett and the Ethics of Elegy', 16.1 & 2 (autumn 2006/winter 2007), pp. 85–96.

1.

Beckett's Papers, Foul and Fair

S. E. Gontarski

'Fair is foul, and foul is fair.' (*Macbeth* 1.1.11–12)

On Publishing and Politics

Among the least theorised subjects of contemporary cultural studies is the relationship between literary or cultural figures (or more broadly themes or historical periods, for that matter) and forms of cultural dissemination like journals dedicated to their production (or to the assessment and critique of larger critical, historical and cultural issues: modernism or post-colonialism, say, or nineteenth-century studies). Is the review, the journal that sits on the library shelf or in the scholar's study, merely a passive entity, a reflection of and so a convenient gathering place for activity that would have emerged in one form or another without it, or do such publications encourage strains of activity, intervene in the cultural process, and so shape, revise or redirect it? What effect does the creation of a journal called *Transnational Studies*, or *Performance Studies*, or *Faulkner Studies*, have on a particular figure or cultural subject? Or how does the establishment of a particular archive, a repository of often ancillary papers, generate interest in a critical approach or research on that particular figure? The purpose of posing such questions is not necessarily to suggest that what follows in the current collection claims to offer answers, but, at very least, to raise the issue in regard to the publication of a group of essays from a journal devoted to a single figure that not only speak for themselves individually but that speak to one another in a conversation different from and more focused than their original appearance.

Certainly, the relationship between a critic or theorist, say, and his or her publication possibilities is related to the much larger issue of the rise and fall of literary reputations and theories of culture, themselves enigmatic and all too underassessed cultural phenomena, especially in a more or less materialist theoretical age where the nature of genius, at one time a convenient explanation for an author's reputation, is so often disparaged, if not ridiculed, in contemporary literary and cultural studies. Remnants of such a master narrative persists, of course: the struggling writer, ahead of his time, perhaps, ignored in his era and thus reduced to penury, enjoys a reversal of such fortune or a posthumous revival. The consequent rise of reputation should thus not only fail to surprise but be deemed inevitable since the writer was 'always a genius'. Such a narrative might be – indeed, has been – applied to Samuel Beckett, of course. But such rags to riches narratives simplify by ignoring culture, that is, the politics and ideology at play, ignoring the role of the marketplace and the power of institutions in the process, especially that of universities or publishers as subsidised or commercial enterprises. Few cultural critics have deemed it meet to return to and critique that master narrative and, particularly from a political perspective, to disclose its contradictions. Writing on the post-World-War-II literary resurgence of William Faulkner, however, Lawrence H. Schwartz has noted that 'in the dozens of books and scores of articles on the novelist's career [up to the book's appearance in 1988, presumably], no cultural historian or literary critic has tried to examine, in a serious, thorough, or scholarly way, the mechanism that came into play to elevate Faulkner': 'ignored in the early 40s . . . proclaimed in the 50s a literary genius, perhaps the best American novelist of the century'.[1] Rather than the ineluctable modality of genius, Schwartz focuses on the critical climate, always important, but also on the marketplace and on institutions that generate and stimulate the marketplace. The complex relationship of Samuel Beckett's to his three major publishers is certainly central to the story of what we might call the Beckett phenomenon, and on a much smaller scale the story of the *Journal of Beckett Studies* – begun as a commercial enterprise by publisher John Calder in 1976 and supported by Beckett, who offered at times *inédit* and first publications, but subsequently supported by universities and university presses – plays a part in that materialist narrative.

Beckett's emergence from obscurity to if not riches at least to become the iconic figure celebrated in Apple computer adverts, parodied in *New Yorker* cartoons and valorised during the centenary of his birth in 2006 – a rise which was fuelled in good part by archives, publishers, institutions, particularly of higher learning, and journals – remains only sporadically examined. Contemporary scholars have begun to explore that relationship, or the relationship between Beckett and the marketplace: Mark Nixon's (ed.) *Publishing Samuel Beckett* (London:

British Library Publications, 2011) and, more controversially, Steven Dilks's *Samuel Beckett in the Literary Marketplace* (Syracuse: Syracuse University Press, 2011) among them, or from the other perspective, that of the commercial publisher, Loren Glass's study of Beckett's primary American publisher, Grove Press, in *Counter Culture Colophon: Grove Press, the Evergreen Review, and the Incorporation of the Avant-Garde* (Stanford University Press), or my own *Grove Press Reader* (New York: Grove Press, 2001), which includes correspondence between publisher Barney Rosset and major Grove Press authors, Samuel Beckett included. Admittedly, a publication like the *Journal of Beckett Studies* plays only a small part in such larger issues of literary reputation and materialist culture, but it can and does have an impact on popularity, on the nature of the literary and cultural study of that author, by altering the critical climate and by demonstrating a receptiveness to certain forms and methods of analysis. In short, like presses, journals themselves have a politics, an ideology, which enters into and shapes the critical discourse, and the current collection of essays details some of that perspective.

Beyond Speculation

The Beckett Critical Reader: Archives, Theories and Translations announces something of its themes, if not its ideology, in its subtitle as it collects and brings into conversation some of the most significant and foundational essays written on Samuel Beckett's work over the past two decades, and makes them available to a broader audience than to subscribers to the *Journal of Beckett Studies* for the first time. The subtitle reflects the scholarly emphases of the *Journal*, particularly between 1992 and 2008, a focus that might be described as something of a renewed or neo-pragmatism, a return to scholarly sources amid the disclosures that emerged with the publication of James Knowlson's authorised biography of 1996, *Damned to Fame: The Life of Samuel Beckett*, and the corresponding growing importance as a repository, a centre for research, of the Samuel Beckett Archive at the University of Reading, founded on a shoestring by Knowlson as an exhibition in 1971, two years after Beckett was awarded the Nobel Prize, and which, with Beckett's full support, developed into a permanent archive thereafter. Mark Nixon outlines the significance of such archival material in his essay in this collection, '"the remains of trace": Intra- and Intertextual Transferences in Beckett's *Mirlitonnades* Manuscripts': Beckett's 'early work, in particular *Dream of Fair to Middling Women*, but also *Murphy*, depended upon what Beckett in letters to [Thomas] MacGreevy called "phrase-hunting" [25 January 1931] or "note-snatching" [(11?) August 1931]'. The fruits of Beckett's labours are, of course, visible in the large corpus of notebooks from the first half of the 1930s – the *Dream* and *Whoroscope* notebooks, as well as the various notes on philosophy, literary history, the visual arts, psychology and so forth. It is this material that has allowed critics to move beyond speculation.' Such documents, what elsewhere I have called 'the grey canon',[2] or what Shakespeareans tend to call 'foul papers' (those documents from which fair copies were subsequently made, the foul papers then, more often than not, relegated to the dustbin), play a central role in the criticism that appears in this collection, and such documents have been subsequently making their way, if slowly, into print. John Pilling's edition of the seminal *Beckett's Dream Notebook* appeared from the Beckett International Foundation in 1999,[3] for instance; Everett Frost's (with Jane Maxwell) dossier on the notes and manuscripts at Trinity College Dublin in *Samuel Beckett Today/Aujourd'hui* (no. 16, 2006) called 'Notes diverse holo: Catalogues of Beckett's reading notes and other manuscripts at Trinity College Dublin, with supporting essays' is an extraordinary resource to primary documents; invaluable as well is Mark Nixon's monograph *Samuel Beckett's German Diaries 1936–1937* that appeared from Continuum Books in 2011, and his edition of the diaries themselves is scheduled to be published by Suhrkamp in Germany and Faber and Faber in London in 2015. Moreover, such neo-empirical research is likely to increase as more scholars are involved in and products begin to emerge from the Beckett Digital Manuscript Project, headed by Mark Nixon and Dirk Van Hulle.[4] And an archival emphasis is maintained in the current iteration of the *Journal of Beckett Studies* as well, with its dossier on Theodor Adorno's 'Notes on Beckett' (XIX.2 (2010), 151–217). A special issue of *Modernism/modernity* (XVIII.4 (November 2011)) is, moreover, devoted to *Beckett: Out of the Archive* with essays and seminars from the conference of that name held at the University of York, 23–26 June 2011. Peter Fifield's introduction to that issue might equally serve as something of an overview, if not the ideology at least the guiding principles, of the *Journal of Beckett Studies* as well as that of the *Modernism/modernity* special issue, which 'assays the value of the archive: it ponders the merits of archival remains, included offcuts, first drafts, notes, proofs, correspondence, and assesses the worth of the research that this material allows'.[5]

The Beckett letters project is now, furthermore, fully under way, volume 1 (1929–40) appearing in 2009, volume 2 (1941–56) in 2011, and these first two instalments (of four) have been both a trove of specific information about what Beckett was writing and when, with unusual insight into his work habits and offering at times overt commentary on his works, and simultaneously disappointing for the opportunities missed, not only in the fact that the letters have been, for many of us, overly selective with no stated principle of inclusion other than what was permissible to publish, but also for the lack of literary or critical sophistication in the annotations. In a letter of 5 January 1933, for example, Beckett describes a Boxing Day walk 'all about Portrane lunatic asylum in the rain' (150). While much documentation is provided in the notes, the connection to the story 'Fingal' is slight, almost an afterthought, even as the comment of the local Beckett engaged during the walk and quoted in the letter, '"That's where Dane Swift came to his motte"', makes it into the story with only minor dramatic alteration; the editors apparently find little to comment on concerning the connection between life and art. In a long paragraph note we are offered the definition of 'motte' – '(Ir. colloq., young woman)' – and told that 'Dane' is substandard Irish pronunciation of Dean – that is, pretty rudimentary stuff – but little is said of Beckett's method of folding the personal, the everyday, into his art. Furthermore, in his letter to Charles Prentice of 14 October 1930, Beckett contemplated adding a few more pages to the end of his *Proust* monograph, 'to develop the parallel to Dostoievski [*sic*] and separate Proust's intuitivism from Bergson's'. The annotation of the line tells us a bit about Proust, Dostoyevsky and Bergson, but no mention is made either of 'intuitivism' as a method or the fact that this was precisely the material Beckett was about to teach at Trinity the following autumn. Beckett reviewed these issues for his class at Trinity College during Michaelmas 1931, where he distinguished between 'Bergsonian conception of intelligence & intuition'; 'B's [Bergson, but 'B' might equally represent Beckett] intuition *is* highest intelligence—*l'intelligence personnelle*'; on the other hand, '*fonctionnement de l'esprit* [that is, function of mind] = lowest form of intelligence, mind doing twice work' (9), Beckett here reiterating Bergson's insistence on the irreconcilability of intelligence and intuition. The problem persists in the second volume where, in a letter to art critic and Beckett collaborator Georges Duthuit, Beckett mounts a defence of his first full-length play, *Eleutheria*, by insisting on Victor Krapp's 'right to be silent', and adds, 'I say confusedly what comes uppermost, like Browning' (97). The annotation tells us from which Browning poem the quotation derives ('Paracelsus') but makes no mention of the fact that this quotation will be central to Beckett's shaping of another play, *Happy Days*, in 1961. Furthermore, what becomes the methodology that develops into 'Three Dialogues with Georges Duthuit', with Bram van Velde as the centrepiece of Beckett's critique, is discussed in Beckett's letter to Duthuit of

17 January 1949: 'I have been thinking of what we are going to do on him [van Velde]. I think it would be better in the form of a dialogue, but written, not spoken. You give me a first nudge, or I you, and so on. Maybe that's a bad idea' (115). Much is detailed in the notes, and excellently so, on the poems Beckett was translating for Duthuit at the time, some of which appeared in *Transition*, some of which did not, but there is no mention of what many have considered a central aesthetic, theoretical text of this time, the 'Dialogues' with Duthuit. The good news is that even with such flaws, the 'selected' letters offer scholars a mass of information hitherto available only through archival visits or with the help of friends and correspondents of Beckett, and scholars can now make the connections the editors have left unmade and so continue the focus on primary documents in the critical discourse of Beckett studies.

How He Used His Original Sources

Many of the essays of *The Beckett Critical Reader* have consistently made use of such documents available in the post-biography era 'to move beyond speculation', and many of them highlight Beckett's penchant for 'phrase hunting' and at times a 'straight lift' or a 'jokey manipulation' of sources, his recycling of phrases from his reading, often multiple times, in letters to friends, and from his own work, what John Pilling refers to as '"touchstone"-type phrases'.[6] Such a method is also discernible through the close reading of texts and through textual comparisons, as Francis Doherty demonstrates for Beckett's punning poem 'Whoroscope', the essay overturning decades of criticism on Beckett's longest poem. As Doherty, countering the 'received critical wisdom', convincingly demonstrates, Beckett relied less on his acknowledged source for details about the quirks of Descartes's life (Baillet) than on a slighter handbook, a source closer to his Irish roots (Mahaffy), from which he freely lifted phrases, which Doherty politely calls 'indebtedness':

> In the business of attributions and indebtednesses, there is no certainty, but it does seem at least interesting that Beckett, in rushing into print to try and gain a £10 prize, might have relied on a short work which contained enough of those details of Descartes's idiosyncratic life history which had already struck him to satisfy his immediate needs. Additionally, it seems only just that an 'Irish' version of Descartes should have been relied on, and that Beckett's use of Mahaffy is almost a tribute to his Trinity College heritage. Beckett certainly had not done what the received critical wisdom believes, namely that during his reading Baillet's *Vie de Des-Cartes* he was so inward with

> Descartes' life that at the drop of a hat he scribbled out his poem. The poem, for all its haste, is a remarkable accomplishment, but it was made all the more possible because of Mahaffy's little book. The poem and its notes can be seen to show a distinct indebtedness to Mahaffy, with sometimes a straight lift, and at others a jokey manipulation of Mahaffy's text. The young Beckett's inventiveness can be seen the more clearly by seeing how he used his original sources, both the grand two-volume 1691 biography and its humbler 1901 successor.

C. J. Ackerley reads closely a single poem, 'Malacoda', to bring to light a musical allusion ignorance of which will mean readers will miss its play as a central motif in the poem and so potentially misread it. Ackerley notes that previous critics have 'overlooked a crucial allusion to Beethoven's final quartet, Opus 135, one motif of which intensifies the tone of anguish and absurdity implicit in the central happening of the poem: the moment when, kneeling in reverence beside the coffin, the undertaker's assistant delicately breaks wind'. Ackerley demonstrates how a financial joke amid the Beethoven household triggered by the phrase '*Muss es sein?*' ('Must it be?') plays into the ending of Beckett's poem. J. D. O'Hara, likewise, while correcting his own monograph,[7] notes of the juvenile short story 'Assumption' in 'From the Lowlands to the Twin Peaks of "Assumption"' that Beckett probably took his inspiration from unsuspected sources, particularly *Louis Lambert* and *Séraphita* by the much maligned (by Beckett) Honoré de Balzac, where 'the escaping seraph's last ideas reach no audience, "ni par la parole, ni par le regard, ni par le geste". That chapter of the novel is titled "L'Assomption".' Phil Baker's 'The Stamp of the Father in *Molloy*' picks up the pun on 'stamp of the father', a parent's imprinting (or stamping) personality traits onto offspring, to examine the implications of the actual stamp in the collection of Jacques Moran *fils*: 'Timor 5 Reis Orange is a real stamp, issued by the Portuguese colony of Timor in 1895. Its primary significance lies in the word "timor", Latin for "fear", which is appropriate to the way that Moran the tyrant father terrorises his son.' Biographer James Knowlson focuses not only on the fact that much work was 'inspired by Beckett's early encounters with art . . . but in seeing how the frescoes in question have been used by Beckett', in particular the 'frescoes painted by Benozzo Gozzoli in the chapel of the Palazzo Medici-Riccardi in Florence in 1459–60'. And my own mathematical corrections to Beckett's calculations in *The Lost Ones* pave the way for a text more accurate than the early, most commonly available ones.

Allusion to music, visual art, philosophy, biography, popular culture and literature permeate Beckett's art, what John Pilling calls 'the literary furniture in his mind', and *The Beckett Critical Reader* makes a cluster of such essays readily available for the first time: major, previously uncollected essays, placed in conversation: David Wheatley's 'Beckett's *Mirlitonnades*: A Manuscript Study' with Mark Nixon's '"the remains of trace": Intra- and Intertextual Transferences in Beckett's *Mirlitonnades* Manuscripts', say; and Mary Bryden's '*Pour finir encore*: A Manuscript Study' with John Pilling's 'Dates and Difficulties in Beckett's *Whoroscope* Notebook', for instance, all of which detail Beckett's methods of composition – as do Ackerley, Knowlson, Baker and Doherty.

As the quantity of available primary documents has increased in the past two decades, published and archival, that is, fair and foul, research based on such documents has correspondingly increased. Beckett's habits of composition were to make fair copies from notes, then again to revise the fair copy to the point where a new fair copy was needed, again and again. Shakespeare evidently routinely discarded his 'foul papers', and so in general they have been lost, except for those retrieved by another, which, according to some bibliographers, formed the basis of the good quartos. Beckett in general saved his 'foul papers' and tended to sell or donate them with an eye toward history. Early collectors certainly saw that they provide unusual insight into the creative process, and many profited from their resale. But Beckett's 'foul papers' differ substantially from those of Elizabethan, Jacobean and even Caroline authors, since the distinction between fair and foul, as the witches of *Macbeth* remind us, is at least fluid, Beckett both disparaging the fair as foul and also retrieving the foul from the trunk to satisfy publication demands and the like, at times even publishing several versions of the same story.[8] Justin Beplate's 'This Little Sound Now in Beckett's *From an Abandoned Work*' looks at a late work in which Beckett announces the fluidity of the distinction or the futility of distinguishing between the fair and the foul, publishing what was previously abandoned. Such linguistic play suggests, of course, a rhetorical strategy and Beplate sees it against Beckett's harsh, self-deprecating assessment in 1937: '*I have never thought for myself.*' Contemporary work on Beckett's 'foul papers' which might be deemed bibliographic is, amid the current critical climate, however, heavily inflected by historical, cultural, psychological and theoretical underpinnings, to the point that Peter Fifield can suggest a strong interconnection or overlap between what we have been calling neo-pragmatism and theory, cultural, philosophical, psychological and historical: 'If there has been a shift from theory-heavy reading to detailed historical, archival, and biographical interpretations, the activity's very rigor and detail has meant that Beckett, more than ever, is a function of his discourse.'[9] Even such neo-pragmatism that might be deemed bibliographic or genetic study, then, is leavened with theoretical, historicist and performance-based methodologies, the author function itself, thus, something of a rhetorical construct.

Intertextual Analysis

The *Journal*'s predilections to a new critical empiricism do not, of course, suggest the abandonment or even the slighting of theory or cultural studies, texts often becoming intertexts. The *Journal*, like Beckett studies as a whole – indeed, like modernist studies itself – has been open to and has welcomed a plurality of approaches. A pair of essays on Beckett's translations of other writers reprinted here serves as a case in point, focusing on the much under-researched subject of Beckett's Italian translations, detailing his 'deep interest in Italian literature that would reveal itself in that thick web of intertextual allusions to Italian poets, narrators, dramatists, philosophers', particularly of Leopardi: Daniela Caselli's 'Beckett and Leopardi' and Norma Bouchard's 'Recovering Beckett's Italian Translations'. As Bouchard concludes,

> Beckett's Italian translations of the 1930s resonate with issues and concerns that were crucial to him at this juncture of his intellectual activity as poet, short story writer, and critical essayist. The translation of Montale's 'Delta' seems to be particularly significant since, as a poem foreshadowing the lyrics of *Occasioni*, it limits the ability of the self to find a more authentic life and therefore comes closer to Beckett's emerging poetics as revealed in his interpretation of Proust.

For Caselli 'intertextual analysis of Beckett's texts is therefore focused not on "how much" Beckett knew and read Leopardi, but on "how" Beckett read him; Leopardi is a good example for understanding how Beckett's texts position themselves in relation to the literary tradition'. She concludes that 'Leopardi's paradoxical and interrogative art fascinated Beckett at the time he was writing *Proust*, and provided him with a model of a tragic art made of repeated rhetorical questions, which Beckett gradually transformed into his art of "rhetorical questions less the rhetoric"', that is, 'pure interrogation', as Beckett quipped in 1938 in his review of Denis Devlin's collection of poetry, *Intercessions* (*Disjecta*, p. 91) – a quip which is, of course, already a rhetorical strategy. Moreover, Beckett's review suggests again his phraseological recycling, his 'note-snatching' on display almost as fully as it is in his letters, 'Davus and the morbid dread of sphinxes' (*Disjecta*, p. 92) making its reprise, of course, amid the 'Addenda' to *Watt*. With such source-hunting we may ourselves be in danger of at times becoming what Beckett ridiculed in the Devlin review as 'the great crossword public', his comment devoid, we might add, of the self-irony of seeing himself thus represented: six across, five letters: 'morbid dread of sphinxes'.

Two seminal essays from the *Journal of Beckett Studies*' special issue *Beckett in France* (4.1 (autumn 1994)), guest edited by Thomas Cousineau, which contains fresh and decidedly Gallic perspectives on Beckett's work, further play on Beckett's rhetorical quip 'rhetorical questions less the rhetoric'. Two theoretically informed essays by major French philosophers, Bruno Clément's 'A Rhetoric of Ill-Saying' (trans. Thomas Cousineau) and Alain Badiou's 'Beckett's Generic Writing' (trans. Alban Urbanas), are of particular note. For Clément,

> Beckett's work was already saying that it was 'ill said', that it was poorly written, that it had no method, as though it were a perpetual improvisation. This rather uncommon phenomenon, whereby the language of the work is repeated by the language of the critical discourse that it elicits, will, in this essay, be investigated as attentively as Beckett's texts themselves.

And Clément includes a 'brief list of rhetorical figures'. Badiou focuses on another set of rhetorical strategies in Beckett's last long work of fiction, the underexplored *How It Is*, which, in Cousineau's summary,

> represents a major breakthrough in that it dismisses a fruitless encounter – between a *cogito* that solicits and a realm of being that maintains its neutrality – and puts in its place the encounter with the figure of the 'Other' that breaks up and dissipates solipsistic enclosure. The first phase alternates between wandering and fixity. This will be progressively replaced by what Badiou calls 'Le poème figural des postures du sujet'. The question of identity, so much at work in *The Unnamable*, is likewise replaced by 'occurrences' of the subject, that is, the enumeration of its possible positions.

Beckett's play with rhetoric and literary genre are picked up in Shane Weller's critique of Beckett's elegiac writing:

> those works by Samuel Beckett that fall squarely within the category of the elegiac in the stricter modern sense of the term are decidedly uncommon – and this despite the fact that, according to both of his major biographers, Beckett's poetry contains his most clearly personal, autobiographical writing. Among the poems that come closest to being elegies proper are 'Malacoda' and 'Da tagte es' – both written shortly after the death of Beckett's father on 26 June 1933, and both included in *Echo's Bones and Other Precipitates* (1935) – and 'Mort de A. D.', written in 1949 in memory of Dr Arthur Darley, a colleague of Beckett's at the Irish Red Cross Hospital at Saint-Lô in northwestern France, where Beckett served as quartermaster and interpreter from August 1945 until early 1946. That each of these poems should take a

male figure as its object of commemoration is far from being a mere coincidence. Indeed, Beckett tends to reserve the more conventionally elegiac mode for the male dead.

In '*Endgame* in the Subjunctive' Paul Lawley examines some of the rhetorical strategies in the drama and suggests that Beckett presupposes

> a spectator who is extraordinarily sophisticated. It may be retorted, of course, that most spectators are engaged, more or less unawares, in reading manoeuvers which, when examined, turn out to be extraordinarily sophisticated, even though they are quite commonplace. However, it is not my impression that many critics, and certainly not many of the early ones, show the agility in reading the action which the playwright supposes he might expect.

Central to the collection, then, is not only how each of the essays is a distinct contribution to Beckett's studies, but how the essays play off each other within *The Beckett Critical Reader* and without, to the Beckett critical reader.

Extraaudenary

We might close at this point by noting, by way of summary, that many of the contributors to the volume are themselves 'Extraaudenary', a neologism Beckett coined for his friend Denis Devlin's poetry, either former editors of the *Journal of Beckett Studies* or directors of the legendary Samuel Beckett Archive at the University of Reading who have led the way in archival research and so were instrumental in setting the research focus of the *Journal*. That group has had, of course, ready access to the primary materials in Reading but as well has recognised and promoted its potential as a source of research about Samuel Beckett's work.

The volume itself is thus designed to supplement existing books and anthologies with essays featuring fresh, archival material, newly discovered sources and hard, close scholarly research, without, at the same time, rejecting or neglecting strong theoretically informed analyses which focus on the philosophy, the rhetorical strategies and the play of language that underpin Beckett's work. The renewed focus on data, on the empirical, on the material, on the archive, on the 'foul papers' is, however, continually developed and presented in combination with philosophical, psychological and performance-based critiques, that is, work on the fair papers, for such an amalgam represents Beckett's own approach to the art of literature. In each case the volume tends to focus on those works underexplored in the Beckett canon and so underrepresented in the critical discourse, on that portion of Beckett's *oeuvre* only lightly or incompletely scrutinised by scholars and critics, certainly on the level of detail developed here, while also making reference to the major works. The collection is designed, then, to stand on its own as a major study with a distinct focus by emphasising Beckett's methods of creation and the strong interconnections among Beckett's works as the essays examine his creative process through the manuscripts, typescripts and letters and his, at times, heavy use of secondary sources, and through rhetorical strategies, all contributing to what some critics see as a single work. The late American novelist John Updike has singularly noted such an interrelationship among Beckett's works in his review of *How It Is*: 'Beckett's work is a single holy book, an absolute of purity and negation by whose light all else in contemporary literature appears somewhat superfluous and unclean' (*The New Yorker*, 1 September 1975, p. 62).

Notes

1. Lawrence H. Schwartz, *Faulkner's Reputation: The Politics of Modern Literary Criticism* (Knoxville: University of Tennessee Press, 1988), p. 1.
2. 'Greying the Canon: Beckett in Performance', in S. E. Gontarski and Anthony Uhlmann (eds), *Beckett after Beckett* (Gainesville: University Press of Florida, 2006), pp. 141–57.
3. See also Pilling's *A Companion to Beckett's 'Dream of Fair to Middling Women'*, which annotates Beckett's first written and last published novel, published as a special issue of the *Journal of Beckett Studies* (12.1 & 2 (New Series), autumn 2002/spring 2003) and subsequently in book form by *Journal of Beckett Studies* Books (2003).
4. Further details available at <www.beckettarchive.org>.
5. 'Samuel Beckett: Out of the Archive: An Introduction', *Modernism/modernity* XVIII.4 (November 2011), p. 674.
6. 'Still Telling the Old Story', *Beckett: Out of the Archive*, *Modernism/modernity* XVIII.4 (November 2011), p. 902.
7. The monograph under attack is O'Hara's own *Hidden Drives*, a fiercely detailed study of Beckett's *Structural Use of Depth Psychology*, as the book's subtitle has it (Gainesville: University Press of Florida, 1997).
8. See my 'From Unabandoned Works: Samuel Beckett's Short Prose' in *Samuel Beckett: The Complete Short Prose, 1928–1989*, edited and with an introduction and notes by S. E. Gontarski (New York: Grove Press, 1996), pp. xi–xxxii.
9. 'Samuel Beckett: Out of the Archive: An Introduction', p. 675.

Foul Papers: Archives and Sources

2.

Mahaffy's *Whoroscope*

Francis Doherty

Everyone seems agreed on the genesis of Beckett's first published work, *Whoroscope*. Characteristic would be Ruby Cohn in her *Samuel Beckett: The Comic Gamut*:

> In 1930 his poem *Whoroscope* won first prize for the best poem on Time, in a contest sponsored by Nancy Cunard's Hours Press in Paris, and it thus became Beckett's first separately published work.[1]

But, apart from these bare facts, what else has been said about the poem can move from the extended analysis in Lawrence E. Harvey's important work on Beckett's poetry, *Samuel Beckett: Poet and Critic* – which John Pilling justly characterises as 'as much extravaganza as exegesis'[2] – to a succinct summary of its speed of composition, its origin in Beckett's reading, followed by some account of the elements of Descartes's biography which are played with in the poem. An example of this explanation would be that in John Fletcher's *Samuel Beckett's Art*:

> His first published poem, 'Whoroscope', came into being almost by chance. He heard one day in Paris that Nancy Cunard and Richard Aldington were offering a prize of ten pounds for a poem, not exceeding 100 lines, on the subject of Time. The closing date was the next day, first mail delivery. He had been reading Adrien Baillet's life of Descartes (1691), and so quite naturally used material from it for his poem, written in a great hurry and carried across Paris at night to ensure its being found in the mailbox the next day . . . Descartes speaks in the first person in *Whoroscope*, which is entirely made up of references to events in his life, some of which are explained in the notes which Beckett later added at Aldington's suggestion. A knowledge of Baillet's book is, however, necessary to clear up several obscurities, but the details need not concern us.[3]

This kind of assurance, and the fact that the poem is both an early one and a jokey Eliotic monologue into the bargain, whose main interest for the critic seems to have been in the tracing of the relationships of later

Beckett texts to Descartes and the post-Cartesian philosophers, might encourage us to leave the matter there. As it is, the idea that a reading of Adrien Baillet (1691) would be a necessary scholarly accompaniment to the poem would in itself be a sufficient deterrent to any reader without a total commitment to source-trawling for a work which lies somehow to one side in the Beckett canon. Later critics are content, understandably, to let sleeping sources lie. But that was not, I believe, exactly how things were.

Beckett, it might be said, relied very heavily on a little, quite unpretentious work which was not only closer to his own time but closer in provenance than that of Baillet, and that was one by his famous Trinity College forebear J. P. Mahaffy, who had produced his *Descartes* in 1901. This was the first of a series of fifteen works intended to introduce the work of philosophers from Bacon to Hegel to the common reader. Beckett did not rely entirely on this little work, but it must have been very handy as an aide-mémoire when he was himself working against the clock for his poem on 'time'.

Some of the footnotes which Beckett gave to the poem seem to be drawn, often verbatim, from Mahaffy, and some of the poem's text could well have been generated from the same source. But it is hard to say, and it is certainly the case that not all the footnotes could have been drawn from Mahaffy, and some quite certainly are generated from Beckett's reading of Baillet, as has always been asserted. However, the amount of material which can unequivocally be said to be from Baillet is small compared to that which can be shown to be taken from Mahaffy. There is sufficient in both text and footnotes (said, variously by commentators, to have been provided for Nancy Cunard or for Richard Aldington) to show Beckett's indebtedness to his great Trinity predecessor. Beckett can be seen to have exploited this source extensively, and to have enjoyed the games that he played with the reader, displaying that erudition at second hand which Mahaffy succinctly offered, especially to the young man fighting time to write a poem on 'time' in an all-night writing session.

We can list, for example, expressions which come from no other source than Mahaffy, and which themselves demand Beckettian footnotes. Such, to quote the first instance, would be the rather puzzling inclusion of 'the brothers Boot' in line three of the poem:

> **By the brothers Boot it stinks fresh.**
> *Note:* 'In 1640 the brothers Boot refuted Aristotle in Dublin.'

We find the answer in Mahaffy:

> Not only with Bruno, Vanini, Campanella on the Continent, and with Bacon in England, but even in Dublin, we find works appearing to show that the current philosophy is confused and false, and must be replaced with a new system—*jam conducendo loquitur de rhetor Thule*.[4]
>
> The brothers Boot, Dutch physicians settled in England, were encouraged by the learned Ussher to publish their refutation of Aristotle, which they had long conceived and worked out in mutual conversation, when Descartes's *Essays* were published. It was printed in Dublin, whither one of them had gone with Ussher in 1640. Probably Descartes's success stopped the printing of the second or positive part of their system, which never appeared.[5]

This must have been a delight to a 'Trinity scholard', a detail which linked Dublin to Descartes, as Beckett himself was doing, and which has no trace in Baillet, but Beckett makes both brothers refute Aristotle in Dublin, rather than the one which Mahaffy says came over.

> **Give it to Gillot.**
> *Note:* 'Descartes passed on the easier problems in analytical geometry to his valet Gillot.'

> He had, moreover, trained a French Huguenot valet named Gillot in his analytic geometry, so as to be better able to explain it than anyone else (Vii. 129). This valet, who must have been a clever youth, was sent abroad with Descartes by his parents to avoid Roman Catholic pressure (Vii. 150, 154), had learned Flemish and some Latin—nay, even (by residence in England) English, which Descartes never knew, and was on such terms with his master that Descartes tells us he treated him *en camarade*; and when mathematical problems of lesser import were sent him, he used to say, *give that to Gillot*.[6]

While Baillet gives a quite extensive account of Gillot, he does so rather to emphasise Descartes's refusal to treat the young man as a valet, and quoting Descartes's advice to a friend:

> mais qu'il ne devoit attendre des sujétions de luy comme d'un valet, parce qu'ayant toujours vécu avec des personnes, qui bien qu'au dessus de luy, navoient pas laissé de le souffrir souvent *comme camarade*, il ne s'étoit jamais accoûtumé à ces assujettissements.[7]

While Gillot is credited with having learned 'sous son Maître dans l'Arithmétique, la Géométrie, & les autres parties des Mathématiques', there is no mention of any instructions to 'give that to Gillot'.[8]

In the second section of the poem (lines 5–10) we have an attack on Galileo which Beckett annotates, but the elements which compose it seem to have been drawn from a variety of places in Mahaffy:

Galileo how are you
and his consecutive thirds!
The vile old Copernican lead-swinging son of a sutler!
We're moving he said we're off—Porca Madonna!
the way a boatswain would be, or a sack-of-potatoey
charging Pretender.
That's not moving, that's moving.

Note: 'Refer to his contempt for Galileo Jr. (whom he confused with the more musical Galileo Sr.), and to his expedient sophistry concerning the movement of the earth.'

> He returned through Florence, where Galileo was then at the summit of his reputation, but tells us expressly in a letter that he never saw him, and even shows a very inaccurate knowledge of his works and a supercilious contempt of them. He thinks Galileo the author of a work of music really written by his father, and professed to have read through his *Dialogues* between Saturday and Monday. He says he found no peculiar merit in them.[9]

> The language in which both he [Voët] and Descartes carried on their controversy is violent and coarse; and when Descartes calls his opponent 'the son of a sutler, brought up among harlots and camp-followers', we are reminded of the ribaldry of Demosthenes and Æschines in their mutual recriminations.[10]

> The work [his earliest treatise, *On Music*, written for Beeckman] is the least important that we possess . . . Yet even here he maintains his originality. He was the first to assert that major thirds were not, as the Greeks held, discords, but concords. As the Greeks were perfectly right, if we assume strict tuning by full tones, which make the thirds so sharp as to be unbearable, the modern temperament, which flattens the third, must have already come into use.[11]

> In his *Principles*, published ten years later, he formally denies that the earth moves, but holds that it is carried along, together with its surrounding water and air, in one of those larger motions of the celestial ether, which produce daily and yearly revolutions of the solar system. The earth indeed did not move, but it was like a passenger in a vessel, who, though he were stationary, and properly said to be at rest, is nevertheless carried along in the motion of the larger system which surrounds him. He makes the most of this distinction, as opposing him to Galileo and to Copernicus, and thinks that he may rather be called a disciple of Tycho Brahe.[12]

The device of explaining illusions of freedom by the case of the ship's passenger who, while the vessel is travelling to the west, may still walk freely to the east but is still being carried to the west, is well known to Beckett scholars. The explorations in Geulincx and Beckett's deformed version of that image (in *Molloy*'s 'I who loved the image of old Geulincx, dead young, who left me free, on the black boat of Ulysses, to crawl toward the East, along the deck') are familiar to us all.[13] This seems to be the first occurrence in Beckett's work.

Beckett's own interests in music and mathematics would, I am certain, have been engaged by Mahaffy's observations on the musical thirds and the difference between ancient and modern accounts of them, and this passage would certainly remain in his memory, to be brought out again in the poem. Baillet makes the surmise that when in a letter of 1 October 1638 Descartes had denied any knowledge of Galileo, and said that the only good thing which he knew that he had written was his work on music, Descartes had confused the son with the father. He also allows Descartes to say that whatever was of interest in the treatise had already been anticipated by himself nineteen years previously. Baillet says nothing about the content of the treatise, only that it was in five dialogues, treated ancient and modern music, and was thought by Joseph Blancanas, an Italian Jesuit, 'nécessaire pour rétablir la Musique des Anciens, & pour corriger celle des Modernes'.[14]

> **Faulhaber, Beeckman and Peter the Red.**
> *Note:* 'He solved problems submitted by these mathematicians.'

> He again joined the active army, but soon turned aside to Ulm, to make trial of his new method of solving problems on Faulhaber and other mathematicians of distinction. The story of Isaac Beeckman is repeated, *mutatis mutandis*, in the case of Faulhaber. He first despised, and then sarcastically challenged, the young inquirer, who on this occasion, however, showed considerable self-confidence, and not only solved the problems proposed, but showed general methods of doing so, and even of determining the solubility of various new problems, or the reverse. He also solved the problems proposed by Peter Roten in reply to a challenge of Faulhaber in his algebra.[15]

Of course, the various accounts of the intellectual challenges thrown out to the young Descartes are given at large in Baillet, but Mahaffy succinctly summarises several dozen pages of Baillet in his few lines, always handy in refreshing memory.

Beckett's playfulness is shown by his 'translating' Peter Roten as 'Peter the Red', and this is a trick which he uses elsewhere, as when he chose to 'translate' in a similar fashion the name of Descartes's brother Pierre de la Bretaillière as 'Peter the Bruiser', allowing a proper distinction to be drawn between the Descartes of the Mind, and his brother of the Body:

> **To think he was my own brother, Peter the Bruiser,**
> **and not a syllogism out of him**
> **no more than if Pa were still in it.**
> **Hey! pass over those coppers,**
> **sweet milled sweat of my burning liver!**
> **Them were the days I sat in the hot-cupboard throwing**
> **Jesuits out of the skylight.**

In order to get 'bruiser' Beckett must have looked up the word *brétailler* in a reference work like Emile Littré, *Dictionnaire de la langue française*, which gives it as 'Tirer l'épée à tout propos; hanter les salles d'armes et s'y escrimer sans cesse', and *brétailleur* as 'Celui qui bretaille. Ce mot se prend presque toujours en mauvaise part, et se dit par mépris'.[16] Beckett, as we know, had a lifelong interest in words, especially the unusual and the low, and in all argots, so this would be an early instance of his assiduous use of dictionaries, though many would have left a name alone and not sought out an etymology. However, according to a recent authoritative work on the French language, *Trésor de la langue française: Dictionnaire de la langue du XIXe et du XXe siècle (1789–1960)*, the word only came into the language in 1752, so Beckett was importing his own jokey but quite inappropriate name for Descartes's brother, going beyond either Baillet or Mahaffy on this occasion.[17]

On the abusive language, Baillet is certainly hard on Descartes's opponents, Voët and Schoockius, but gives no instances and restricts himself to a general smear, letting Descartes off completely:

> Voetius & Schoockius, que les Hollandois ne prendront jamais pour des modéles de politesse dans l'art de dire des injures, ont été les principaux instrumens, dont il plut à Dieu de se servir, pour donner de l'exercise à cette vertu. Les ordures & les brutalitez qu'ils employérent dans leurs libelles firent bien voir qu'ils n'avoient pas été élevez dans son école: mais la réponse qu'il leur fit est l'un des plus beaux monumens que nous avons de la modération, qui paroît victorieuse à chaque page.[18]

Baillet spends a great deal of time on the maladministrations of Descartes's elder brother, and we would not need to rely on Mahaffy's summary necessarily, perhaps just because Baillet is so detailed and angry on Descartes's behalf. But there is the other feature of Beckett's lines about throwing Jesuits out of the skylight. This might possibly be explained by the fact that Baillet, while discussing Descartes's education at La Flèche with the Jesuits, shows how Descartes came to streamline the teachings on Logic to which he was subjected as a boy, something drawn, of course, from the later *Discourse on Method*, but given chronologically in the account of the schooldays.

> De tout ce grand nombre de préceptes qu'il a reçeus de ses Maîtres dans la Logique, il n'a retenu dans la suite que les quatres Régles qui ont servi de fondement à sa nouvelle Philosophie. La première de ne rien recevoir pour vrai qu'il ne connût être tel évidemment. La seconde, de diviser les choses le plus qu'il seroit possible pour le mieux résoudre. La troisième, de conduire ses pensées par ordre, en commençant par les objets les plus simples & les plus aisez à connoître, pour monter par dégrez jusqu'à la connoissance des plus

composez. La quatriéme, de ne rien omettre dans le dénombrement des choses dont il devoit éxaminer les parties.[19]

His elder brother, Pierre, called after his property M. de la Bretaillière, turned out a narrow-minded country squire, who thought that René was rather disgracing his origin by adopting the profession of letters, and squandering his patrimony in eccentric scientific experiments. Hence he endeavoured to secure as much of the family property as he could in the settlement after their father's death. Our Descartes speaks with great annoyance of his conduct, and when settled abroad, appointed the Abbé Picot and other friends as his representatives in money matters, to the exclusion of M. de la Bretaillière, who in his turn felt offended.[20]

In his tract *On the Formation of the Foetus*, and *On Man*, as well as through several of his finished works, he develops a mechanical theory of the formation of the human body, like that of the other animals, starting from the fermentation produced in generation, which causes heat and expansion, so forming the heart, and next producing a motion of the subtler matter there found towards the locus which becomes the base of the brain, with a consequent return of the grosser matter into the places thus vacated.[21]

They ['animal spirits'] were adopted from Galen, whose *natural spirits* in the liver, and *vital spirits* in the heart, Descartes rejected.[22]

Descartes proposes to reject all such principles derived from mere authority; and he perceives that syllogism, however useful for expounding and explaining, is idle for the purpose of adding to knowledge. What we want is, first, clear principles, and then a process of deducing from them sure consequences.[23]

Who's that? Hals?
Let him wait.
Note: 'Franz Hals.'

His friends at the Hague insisted on having his portrait taken, apparently by Franz Hals, and this fine picture is engraved as the frontispiece of Baillet's *Life*.[24]

There is no need to invoke Mahaffy here, perhaps, as the portrait is indeed fine, yet not much is made of it within the *Life* itself.

Part of Beckett's playfulness with language might be said to imitate the playing of the young Descartes with his childhood friend, and three of eight words in the two lines which record this are either neologisms or unusual:

My squinty doaty!
I hid and you sook.

'Squinty' is recorded in the *Oxford English Dictionary* as obsolete and meaning 'oblique', while the word which Beckett might have used would have been one with a longer second vowel, 'squint-eye', 'a person who has squinting eyes'. 'Doaty' does not appear in that dictionary in the sense required by the context, but the verbal form 'dote, doat', sense 3, 'to be infatuatedly fond of; to bestow excessive love or fondness on; to be foolishly in love', gives rise to other substantives, like 'doter', and verbal forms like 'doting, doating'. 'Doty' is, however, given as a dialect word related to sense 4 of 'dote, doat', 'to decay as a tree', so meaning 'decayed'. Beckett is making his own meanings. Just so, he makes his own impossible verbal form, 'sook', a new-minted past tense of 'seek', related to 'sought', of course, but perhaps with attention to the squinted way in which the seeking was done.

> *Note:* 'As a child he played with a little cross-eyed girl.'

> We know nothing more of the first eight years of his life, except that he was nurtured in the gardens of southern Touraine, where he had as a playmate a little girl with a squint, whose early friendship made him regard this defect, whenever he met it, with favour—as he observes somewhere in illustrating the association of his ideas.[25]

There is no account in Baillet of Descartes's life up to the age of eight before he went to La Flèche or of any playmate, squint or no squint, so Beckett appears to have relied on Mahaffy for this detail.

The death of the other child in the poem, Descartes's only child, a sad and perplexing story, is given in the lives of Descartes, as it is so singular and noteworthy. However, Beckett's note says that she was six when she died, but simple arithmetic and Mahaffy's dates would give her age as five. The second date which he gives, however, the date noted on the fly-leaf of a book of the date of her conception in October of the year before she was born, would give the six years.

> **And Francine my precious fruit of a house-and-**
> **parlour foetus!**
> **What an exfoliation!**
> **Her little grey flayed epidermis and scarlet**
> **tonsils!**
> **My one child**
> **scourged by a fever to stagnant murky blood—**
> *Note:* 'His daughter died of scarlet fever at the age of six.'

> There was born to him on the 19th July 1635, at Deventer, a daughter, the events of whose brief life he noted on the fly-leaf of a book. 'Concepta fuit Amstelodami die Domini 15mo Oct. 1634',—that is to say, while he was specially engaged with his physiological researches. Though he became tenderly attached to this child, called Francine—who died of scarletina in 1640, and whose death, together with that of his father about the same time, he deplored as the loss of the two persons he loved best in the world—there is the most profound and absolute silence about her mother.[26]

Baillet gives no cause of death, saying only that she died on the third day of her illness, on 7 September 1640, 'ayant le corps tout couvert de pourpre', and that Descartes was inconsolable:

> Il la pleura avec une tendresse qui lui fit éprouver que la vraye philosophie n'étouffe point le naturel. Il proteste qu'elle luy avoit laissé par sa mort le plus grand regret qu'il eût jamais senti de sa vie: ce qui étoit un effet des éxcellentes qualitez avec lesquelles Dieu l'avoit fait naître.[27]

It is Beckett who decides that the little girl died from scarlet fever (certainly a step up from Mahaffy's less virulent 'scarletina'), and it is he who supplies the physical details of the sufferings which led to her death.

> **blood!**
> **Oh Harvey belovèd**
> **how shall the red and white, the many in the few,**
> **(dear bloodswirling Harvey)**
> **eddy through that cracked beater?**
> *Note:* 'Honoured Harvey for his discovery of the circulation of the blood, but would not admit that he had explained the motion of the heart.'

> There was a fourth and a most important illustration in physiology embodied in the opening Discourse. It was the theory of the circulation of the blood. Although he could not refrain from claiming originality here also, and denying that anyone else had explained the motion of the heart in the way he now proposed, yet he here—and here only, perhaps, in all his works—concedes to another the honour of a great discovery, and tells us that Harvey deserved the credit of being its pioneer.
> 'Do you know in London,' he said in a letter (ix 360), 'a celebrated physician named Harvey, author of a book *De motu cordis et circulatione sanguinis*? What sort of person is he? As to the motion of the heart he has said nothing not found in other books, and I do not quite approve of it; but as to the circulation of the blood, there he has his triumph and the honour of first discovering it, for which medicine owes him much.'[28]

> **And the fourth Henry came to the crypt of the arrow.**
> *Note:* 'The heart of Henri IV was received at the Jesuit college of La Flèche while Descartes was still a student there.'

There is no detail in either Baillet or Mahaffy to suggest that the crypt of the college was where the heart of Henry IV was placed. Baillet gives elaborate details of the procession and of the ceremonies involved in the bringing of Henry's heart to La Flèche, describing a large arch which was constructed in the middle of the courtyard, through which the procession made its way to the large inner hall of the college, and the final mention of the heart is that it was placed before the main altar of the Church of St Thomas:

Le Héraut monté sur l'échaffaut le reçut des mains du Duc de Montblazon, l'éleva pour le faire voir à toute l'assemblée, aprés le cry répété par trois fois, il le posa sur le fleuron pour y demeurer, jusqu'à ce qu'on eût achevé l'urne dans laquelle il devoit être mis devant le maître autel de l'Eglise.[29]

These were the Jesuits, who had just been re-established by Henri IV, in one of his ancestral palaces at La Flèche, in Anjou . . . Had he lived longer, his influence might have produced a better effect. But at the time of his death, when his heart was brought to be buried at La Flèche, there were only twenty-four sons of *gentilshommes* in the procession, while there were 1200 ordinary students.[30]

A wind of evil flung my despair of ease
against the sharp spires of the one
lady:
not once or twice but . . .
(Kip of Christ hatch it!)
in one sun's drowning
(Jesuitasters please copy).
So on with the silk hose over the knitted, and the
morbid leather—
what am I saying! the gentle canvas—
and away to Ancona on the bright Adriatic,
and farewell for a space to the yellow key of the
Rosicrucians.
Note: 'His visions and pilgrimage to Loretto.'

Descartes's dreams/visions of the night of 16 November 1619 are elaborately given in Baillet, while Mahaffy underplays the sense of evil which Descartes obviously felt to be involved in the dreams, something which Beckett certainly includes in his 'wind of evil'. However, there are details in this section which can only come from Mahaffy, even when the Baillet rendering of the dream/vision is taken into account. These dreams obviously impressed Beckett greatly, and we remember the strange description of the linoleum in *Murphy* as 'dream of Descartes linoleum'. At least one critic believes that Murphy himself is constructed in part on a parody of these famous Cartesian dreams:

Nevertheless, an ironic sort of divine spark illuminates the last movement of Murphy's quest. Like Descartes' bedchamber, Murphy's garret is filled with sparks of fire. And with the ultimate separation of mind and body Murphy finally experiences an ironic counterpart of Descartes' vision of eternal harmony, as his ashes are dispersed throughout the big world, thereby uniting macro- and microcosm.[31]

It is certainly Baillet whom Beckett follows as Descartes encounters 'quelques fantômes qui se présentérent à lui' which force him to change the direction in which he is walking:

> Etant honteux de marcher de la sorte, il fit un effort pour se redresser: mais il sentit un vent impétueux qui l'emportant dans une espéce de tourbillon lui faire trois ou quatre tours sur le pied gauche. Ce ne fut pas encore ce qui l'épouvanta.[32]

Descartes's interpretation of the dream was of an evil spirit working on him, as the poem records:

> Le vent qui le poussait vers l'Eglise du collége, lorsqu'il avoit mal au côté droit, n'étoit autre chose que le mauvais Génie qui tâchoit de le jetter par force dans un lieu, où son dessein étoit d'aller volontairement.

He prayed to the Virgin and vowed to make a pilgrimage to the shrine of Loretto, circumstances which Baillet obviously makes much of (and which Mahaffy, as a good Protestant, treats as superstitious nonsense):

> Il s'addressa ensuite à la sainte Vierge pour luy recommander cette affaire, qu'il jugeoit la plus importante de sa vie. Et pour tâcher d'intéresser cette bien-heureuse Mére de Dieu d'un maniére plus pressante, il prit occasion du voyage qu'il méditoit en Italie dans peu de jours, pour former le voeu d'un pélerinage à Nôtre-Dame de Lorette.[33]

It is Mahaffy, though, who foregrounds the word 'key' in his account of the dreams and their aftermath, and this gets into Beckett:

> In the words of his epitaph, written by his intimate friend Chanut, with whom he had often talked over his mental history— 'In his winter furlough comparing the mysteries of nature with the laws of mathematics, he dared to hope that the secrets of both could be unlocked with the same key.'[34]

Baillet spends a good deal of energy on Descartes and the Rosicrucians, so we need not credit Mahaffy with being the source there. But other details from the poem come from Mahaffy. For example, the word 'Jesuitaster' does not appear in Baillet, but rather in Mahaffy:

> In these pamphlets Descartes was no longer the unique Archimedes and Atlas of science, but *Jesuitaster*, atheist, a second Vanini, a Cain, a vagabond, impious, and profligate of life.[35]

And Mahaffy summarises Descartes's choice of dress:

> In Holland he affected plain black cloth, though always adhering to the use of silk hose.[36]

One of the more curious uses of Mahaffy is in the poem's account of Descartes on Transubstantiation. Here there is not only a turning of Mahaffy into verse, but the pillaging of Mahaffy's quoting of St

Augustine's 'Fallor, ergo sum', which is quoted in turn by Beckett in line seventy-three.

> **They don't know what the master of them that do**
> **did,**
> **that the nose is touched by the kiss of all foul and**
> **sweet air,**
> **and the drums, and the throne of the faecal inlet,**
> **and the eyes by its zig-zags.**
> **So we drink Him and eat Him**
> **and the watery Beaune and the stale cubes of Hovis**
> **because He can jig**
> **as near or far from His Jigging Self**
> **and as sad or lively as the chalice or the tray**
> **asks.**
> **How's that, Antonio?**
>
> *Note*: 'His Eucharistic sophistry, in reply to the Jansenist Antoine Arnauld, who challenged him to reconcile his doctrine of matter with the doctrine of transubstantiation.'

> We turn to the fourth objections, made by the celebrated Anthony Arnauld, then a man of twenty-eight, shortly afterwards a doctor of the Sorbonne, and the greatest of all the Jansenists at the new *Oratory of Jesus*, founded by Cardinal Bérulle in 1614. His remarks open by showing that S. Augustin had forestalled Descartes by his *Fallor, ergo sum* . . . He adds some difficulties which he apprehends will be made by theologians, especially in explaining the doctrine of Transubstantiation on Descartes's principles . . . The explanation of the doctrine of the Eucharist is a masterpiece of subtlety on Descartes's part, and shows what a splendid scholastic theologian he would have made.[37]

> The cause why bread appears to us bread is, then, merely because the minute particles which compose it are differently arranged from the particles of other substances, have different interstices filled with air, moisture, &c., and a different amount of motion in these parts; for Descartes held that all substances, not merely liquid ones, contained some constant motion of their parts. If, says he, the body and blood of Christ should be conceived as occupying exactly the same minute places as the particles of bread and wine occupy, then though a new substance were substituted for the old, it would produce in us exactly the old sensations. Thus the body of Christ would produce in us sensations exactly the same in kind as were produced by the elements, and the accidents might be said to remain, while the substance was changed.[38]

> Among his most notable friends were MM. Hardy, De Beaune, Des Argues, Claude Picot . . .[39]

What Baillet says about the use of Augustine is simply to quote the comment made to Descartes by Arnauld, who complimented him for two things especially, and the second of them was that Descartes had quoted Augustine in his own work:

> L'autre étoit de l'avoir fortifié d'un grand secours en le munissant de l'autorité de S. Augustin. En effet, la prémiére chose que M. Arnauld prétendoit avoir trouvée dans ces Méditations Metaphysiques qui luy parût digne de remarque étoit de voir M. Descartes établit pour fondement & pour prémier principe de toute sa Philosophie, ce qu'avant luy S. Augustin avoit pris pour la base & le soutien de la sienne.[40]

There is no mention here of 'Fallor, ergo sum'.

One place which shows distinctly how Beckett relied on Mahaffy is when he incorporates Mahaffy's own illuminating reflection on Francis Bacon but makes his own jokey 'Bacon and Egg' routine out of it, turning a philosophical observation into breakfast.

> **In the name of Bacon will you chicken me up that**
> **egg.**
> **Shall I swallow cave-phantoms?**

> In fact, he failed to notice that the *impetus spontaneus*, which he evidently distinguished from *lumen naturale*—as being unreflective and, as it were, instinctive—might also arise from over-subtlety, and be (as Bacon has it) a *phantom of the cave* as well as *phantom of the marketplace*.[41]

Certainly there is comment in Baillet on Descartes's views on Bacon, but certainly not on the 'phantoms', Mahaffy's own incorporation.

When Mahaffy turns aside from the standard life of Descartes and wants to incorporate a few details from a more recent biography, we can see that Beckett has followed in his footsteps and used the same material in the poem. This is the case with regard to Anna Maria Schurmann of Utrecht, whom Beckett calls 'the Dutch blue-stocking'.

> **Anna Maria!**
> **She reads Moses and says her love is crucified,**
> *Note:* 'Schurmann, the Dutch blue-stocking, a pious pupil of Voët, the adversary of Descartes.'

> . . . the great female savant of Holland was Anna Maria Schurmann of Utrecht, of whom we hear the most wonderful accounts.[42]

> With all these accomplishments, she was of a deeply pious and modest mind, given to prayer and study, avoiding all worldly delights, adopting a vow of virginity with the touching motto of S. Ignatius, *amor meus crucifixus est*.[43]

So far, that accounts for Beckett's 'Anna Maria!' and 'She . . . says her love is crucified', and Baillet is fulsome in his description of her intellectual abilities and attainments, with his emphasis, however, not especially on her knowledge of Hebrew, but rather on the multiplicity of languages, western and oriental, which she was mistress of:

Elle possédoit un trés-grand nombre de Langues qu'elle sçavoit parler & écrire également. Elle n'ignoroit aucune de celles qui sont vivantes ou vulgaires en Europe, sous en excepter le Turc. Parmi celles de l'Orient elle s'étoit appliqué particuliérement à l'Ebreu, au Syriaque, au Chaldéen, & à l'Arabe.[44]

And Baillet gives the motto from St Ignatius, Martyr: *Amor meus crucifixus est*. But it is the other detail which could only have come from Mahaffy:

In M. Foucher de Careil's recent book on Descartes and the princess [Elizabeth], we have this interesting fact, that Mdlle. Schurmann came to have a horror of Descartes, which we should think natural enough in a pious pupil of Voët; but there is added the anecdote, that he once, on visiting her, found her occupied with the study of the Hebrew Scriptures, and expressed his wonder that so clever a person should be occupied with such trivialities. Upon her protesting that no study could be more profitable, he told her he too had once been very curious to know exactly what Moses had said on the subject of the creation, and had even learned Hebrew to judge for himself in the original, but finding that Moses had said nothing *clare et distincte*, he had laid him aside as affording no light in philosophy. She afterwards used to thank God she had escaped from the influence of so profane and impious a person. It was no doubt this spirit which alarmed orthodox Protestants like Voët, and caused them to see in Descartes not only a disguised Jesuit but an atheist.[45]

Beckett transfers to her a piece of Descartes's abuse of Petit, out of Mahaffy, making his own use of the sources for his own jokes.

Lieder! Lieder! she bloomed and withered,
a pale abusive parakeet in a mainstreet window.
Also on Petit he says: 'I think no more of him than I do of the abuse given me by a parrot hanging in a window as I pass in the street' (vii. 149–51).[46]

What Beckett gives as his note to lines 73–6, 'Saint Augustin has a revelation in the shrubbery and reads Saint Paul', is puzzling enough, but his 'Fallor, ergo sum' appears, as I noted earlier, in Mahaffy.

Failor, ergo sum!
The coy old frôleur!
He tolle'd and legge'd and he buttoned on his redemptorist waistcoat.
Note: 'Saint Augustin has a revelation in the shrubbery and reads Saint Paul.'

Mahaffy (in pages 96–7) contains the only mention of St Augustine's 'Fallor, ergo sum' in connection with Arnauld – but, as Ruby Cohn points out, Augustine's actual words were 'Si enim fallor, sum'.[47] So, it seems that here again, rather than another source for his remarks on St Augustine, Beckett is indebted to Mahaffy.

The other details from Descartes's life in the poem are so well known and so memorably presented in Baillet that all we can add is that because those details are so succinctly given in Mahaffy, they might, as in other cases, have been used as an aide-mémoire, but only as a secondary source.

There might be a final echo from Mahaffy in the 'Notes' on casting nativities:

> 'He kept his own birthday to himself so that no astrologer could cast his nativity.'
>
> He objected to his birthday being noted under his picture, because it exercised idle people in superstitions about his horoscope.[48]

In Baillet's index the relevant comments are noted under 'horoscope', and we can see that Beckett saves the word 'horoscope' for his own poem and substitutes 'nativity'. It is also clear from Baillet that he thinks that Descartes's declaration about his apparent superstition really concealed a different kind of concern altogether, even though he quotes Descartes's actual words to someone who wished to publish a portrait of Descartes which had been made in Holland:

> Nous avons encore la lettre qu'il en écrivit à cet homme pour prier de ne point laisser paraître ce Portrait: ou s'il ne pouvoit obtenir de lui cette faveur, d'en faire ôter ou moins ces mots, *Natus die ultimo Martii* 1598 *parce*, dit-il, *qu'it avoit aversion pour les faiseurs d'horoscope, à l'erreur desquels on semble contribuer quand on publie le jour de la naissance de quelqu'un.* C'est moins une raison qu'un pretexte qu'il alleguoit pour tâcher d'éviter la confusion ou la gloire de se voir produit au Public, même en peinture.[49]

Had close attention been paid to Baillet, then, it is hard to extract the bald statement that Descartes was superstitious about having his 'nativity' cast, as Mahaffy (and Beckett) had done.

In the business of attributions and indebtednesses, there is no certainty, but it does seem at least interesting that Beckett, in rushing into print to try and gain a £10 prize, might have relied on a short work which contained enough of those details of Descartes's idiosyncratic life history which had already struck him to satisfy his immediate needs. Additionally, it seems only just that an 'Irish' version of Descartes should have been relied on, and that Beckett's use of Mahaffy is almost a tribute to his Trinity College heritage. Beckett certainly had not done what the received critical wisdom believes, namely that during his reading of Baillet's *La Vie de Monsieur Des-Cartes* he was so inward with Descartes's life that at the drop of a hat he scribbled out his poem. The poem, for all its haste, is a remarkable accomplishment, but it was made all the more possible because of Mahaffy's little book. The poem and its notes can be seen to show a distinct indebtedness to Mahaffy, with sometimes a straight lift, and at others a jokey manipulation of Mahaffy's text. The young Beckett's inventiveness can be viewed more clearly by seeing how he used his original sources, both the grand two-volume 1691 biography and its humbler 1901 successor.

Notes

1. Ruby Cohn, *Samuel Beckett: The Comic Gamut*, p. 11.
2. John Pilling, *Samuel Beckett*, p. 160.
3. John Fletcher, *Samuel Beckett's Art*, p. 26.
4. J. P. Mahaffy, *Descartes*, p. 147.
5. Ibid. p. 147 ff.
6. Ibid. p. 77.
7. Adrien Baillet, *La Vie de Monsieur Des-Cartes*, Vol. 1, p. 394.
8. Ibid. Vol. 2, pp. 456–7.
9. Mahaffy, *Descartes*, p. 35.
10. Ibid. p. 105.
11. Ibid. pp. 21–2.
12. Ibid. p. 61.
13. Samuel Beckett, *Molloy*, p. 51.
14. Baillet, *La Vie de Monsieur Des-Cartes*, Vol. 1, pp. 124–5.
15. Mahaffy, *Descartes*, p. 32.
16. Emile Littré, *Dictionnaire de la langue française*, Vol. 1, p. 1242.
17. *Trésor de la langue française*, Vol. 4, p. 940.
18. Baillet, *La Vie de Monsieur Des-Cartes*, Vol. 2, p. 493.
19. Ibid. Vol. 2, pp. 24–5.
20. Mahaffy, *Descartes*, p. 8.
21. Ibid. p. 174.
22. Ibid. p. 176.
23. Ibid. p. 145.
24. Ibid. p. 132.
25. Ibid. pp. 10–11.
26. Ibid. p. 62.
27. Baillet, *La Vie de Monsieur Des-Cartes*, Vol. 2, pp. 89–90.
28. Mahaffy, *Descartes*, pp. 67–8.
29. Baillet, *La Vie de Monsieur Des-Cartes*, Vol. 1, pp. 23–4.
30. Mahaffy, *Descartes*, p. 11.
31. Robert Harrison, *Samuel Beckett's* Murphy, p. 68.
32. Baillet, *La Vie de Monsieur Des-Cartes*, Vol. 1, p. 85.
33. Ibid. Vol. 1, pp. 85–6.
34. Mahaffy, *Descartes*, p. 27.
35. Ibid. p. 102, emphasis in original.
36. Ibid. p. 138.
37. Ibid. pp. 96–7.
38. Ibid. p. 119.

39. Ibid. p. 36.
40. Baillet, *La Vie de Monsieur Des-Cartes*, Vol. 2, p. 126.
41. Mahaffy, *Descartes*, p. 92.
42. Ibid. p. 84.
43. Ibid. pp. 85–6.
44. Baillet, *La Vie de Monsieur Des-Cartes*, Vol. 2, p. 60.
45. Mahaffy, *Descartes*, pp. 85–6.
46. Ibid. p. 73.
47. Cohn, *Samuel Beckett: The Comic Gamut*, p. 15.
48. Mahaffy, *Descartes*, p. 9.
49. Baillet, *La Vie de Monsieur Des-Cartes*, Vol. 1, p. 8.

Bibliography

Baillet, Adrien, *La Vie de Monsieur Des-Cartes*, 2 vols (Paris: Horthemels, 1691).

Beckett, Samuel, *Molloy* (London: John Calder, 1959).

Cohn, Ruby, *Samuel Beckett: The Comic Gamut* (New Brunswick, NJ: Rutgers University Press, 1962).

Fletcher, John, *Samuel Beckett's Art* (London: Chatto and Windus, 1971).

Harrison, Robert, *Samuel Beckett's* Murphy*: A Critical Excursion* (Athens, GA: University of Georgia Press, 1968).

Harvey, Lawrence E., *Samuel Beckett: Poet and Critic* (Princeton: Princeton University Press, 1970).

Littré, Emile, *Dictionnaire de la langue française*, 4 vols (Paris: Jean-Jacques Pauvert, 1956).

Mahaffy, J. P., *Descartes (Philosophical Classics for English Readers)* (Edinburgh: William Blackwood, 1901).

Pilling, John, *Samuel Beckett* (London: Routledge and Kegan Paul, 1976).

Trésor de la langue française: Dictionnaire de la langue du XIXe et du XXe siècle (1789–1960), 16 vols, ed. Paul Imbs (Paris: Editions du Centre national de la recherche scientifique, 1975).

3.

Beckett's 'Malacoda': or, Dante's Devil Plays Beethoven

C. J. Ackerley

This short chapter offers a reading of Samuel Beckett's poem 'Malacoda', written in response to the death of his father in 1933. Its point of reference is the detailed interpretation by Lawrence E. Harvey in his *Samuel Beckett: Poet and Critic* (1970), and I acknowledge with gratitude many of the fine comments Harvey makes.[1] However, I contend that his overall sense of the poem is wrong, particularly when he argues that the final 'nay' negates what has gone before, so that mourning is rejected and death seen as a welcome release from life. Specifically, I suggest that Harvey has overlooked a crucial allusion to Beethoven's final quartet, Opus 135, one motif of which intensifies the tone of anguish and absurdity implicit in the central happening of the poem: the moment when, kneeling in reverence beside the coffin, the undertaker's assistant delicately breaks wind.

The title 'Malacoda' derives, of course, from Canto XXI of Dante's *Inferno*, where, in the fifth bolgia of the eighth circle, Dante and Virgil look down on the Barrators and Peculators who are plunged into boiling pitch by devils known as Malebranche ('Evil-claws'), armed with long hooks. These threaten the poet, until Virgil appeases their leader, Malacoda ('Evil-tail'), who prevents Scarmiglione from harming them, and appoints ten of his band to guide them from that place. The canto concludes with the celebrated reply of Malacoda to the devils gnashing their teeth: 'ed egli avea del cul fatto trombetta'/'and of his arse he made a trumpet'.[2]

The poem begins:

> thrice he came
> the undertaker's man
> impassible behind his scutal bowler[3]

This is the modern Malacoda, the undertaker's assistant in his long black tails, incapable of feeling, shielded by his bowler hat. He comes *thrice*, and that recurrence of Dante's number informs Beckett's orchestration: 'to measure . . . to coffin . . . to cover'.[4] There are three images of death: the devils, the flowers and the ship of death. Major phrases are developed in triads: 'hear she may . . . hear she must . . . hear she must'; 'see she need not . . . see she need not . . . see she must'; 'find the weeds . . . find the weeds . . . lay this Huysum on the box'.[5] Minor motifs are also reiterated in parallel thirds: 'cover . . . cover . . . cover'; 'stay . . . stay . . . stay'.[6] And the inevitability of death is articulated as the phrase 'must it be it must be it must be' is echoed and transposed in the coda: 'aye aye / nay'.[7]

The first theme is developed:

to measure
is he not paid to measure
this incorruptible in the vestibule
this malebrancha knee-deep in the lilies
Malacoda knee-deep in the lilies
Malacoda for all the expert awe
that felts his perineum mutes his signal
sighing up through the heavy air
must it be it must be it must be
find the weeds engage them in the garden
hear she may see she need not[8]

Note the orchestration, to be repeated twice more: the introduction by the infinitive ('to measure'); a striking image of death (Malacoda amidst the lilies); the flowers ('the weeds'); and the suffering as the son tries to shield the mother from distress ('hear she may see she need not'). Note also the enormity of the event described, the indefinable tone of pain and irreverence as the son hears the faint fart and, in a moment of anguished insight, associates it with the motif: 'must it be it must be it must be'. And note finally the modulation as Malacoda's signal to his fellow demons is at the perineum[9] muted, or *felted*, before passing forth (one thinks of the Galls, father and son).[10]

Harvey comments that line twelve of the poem ('must it be it must be it must be') is especially worthy of note, 'because it exemplifies the tension (weighted on the side of acceptance) between revolt and resignation so typical of much of Beckett's work'.[11] I fear he has missed the point of the musical echoes noted above, which culminate in a specific reference to Beethoven's last quartet, Opus 135 in F Major, the dominant motif of which is known traditionally as '*Muss es sein*?' ('Must it be?'). While I stop short of suggesting that Beethoven's Opus 135 is Beckett's model for the poem, I contend nonetheless that the echo of this quartet is meant to be heard, and I point to the intuitively apprehended similarity between the two works in terms of their spare contrapuntal structure, their compelling orchestration and their association with death. But some further evidence is needed.

In *The Life of Ludwig van Beethoven*, Alexander Wheelock Thayer recounts an anecdote to the effect that Herr Dembscher, wishing to produce a quartet, was unable to get the manuscripts from Beethoven because he had neglected to subscribe to a concert.[12] Told that the first step to restore himself to Beethoven's good graces would be to send the price of the subscription, Dembscher laughingly asked, 'Must it be?' ('*Muss es sein*?'): 'When the incident was related to Beethoven he too laughed and instantly wrote down a canon on the words: "It must be! Yes, yes, yes, it must be. Out with the purse!"'[13] Thayer notes that the joke was repeated frequently when Beethoven's housekeeper came to him of a Saturday for the weekly house money, and that it played a part in his conversations for some time: 'Out of this joke in the late fall of the year [1826] grew the finale of the last of the last five quartets, that in F major, Op. 135, to which Beethoven gave the superscription: "The difficult resolution" (*Der schwergefasste Entschluss*).'[14]

The Quartet in F was completed at Gneixendorf on 30 October 1826, and differs from the other late quartets in its shortness and its bare, spare contrapuntal writing. Strictly speaking, it was not Beethoven's last work, for the new finale for the Quartet in B-flat (Op. 130) was written after that, but in popular mythology Opus 135 represents his questioning acceptance of death, for the last part of the last quartet, its final passage, is the coda based on the melodic inversion of the '*Muss es sein*?' motif, '*Es muss sein*':[15]

In the popular imagination, then, this is Beethoven's last word, his final statement, a musical joke that nevertheless accentuates the inevitable (he died a few months later, on 26 March 1827). And it is to this coda, in his bare, spare poem with its intricate music and difficult resolution, that Beckett is attuned.

The poem continues:

to coffin
with assistant ungulata
find the weeds engage their attention
hear she must see she need not[16]

This constitutes a short movement, a simple restatement of the essential themes, with the curious depiction of the undertaker's other men, placing the corpse into the coffin, as 'assistant ungulata', that is, of the demonic, hence hoof-footed, order. And there is the repeated impulse (through the modulation from flowers to a widow's weeds) to engage the mother's attention, to shield her from pain.

That pain is felt more intensely in the next movement, which also recapitulates the major themes:

> to cover
> to be sure cover cover all over
> your targe allow me hold your sulphur
> divine dogday glass set fair
> stay Scarmilion stay stay
> lay this Huysum on the box
> mind the imago it is he
> hear she must see she must[17]

Beckett dramatises the plaintive impulse towards helping and a wish for decorum: cover him up properly, let me hold your hat, please don't fart,[18] yes, it's devilishly hot today. He anticipates the seafaring image that will be picked up in the coda, and voices a muted plea for a 'stay' before the coffin is taken away; as Harvey notes, this is a direct translation of Dante's 'Posa, posa, Scarmiglione'.[19] The key image, however, is that of the flowers, imaginatively transformed into a painting by Jan van Huysum, the eighteenth-century Dutch master, whose magnificent floral creations are so often emblematic of the certainty of death, the flowers depicted in conjunction with a clock, skull, worm or other *memento mori*. As Harvey informs us, after his essay had been written Beckett pointed out that his source for the imago was a butterfly posed on a flower in a Huysum painting.[20] Harvey also notes, most pertinently, that while the word 'imago' refers to the adult stage in an insect's life, it is at the same time in psychological terminology 'the idealised image of the father retained from childhood by the son'.[21] The placing of flowers upon the coffin is thus both a complex recognition of the inevitability of death and a simple act of devotion from son to father.

The poem concludes:

> all aboard all souls
> half-mast aye aye
> nay[22]

The final image is the traditional one of the death-ship, of the soul setting forth to regions unknown, in a flurry of departure: all aboard who are going aboard, flag at half-mast, aye aye sir . . . the coffin departs. And then, the final 'nay'. As Harvey suggests, it constitutes 'a kind of refusal that is aware of its own futility in the face of what is unacceptable and at the same time inevitable'; but I cannot reconcile this with his earlier contention that 'Malacoda' is an ambivalent title, death being 'not a penalty but a welcome release from life . . . not an evil but a blessing. Logic, of a kind, has come to the aid of art, and together they have tamed the monster.'[23] Such a reading, I suggest, ignores the accumulated weighting and reiteration of the word 'must', the entire impact of the Beethoven allusion, and the rhetorical force of the final melodic inversion, whereby 'aye aye' is negated absolutely. The final emphasis is upon suffering; the only acceptance that of existential inevitability. 'Evil coda' or not, *it must be*. Beckett's strategy here is similar to that at the end of 'Dante and the Lobster', where, after a prolonged struggle with Dante's paradoxes of pity and piety, Belacqua comforts himself with the thought, God help us all, that it's a quick death, only to experience the sudden and unexpected authorial intrusion 'It is not'.[24] In both works, dating from roughly the same time, any easy consolation is deliberately withheld, and the final impression is that of the cruel absurdity of death. And, in the poem, the lasting image is that of the undertaker's man, in an act of irreverence that only the anguished Beckett can detect, passing into the air his quiet breath. It is desperately funny, but in the end (as it were), it is not a joke.

Notes

1. Lawrence E. Harvey, *Samuel Beckett*, pp. 108–12.
2. Dante Alighiere, *Inferno*, XXI.139.
3. Samuel Beckett, 'Malacoda', lines 1–3.
4. Ibid. p. 26.
5. Ibid. p. 26.
6. Ibid. p. 26.
7. Ibid. p. 26.
8. Ibid. lines 4–14.
9. The perineum, as defined by the *Oxford English Dictionary*, is 'The region of the body between the anus and the scrotum'; or, as a further gloss would have it, 'the Ligamentous Seam betwixt the Cod and the Fundament'.
10. See Samuel Beckett, *Watt* (New York: Grove Press, [1953] 1959), pp. 70–80, for the 'incident of note' concerning the felts of Mr Knott's piano (note, in the poem, how the piano effects the transcription from Dante's trumpet to Beethoven's strings).
11. Harvey, *Samuel Beckett*, p. 110.
12. Alexander Wheelock Thayer, *The Life of Ludwig van Beethoven*, p. 224. This is an unabridged reprint of the Krehbiel edition, in Beckett's day the standard authority.

13. Ibid. p. 225.
14. Ibid. p. 224.
15. Philip Radcliffe, *Beethoven's String Quartets*, p. 170.
16. Beckett, 'Malacoda', lines 15–18.
17. Ibid. lines 19–26.
18. I cannot accept Harvey's reading that 'the son assists by holding Scarmilion's hat and his sulphur' (*Samuel Beckett*, p. 110).
19. Harvey, *Samuel Beckett*, p. 110 n. 55; Alighiere, *Inferno*, XXI.105. Henry Cary's well-known translation of *The Divine Comedy* uses 'Stay, stay thee, Scarmiglione!', but mutes the final indecency to 'Which he with sound obscene triumphant gave'.
20. Harvey, *Samuel Beckett*, p. 111 n. 56. The painting is likely to be the large canvas (52½" x 36") depicting fruit and flowers, dated 1736–7, and now in the National Gallery, London; on a terracotta vase, in the midst of the flowers, there is a small Red Admiral butterfly.
21. Ibid. p. 111.
22. Beckett, 'Malacoda', lines 27–9.
23. Harvey, *Samuel Beckett*, p. 160; p. 112.
24. Beckett, 'Dante and the Lobster', p. 21. Note, too, the words of Belacqua's aunt: '"Have sense," she said sharply, "lobsters are always boiled alive. They must be." She caught up the lobster and laid it on its back. It trembled. "They feel nothing," she said' (p. 22).

Bibliography

Alighiere, Dante, *Inferno*, in Dr E. Moore (ed.), *Tutte le opere di Dante Alighiere*, 3rd edn (Oxford: Oxford University Press, [1894] 1904), pp. 1–51.

Beckett, Samuel, 'Dante and the Lobster', in *More Pricks Than Kicks* (London: Calder and Boyars, [1934] 1970), pp. 9–24.

Beckett, Samuel, 'Malacoda', in *Collected Poems 1930–1978* (London: John Calder, 1984), p. 26.

Harvey, Lawrence E., *Samuel Beckett: Poet and Critic* (Princeton: Princeton University Press, 1970).

Radcliffe, Philip, *Beethoven's String Quartets* (London: Hutchinson, 1965).

Thayer, Alexander Wheelock, *The Life of Ludwig van Beethoven*, Vol. 3 (London: Centaur Press, [1921] 1960).

4.

Beckett's *Mirlitonnades*: A Manuscript Study

David Wheatley

The reader coming upon Beckett's *mirlitonnades* notes and drafts for the first time might be forgiven for thinking initially that he had caught the poet off his guard in that most unBeckettian of modes: travel-writing. The 'scraps of paper' of which the note to the *mirlitonnades* speaks in the 1984 Calder *Collected Poems 1930–1978* range from diary pages and train timetables to UNESCO and, more humbly, café notepaper. From them we can confirm, for instance, that 'ne manquez pas à Stuttgart' dates from Beckett's trip to that city in June 1977 for the Süddeutscher Rundfunk production of *Geistertrio*, while in similarly sepulchral vein 'ne manquez pas à Tanger' and 'plus loin un autre commémore' date from a vacation in Tangier later the same summer. It is from a Morocco vacation too that 'noire soeur' derives – perhaps in response to another of the djellaba-clad figures that inspired *Not I*. The polite disclaimer of 'Nothing dated' (the Calder *Collected* again) may thus be profitably laid aside; the drafts for the *mirlitonnades* are in fact unique in the corpus of Beckett's poetry in the virtual completeness of reconstruction they allow. Deposited in the Beckett archive of University of Reading Library, they form two separate groups: the 'scraps of paper' themselves, UoR MS 2940, and the *mirlitonnades* 'Sottisier', a leather-spined 9 cm x 12 cm notebook, UoR MS 2901, which one's first suspicion would have been that Beckett reserved for finished items – though, as we shall see, the relationship between drafts and 'Sottisier' is far less clear cut than this. In addition to poems, UoR MS 2901 earns its 'Sottisier' status through the inclusion of much further miscellaneous material: quotations from favourite authors, notes on classical mythology, and the contemporaneous prose piece *The Voice* (UoR MS 2910), referred to as *Verbatim*. My study of this material comes under three headings: the *mirlitonnades* as a sequence, establishment of the text and, lastly, a close reading of the individual items.

Following the text of the Calder *Collected Poems 1930–1978* the sequence of the *mirlitonnades* is as follows:

1. en face
2. rentrer
3. somme toute
4. fin fond du néant
5. silence tel que ce qui fut
6. écoute-les
7. lueurs lisières
8. imagine si ceci
9. d'abord
10. flux cause
11. samedi répit
12. chaque jour envie
13. nuit qui fais tant
14. rien nul
15. à peine à bien mené
16. ce qu'ont les yeux
17. ce qu'a de pis
18. ne manquez pas à Tanger
19. plus loin un autre commémore
20. ne manquez pas à Stuttgart
21. vieil aller
22. fous qui disiez
23. pas à pas
24. rêve
25. morte parmi
26. d'où
27. mots survivants
28. fleuves et océans
29. de pied ferme
30. sitôt sorti de l'ermitage
31. à l'instant de s'entendre dire
32. la nuit venue où l'âme allait
33. pas davantage
34. son ombre une nuit
35. noire soeur

Even before manuscript evidence is taken into account, however, the picture becomes complicated; current Minuit editions of *Poèmes suivi de mirlitonnades* (prepared after Beckett's death) conclude the sequence with 'le nain nonagénaire' and 'à bout de songes un bouquin' despite their appearing separately, among the *Poèmes*, in the original 1978 printing. Though occurring in both the *mirlitonnades* drafts and 'Sottisier', the canonicity of these pieces would thus appear to be in some doubt. In support of this reservation one could adduce the fact that a numbered sequence is clearly identified throughout the various poems and drafts that make up the 'Sottisier', corresponding almost exactly to the eventually published items.[1] With very few exceptions, the unnumbered items occur *en masse* at the end of the notebook, which would suggest that the selection process had already been made before entries were logged rather than as the result of subsequent reflection on Beckett's part. The details of the sequence – taking no account for the moment of the (on occasion, widely) different versions in which these poems occur – are as follows: beginning with 'rentrer', numbered I, Beckett reverts to Arabic numeration for items 2 to 16, 'somme toute' to 'ce qu'a de pis'; these correspond to items 3 to 17 of the Calder sequence. 'Noire soeur', the last of the Calder *mirlitonnades*, then occurs as number 17, with 'ne manquez pas à Tanger' and 'ne manquez pas à Stuttgart' providing items 18 and 19, knocking 'plus loin un autre commémore' out of sequence. Items 20 to 26, 'vieil aller' to 'mots survivants', then correspond to items 21 to 27 in Calder, 'plus loin un autre commémore' turning up next as number 27, or alternatively (in parentheses) 19. The remaining numbers in the sequence are:

28. fleuves et océans
29. [x du tiers oeil revenu sur terre x][2]
29 (1). en face
30. de pied ferme tout en
31. sitôt sorti de l'ermitage
32. à l'instant de s'entendre dire
33. ne verra-t-il jamais
34. pas davantage

Only one unpublished poem – 'ne verra-t-il jamais' is a preliminary version of 'la nuit venue où l'âme allait' – has been numbered; numbers 28, 30, 31, 32 and 34 are in the Calder sequence order; 'en face' has been restored in an afterthought to number 1. The unnumbered items grouped after 'pas davantage' that form recognisable poems are as follows:

[a] son ombre une nuit
[b] la nuit venue où l'âme allait
[c] c'est l'heure
[d] comme un / berceau
[e] le nain nonagénaire
[f] lui / à son âge
[g] à bout de songes un bouquin
[h] par une faille dans l'existence
[i] there / the life late led
[j] head on hands
[k] let ill alone
[l] nothing blest
[m] ashes burning more than all

– with these last, English-language items being frequently no more than a half-dozen words in length. From the drafts, by contrast, one may reconstruct, as far as Beckett's dating will allow, the following sequence (dates, where applicable, being those of final versions, with undated items given in the order of their manuscript occurrence):

[1.] rentrer [(uniquely) titled 'retard'] (Paris 24.11.76)
[2.] somme toute (13.2.77)
[3.] lueurs lisières (22.2.77)
[4.] imagine (Ussy 26/27.2.77)
[5.] flux cause (U. 7.3.77)
[6.] samedi répit (U. 7.3.77) (a Monday, incidentally)
[7.] chaque jour envie (U. 10.3.77)
[8.] rien nul (P. 21.3.77)
[9.] à peine à bien mené (Ussy 29.3.77)
[10.] noire soeur (Tanger 21.4.77)
[11.] nuit qui fais tant
[12.] silence vide une
[13.] d'abord
[14.] ne manquez pas à Tanger (T. 2.5.77)
[15.] ne manquez pas à Stuttgart (Stuttgart 20.6.77)
[16.] rêve (Ussy juillet 77)
[17.] d'où vient (P. 18.7.77)
[18.] un autre plus loin commémore (août 77)
[19.] mots survivants (Tanger août 77)
[20.] pas à pas
[21.] fleuves et océans
[22.] la nuit venue où l'âme allait
[23.] en face (P. 12.11.77)
[24.] de pied ferme (P. 13.11.77)
[25.] la nuit où il s'entendait dire (U. 17.1.78)
[26.] son ombre une nuit
[27.] [x minuit mille ans d'ici x]
[28.] qu'à lever la tête
[29.] c'est l'heure (P. 2.8.78)
[30.] la nain nonagénaire (Paris 9.9.78)
[31.] à bout de songes un bouquin (Tanger 21.12.78)
[32.] par une faille dans l'inexistence (Ussy 5.7.79)
[33.] à quelques centimètres
[34.] [x du tiers oeil revenu sur terre x] (Ussy 5.11.79)
[35.] fin fond du néant
[36.] silence tel que ce qui fut
[37.] navette entre deux lueurs
[38.] d'une lueur l'autre
[39.] écoute-les
[40.] comme au
[41.] [x gone with what x] (Paris 7.9.81)

Even at draft stage, though, Beckett appears to have given thought to the possibilities of ordering these poems into sequence form: a list of thirty-three titles placed at the beginning of the manuscript contains all but four of the Calder sequence – the exceptions being 'fin fond du néant', 'écoute-les', 'plus loin un autre commémore' and 'son ombre une nuit' – but in the absence of any date (not to mention the editorial foresightedness that allows Beckett to have already excluded any of the unpublished pieces), the list must be treated with a certain degree of caution.[3]

I have delayed giving the dates for the 'Sottisier' entries so as not to be distracted by the question of the sequence order. Here then are the dates we find in UoR MS 2901:

1. rentrer (76)
2. somme toute (2.2.77)
3. fin fond du (9.2.77)
4. silence tel que ce qui fut (18.2.77)
5. écoute-les (20.2.77)
6. lueurs lisières (21.2.77)
7. imagine si ceci (Ussy 26.2.77)
8. d'abord (U. 26/7.2.77)
9. flux cause (U. 7.3.77)
10. samedi répit (7.3.77)
11. chaque jour envie (U. 19.3.77)
12. nuit qui fais tant (P. 19.3.77)
13. rien nul (-)
14. à peine à bien mené (U. 29.3.77)
15. ce qu'ont les yeux (U. 30/1.3.77)
16. ce qu'a de pis (U. 31.3.77)
17. noire soeur (Tanger 21.4.77)
18. ne manquez pas à Tanger (T. 1.5.77)
19. ne manquez pas à Stuttgart (S. 20.6.77)
20. vieil aller (S. 26.6.77)
21. fous qui disiez (-)
22. pas à pas (-)
23. rêve (U. 14.7.77)
24. morte parmi (P. 17.7.77)
25. d'où (P. 18.7.77)
26. mots mourants (Tanger 27.7.77)

27 (19). plus loin un autre commémore (Tanger août 77)
28. fleuves et océans (Ussy Toussaint 77)
29. [x du tiers oeil revenu sur terre (U. 5.11.77) x]
29 (1). en face (P. 12.11.77)
30. de pied ferme tout en (P. 21.11.77)
31. sitôt sorti de l'ermitage (P. 22.11.77)
32. à l'instant de s'entendre dire (P. 13.1.78)
33. ne verra-t-il-jamais (U.)

34. pas davantage (T. 8.2.78)
[a] son ombre (P. 11.6.78)
[b] la nuit venue (-)
[c] c'est l'heure (P. 2.8.78)
[d] comme au / berceau (Tanger août 78)
[e] le nain nonagénaire (P. Sept. 78)
[f] lui / à son âge (U. Nov. 78)
[g] à bout de songes un bouquin (T. 27.12.78)
[h] par une faille dans l'inexistence (U. juillet 79)
[i] there / the life late led (23.3.81)
[j] head on hands (P. 26.5.81)
[k] let ill alone (Stuttgart June 81)
[l] nothing blest (-)
[m] ashes burning more than all (Courmayeur June 81)

Comparison of the drafts and 'Sottisier' dates now establishes, bizarrely enough, the almost uniform precedence of the 'Sottisier' versions, even if only by a single day, while in the case of 'somme toute', 'de pied ferme', 'à l'instant de s'entendre dire' and 'à bout de songes un bouquin' the interval has expanded to anything from four to eleven days. And with crowning irony, the later versions of 'à l'instant de s'entendre dire' and 'à bout de songes un bouquin', it emerges, both move further away from rather than closer to their finally published versions than the 'Sottisier' had already come, while in the case of 'somme toute' the crucial variant of the *Collected Poems* version appears in neither. In tracing the development of the text, one is thus obliged to shuttle between drafts and 'Sottisier' in the spirit of 'lueurs lisières / de la navette', trusting wholly in neither one nor the other:

halte plutôt
loin des deux
chez soi sans soi
ni eux

It is to this task together with a close reading of the poems that I now turn, following as far as possible the order of the 'Sottisier' entries.

'Rimailles/Rhymeries/Versicule(t)s': such, jotted inside the copy of a small leather notebook, UoR MS 2901, is Beckett's own description of the short poems now known as *mirlitonnades* that he composed between December 1976 and December 1978. A *mirliton* is a kazoo, and a *vers de mirliton*, according to Robert's dictionary, being a poem 'du genre de ceux qui sont imprimés sur les bandes de papier entourant en spirale les mirlitons', a 'mauvais vers', it seems probable that at no stage did Beckett intend venturing beyond 'wee bit songs', to use a phrase of Hugh MacDiarmid's.[4] The first of the *mirlitonnades* composed seems to have come to Beckett as a *poème donné*, occurring as printed in both the 'Sottisier' and the drafts –

rentrer
à la nuit
au logis
allumer

éteindre voir
la nuit voir
collé à la vitre
le visage[5]

– a fact which may have lent it added authority in Beckett's mind as an indication of the shape that subsequent poems should take. Unrhymed, it displays an interesting vowel patterning, with two repeated groups in each of the verses ('rentr*er*'/'allum*er*', 'nu*it*'/'log*is*', 'v*oi*r'/'v*oi*r' and 'v*i*tre'/'v*i*sage'), and states for the first time what will be one of the most insistently explored themes of the sequence: light and dark. A constant feature of the poetic grammar of the *mirlitonnades* is the avoidance of indicative verbal statement and pronomial identification. The verbal infinitives here suggest the flexible neutrality of the Greek middle voice; the vision involved in 'voir' seems to pass from poet to the surrounding night in the second quatrain – 'éteindre voir / la nuit voir / collé à la vitre / le visage' – as though the poem had executed a *Film*-like about-turn from object to eye, the eye becoming an object in its own right, 'collé à la vitre' like a photographic image traced in light.

Our appreciation of the next poem, 'somme toute', is considerably enhanced by the jottings and quotations on the subject of time and decay with which it is accompanied in both the 'Sottisier' and drafts. In the drafts, Beckett has calculated the number of days in seventy years (excluding leap years) – 25,550 – which, rounded up to the more convenient 26,000, he then multiplies by twenty-four for the number of hours: 624,000, '3 and ½ million minutes' (though only 'deux millions et demi' in the drafts; the truer figure is closer to thirty-seven and a half million, but Beckett soon realises his mistake, clarifying that the units he has in mind are *quarts d'heure*).[6] In the printed version:

somme toute
tout compte fait
un quart de milliasse
de quarts d'heure
sans compter
les temps morts

A *milliasse* means merely any enormous number, as against the more common *milliard*, a thousand million; the subdivision in four of the vague 'milliasse' to give the desired result here carries a comic specificity. An original second line ('x peu s'en faut x') becomes 'bon poids' in the 'Sottisier' before assuming the form in which we now find it. Where Proust's time was lost, Beckett's is dead: 'sans compter / les temps morts'. The suggestion that what he has just surveyed were, by contrast, 'temps vives' one may feel entitled to take with the usual grain of Beckettian salt.

Like the two previous poems, 'fin fond du néant' enacts a pursuit of a 'something there' that the final line assures the poet 'ne fut que dans ta tête'. In its printed version:

fin fond du néant
au bout de quelle guette
l'oeil crut entrevoir
remuer faiblement
la tête le calma disant
ce ne fut que dans ta tête

and in the 'Sottisier' version:

au ^[fin fond du] loin dans le néant
au bout de quelxx affût <[quelle guette]
l'oeil crut <[croit] entrevoir
remuer un instant
la tête le calm/a <[e] disant
<[x n'est x] ce ne fut <[n'est] que dans ta tête

The change of tense from present to past has vaguened the sense of drama, the replacement of 'ce n'est que dans ta tête' by 'ce ne fut que dans ta tête' leaving not even the presence of the mirage, but only the ghost-forsaken mind to administer its salve and solace *in vacuo*, while the more passive 'guette' for 'affût' places a vigil where previously there has been a hunt. Syntactically, too, the poem is unusual in beginning as it does with the noun-clause; disambiguated into prose the sequence would presumably be 'l'oeil crut entrevoir remuer faiblement [le] fin fond du néant au bout de quelle guette'.

In item four, 'silence tel que ce qui fut', 'déchiré' by the 'murmure' of its own language, the poem contracts to a timeless 'parole sans passé'. As printed:

silence tel que ce qui fut
avant jamais ne sera plus
par le murmure déchiré

d'une parole sans passé
d'avoir trop dit n'en pouvant plus
jurant de ne se taire plus

In the drafts we find the following variants on the opening:

[x trouver que x]
ne trouver qu'à dire
ce son

xxxxxxx ^[silence] tel qu'avant
ce qui fut [x n'est plus x] ne fut ^[sera] plus
par le murmure rompu

and

silence tel que ce qui fut
avant lui <[auparavant] ne sera plus
par le murmure déchiré

But neither here nor in the 'Sottisier' does the puzzling 'avant jamais' of the printed version appear. Does 'ce qui fut' become liable once more to the depredations of a 'parole sans passé' on the arrival of the hypothetical 'jamais'? Or, as seems more likely, should the lines be unconsciously recast to read as follows:

silence tel que ce qui fut avant
jamais ne sera plus [. . .]

As printed, and with no discernible gain from the ambiguity it causes, the word order is certainly odd. But the play of present, past and future, of voice and silence, and the last line so reminiscent of that of 'musique de l'indifférence' from the 1937–9 French sequence, are more recognisably *mirlitonnades* fare. The dangerous 'parole sans passé' is kept at bay by a silence which earths the poet's utterance to a condition of primal pastness, beyond the impotent efforts of articulation ('déchiré / [. . .] d'avoir trop dit n'en pouvant plus / jurant de ne se taire plus').

In the fifth item, 'écoute-les', the theme of time is taken up again in another meditation on the temporal dimension of the poetic act, amassing word upon word as Clov in *Endgame* did his 'Grain upon grain':

écoute-les
s'ajouter
les mots
aux mots
sans mot

les pas
aux pas
un à
un[7]

The paradox of the example from *Endgame*, variously credited to Zeno of Elea, Sextus Empiricus and Eubulides of Miletus, is the inability of a halved pile of millet to become the 'impossible heap' again through having fractions of one portion added to the other in diminishing sequence. At no point does one pile unequivocally become the other; part and whole are not commensurable.[8] The individual words are added 'un à / un' to make the unit of the poem, but 'sans mot', imperceptibly. A practical illustration of this logic of denial is that, in the drafts, we find a longer poem, whose opening lines –

s'ajoutent les mots
[. . .]
l'un après l'autre
les mots aux mots s'ajoutent
et sur la route seul son
de l'un silence à l'autre
les pas aux pas

– Beckett has chosen to eliminate. Gone is the auto-referential 'route' on which the words form the only sound, bearing out the verdict of Proust that – even where the theme is the creative act – 'The artistic tendency is not expansive, but a contraction' (*Proust and Three Dialogues*, p. 64).

In 'lueurs lisières', the 'Sottisier' once again provides us with a close approximation to the printed text, only the circled 'mort [x des x] aux deux' of its seventh line separating it from the final version:

lueurs lisières
de la navette
plus qu'un pas s'éteignent
demi-tour remiroitent

halte plutôt
loin des deux
chez soi sans soi
ni eux

'Lisière' here translates as 'selvage', an edge of cloth specially woven to prevent its unravelling, or (alternatively) the finish along an edge of cloth intended to be torn off or concealed; 'pas' is a 'step', but possibly also the unfamiliar usage as 'thread'. The poem thus describes an act of stitching, with the thread knitting in and out of visibility in the third and fourth lines. The first quatrain, however, we learn from the drafts, caused Beckett considerable problems, occurring as

[x lueurs lisières
de la navette
atteintes s'éteignent
demi-tour remiroitent x]

and (incorporating the second quatrain)

navette entre deux lueurs
les xxxx atteindre les éteint
s'en détourner les rallume
halte mi-chemin
sans soi sans l'autre

and

d'une lueur l'autre
va-et-vient
les atteindre
les éteint

and

d'une lueur l'autre
deux lueurs
va-et-vient
atteintes
[x s'éteignent eteintes x] s'éteignent
demi-tour
[x se rallument reluisent x] remiroitent

– each version like a separate exposure of the moment of illumination being described. Unable to make up its mind between light and dark, the poem concludes with the already quoted self-subtracting cessation:

halte plutôt
loin des deux
chez soi sans soi
ni eux

In item seven, the hesitations of 'écoute-les' and 'lueurs lisières' recur in the stuttering effect with which imagination contemplates its decease:

imagine si ceci
un jour ceci
un beau jour

imagine
si un jour
un beau jour ceci
cessait
imagine[9]

The changes recorded in the 'Sottisier' are minimal but significant: the first line originally stops short at 'imagine si'; the fifth line has discarded a 'beau'– 'un beau jour'; while lines six and seven of the printed version are much improved from the '[si un beau jour /] ceci pouvait / s'atténuer' of Beckett's first thoughts. In pieces like 'imagine', the *mirlitonnades* approach a poetics of pure onomatopoeic effect: conventional syntax, for instance, has given way to a series of discrete verbal units fashioned into a whole by the merest phonological pretence.

In 'd'abord', too, onomatopoeia plays its part. The tone is apodictic and self-assured, as if giving directions to be followed:

d'abord
à plat sur du dur
la droite
ou la gauche
n'importe

ensuite
à plat sur la droite
ou la gauche
la gauche
ou la droite

enfin
à plat sur la gauche
ou la droite
n'importe
sur le tout
la tête

Recalling Macmann's earthy prostrations in *Malone Dies*, the poem is perhaps closest in style to the English poem of 1974, 'something there'. The 'à plat sur du dur' of the second line, like the 'pressé contre ma vieille planche vérolée du noir' of 'Mort de A. D.', reminds us of the Beckettian predilection for deriving speech from uncomfortable physical positions.[10] The purposive tripartite structure, though – 'd'abord', 'ensuite', 'enfin' – should not blind us to the vagueness of the instructions themselves, turning finally from the vagaries of left and right ('la droite / ou la gauche / n'importe') to the unfortunate head ('n'importe / sur le tout / la tête'). But where its composition is concerned, the poem seems to have been in no doubt whatever, coming to Beckett entire, with only the most minimal of redrafting.

The same, oddly enough for so Heraclitean a poem in its espousal of 'flux', goes for 'flux cause', to judge by the 'Sottisier', from whose version only the 'même' in line six of the printed text is missing:

flux cause
que toute chose
tout en étant
toute chose
donc celle-là
même celle-là
n'est pas
parlons-en

The drafts are somewhat more disordered. There the first version occurs on a page of doodles with, in a corner, the intriguing query 'qui fut le fou / l'optimiste / 6 siècles avant Christ'. Since Democritus was born in 460 BC the identity of this unbalanced meliorist must remain an open question. An undated, scored-through version of the poem on the same page modifies 'n'est pas' to the more forbidding 'n'est jamais', whereas another version on a separate page, dated '5.3.77', numbers its nine lines in accordance with what appears to be a rhyme scheme:

[x flux cause	a1
que toute chose	a2
tout en étant	b1
toute chose	a3
donc celle-là	c1
(tout en étant)	
celle-là	c2
tout en étant	b2
n'est pas	c3
parlons-en	b3 x]

The close attention to the question of time continues: the repetition in line four, for instance ('toute chose / tout en étant / toute chose'), harmonises expertly with the mood of Heraclitean non-self-identity, since the form of being at issue, however reinforced, still disappears in the penultimate line ('n'est pas').

Of the next group of four shorter pieces – 'samedi répit', 'chaque jour envie', 'nuit qui fais tant' and 'rien nul' – only the first seems to have given Beckett any trouble. In the 'Sottisier', the last line of 'samedi répit' –

samedi répit
plus rire

depuis minuit
jusqu'à minuit
plus pleurer

– reads 'pas pleurer', while in the drafts 'répit' replaces the less attractive 'ataraxie':

samedi ^[répit] [x ataraxie x]
trop tard pour rire
trop tôt pour pleurer

The printed four-line version of 'chaque jour envie' occurs in both drafts and 'Sottisier' after a(n in both cases identical) six-line preliminary draft, giving a separate line to 'en vie' and 'né', with, further, 'd'être un jour / né' where we now find 'un jour d'être né'. As in 'flux cause', the temporal dimension is ambiguous. Does the speaker hope to be at last 'en vie' in some unspecified future ('un jour'), or, mayfly-like, for the duration of a single day ('un jour')? The rearrangement noted in the fourth line creates similar difficulties. Is the regret at having been born directed backwards at the event ('regret / d'être un jour né') or – more unlikely maybe, but otherwise why the change? – being distantly anticipated on the hypothetical 'jour en vie' when the life-force will at last have become active enough to require the obligatory Beckettian anathema?

Of item twelve, 'nuit qui fais tant', it will suffice to point out the resemblance to Baudelaire's 'Recueillement', so memorably excerpted by Hamm in *Endgame*, and the slight syntactic tinkering it has undergone in the revision from

[x de grâce nuit
qui fais tant
implorer l'aube
tombe x]

(drafts), to

nuit qui fais tant
implorer l'aube
nuit de grâce
tombe

('Sottisier' and printed text) – a level of elaboration quite in excess of that surrounding 'rien nul', another *poème donné*. Printed text:

rien nul
n'aura été
pour rien

tant été
rien
nul

The musical resonance of 'pour rien' – as in 'mesure pour rien' – may be of some assistance here. One might read the double nothing of 'rien nul' as not having been 'pour rien', in vain, if, accepting the *parti pris* of 'flux cause', we agree to see in nothingness a reserve of existential energy and not mere non-existence. The 'tant' of line four would then be equivalent in force to 'aussi longtemps que' – nothing has been in vain as long as nothing ('rien') has been merely 'nothing' ('nul'), or seen as such. Eleven words: a *tour de force* of poetic economy even by Beckett's own standards.

Item fourteen too, 'à peine à bien mené', needs no reconstruction, occurring as printed in both 'Sottisier' and the drafts. Dragging its physical and metrical feet, 'comme le veut l'usage / enfin jusqu'à présent', 'à peine à bien mené':

à peine à bien mené
le dernier pas le pied
repose en attendant
comme le veut l'usage
que l'autre en fasse autant
comme le veut l'usage
et porte ainsi le faix
encore de l'avant
comme le veut l'usage
enfin jusqu'à présent

Items fifteen and sixteen, 'ce qu'ont les yeux' and 'ce qu'a de pis', form a diptych, informed perhaps by the notes on the Fates, or Moirai, 'Ministers of Pluto, sitting at foot of his throne', which Beckett makes on page ten of the 'Sottisier' immediately following the poems. There is one variant: 'les mains' for 'les doigts' in a first version of 'ce qu'ont les yeux'; there are no surviving drafts. 'Ce qu'ont les yeux':

ce qu'ont les yeux
mal vu de bien
les doigts laissé
de bien filer
serre-les bien
les doigts les yeux
le bien revient
en mieux

and, with its immediate retort, 'ce qu'a de pis':

ce qu'a de pis
le coeur connu
la tête pu
de pis se dire
fais-les
ressusciter
le pis revient
en pire

Item seventeen – whose indebtedness to the Moroccan holiday on which it was written I have already implied – similarly portrays an Atropos-like figure ('Atropos – death – scissors / dressed in black'):

noire soeur
qui es aux enfers
à tort tranchant
et à travers
qu'est-ce que tu attends

The familiar second-person address resembles that of 'nuit qui fais tant', ending (as 'd'où' alone of the *mirlitonnades* also does) with an invocatory question, although without a question mark – 'qu'est-ce que tu attends'; a feature which may have been behind Beckett's decision to move it to the end of the sequence it occupies in the *Collected Poems* printing. The throne of Pluto just referred to turns up in the most interesting of the drafts, confirming the Atropos connection:

[x accomplice [¿ aux nus pieds ?]
du trône elle coupe
toute de noir vêtue
qu'est-ce que tu attends x]

'Ne manquez pas à Tanger', 'ne manquez pas à Stuttgart' (items eighteen and nineteen) and 'plus loin un autre commémore' (twenty-seven) so obviously belong together that, following Beckett's second thoughts in having placed a '19' in brackets after the last of the three in the 'Sottisier', I will examine the three together. Beckett's interest in graveyards and inscriptions was, like Cooper's acathisia in *Murphy*, of long standing, sometimes taking the most unusual forms, as in the fascinating 'Été 56' notebook, where work on *Krapp's Last Tape* is interrupted to allow Beckett to copy out three whole pages of newspaper 'In Memoriam' notices. In the first poem, the Saint-André cemetery in Tangier ('[¿ bonde ?] de britanniques', a draft informs us) is agreeably contemplated from a bench inscribed to the memory of Arthur Keyser:

ne manquez pas à Tanger
le cimetière Saint-André
morts sous un fouillis
de fleurs surensevelis
banc à la mémoire
d'Arthur Keyser
de coeur avec lui
restes dessus assis

A cancelled opening of a draft version fellow-feelingly depicts the poet 'mort . . . de fatigue':

aux ¾ mort
le quart qui reste
de fatigue d'avoir
tant grimpé

mort seulement
de fatigue

This is a quite distinct sort of poetry from the *mirlitonnades* we have looked at up to now; a poetry of statement, free of verbal effect. 'Plus loin un autre commémore', written on an envelope in the drafts, memorialises 'Caroline Hay Taylor morte en Irlande August 32', as the 'Sottisier' macaronically notes:[11]

plus loin un autre commémore
Caroline Hay Taylor
fidèle à sa philosophie
qu'espoir il y a tant qu'il y a vie
d'Irlande elle s'enfuit aux cieux
en août mil neuf cent trente-deux

Moving to Stuttgart, we find one of the most perfect of the *mirlitonnades*, 'ne manquez pas à Stuttgart', regrettably disfigured by the omission in the Calder *Collected Poems* of the article in line three:

ne manquez pas à Stuttgart
la longue Rue Neckar
du néant là l'attrait
n'est plus ce qu'il était
tant le soupçon est fort
d'y être déjà et d'ores

Like its two companion pieces, this poem has the distinction of being written in French to what one might very fancifully take for an English metre, in this case iambic trimeter. The syllable count for each line is seven, six, six, six, six, seven (counting 'longue' in line two as two syllables); an anglophone ear by contrast hears the trimeter pattern suggested with trochaic reversals in the last feet of lines two, three and four, in the second foot of line four, and in the first of line five, with an anapest at the end of line six (eliding the second syllable of 'd'ores').

Neither 'vieil aller' nor 'fous qui disiez', numbered twenty-one and -two in the 'Sottisier', is preserved in draft form. A reflexive 's' in brackets before 'arrêter' in line six constitutes the only variant in the text of 'vieil aller':

vieil aller
vieux arrêts

aller
absent
absent
arrêter

This piece can be grouped with 'd'abord' and 'à peine à bien mené' as one of the poems of movement, with the familiar adjectival wordplay seen here on 'absent' conveying a sense of movement before our eyes, within the poem itself.[12] 'Fous qui disiez', too, has the impetus of verbal repetition. Printed text:

fous qui disiez
plus jamais
vite
redites[13]

as revised from:

[x mots qui disent
silence finis
absence
vite dites x]

– words, it emerges, being the 'fous' of the printed version for trying to articulate the 'silence'; the vow of 'plus jamais' a tribute to the impossibility of silence (and as a noun, *redites* = needless repetition).

With 'pas à pas', item twenty-two, the analogy is with 'écoute-les', for its sense of incremental movement forward, and 'rien nul', for the play it makes of negative particles:

pas à pas
nulle part
nul seul
ne sait comment

petits pas
nulle part
obstinément

as revised in the 'Sottisier' from:

[x aller xxxxxxxx avant de l'avant
nulle part
Dieu sait
comment
obstinément " " " x][14]

Poems twenty-three and -five, 'rêve' and 'd'où', continue the existential strain of 'rien nul', while poem twenty-four, 'morte parmi', is a perfectly observed descriptive piece: 'rêve':

rêve
sans fin
ni trêve
à rien

'morte parmi':

morte parmi
les mouches mortes
un souffle coulis
berce l'araignée

and 'd'où':

d'où
la voix qui dit
vis

d'une autre vie

Of the three, only the last goes through more than one version. In the drafts for 'd'où' the unanswered question of the printed text is answered for us as follows:

[x d'où vient
la voix qui dit
vis
elle vient
d'une autre vie x]

At this preliminary stage it is not 'd'une autre vie' that we are being asked to live, merely to live.

What stops the poet from doing so, the drafts of item twenty-six, 'mots mourants', identify:

[x finie
ou peu s'en faut
la vie

. . .

sa vie
morte sous les mots

. . .

vie
morte de mots . . . x]

The printed version, not for the first time in these poems, has performed an about-turn, words now having become the agency of survival, not destruction. The poem is found in the drafts with only the variant of 'tenez-nous' for 'tenez-lui', and similarly in the second 'Sottisier' version:[15]

mots survivants
de la vie
encore un moment
tenez-lui compagnie

With 'fleuves et océans', dated 'Ussy Toussaint 77', we return to the imagistic poetry of place we have seen in the Tangier and Stuttgart graveyard poems. Apart from the occurrence of lines four and three, both scored through, before line one in the 'Sottisier' (originally intended as lines one and two?), no draft variants survive. 'Fleuves et océans':

fleuves et océans
l'ont laissé pour vivant
au rue de Courtablon
près la Mare-Chaudron

A 'ru' is an archaic form for a streamlet. The Mare-Chaudron and its attendant 'ru' are in Ussy, site of Beckett's 'hole in the Marne mud'.

Number twenty-nine in the sequence, as I have previously signalled, is initially allocated to the unpublished 'du tiers oeil revenu sur terre' before passing to 'en face' – before second thoughts here too award that poem the privilege of beginning the sequence, as it now does in the trade editions. 'Du tiers oeil revenu sur terre' is close to the English 'dread nay' as one of Beckett's 'eye' poems, and the other unpublished poems 'par une faille dans l'inexistence' and 'à quelques centimètres'.[16] A mysterious third eye (though compare the second version below) offers the poet the possibility of revisiting his tomb. Two 'Sottisier' drafts, both crossed out diagonally:

[x du tiers oeil revenu sur terre
il fixe son tombeau jusqu'à ce
qu'en soit perdue toute trace
puis clot la tierce paupière x]

and

[x d'un ^[sale ou][17] seul oeil revenu sur terre
il fixe son tombeau jusqu'à ce
que s'en efface toute trace
puis lâche la lourde paupière x]

Next, in marker in the 'Sottisier' where the other entries are in ink as a rule, 'en face', without revisions. Without further comment, 'en face':

en face
le pire
jusqu'à ce
qu'il fasse rire[18]

'De pied ferme', item thirty, is another poem of movement. The first line seems to have been an afterthought, replacing the 'lui debout' of the first of the drafts:

de pied ferme
tout en n'attendant plus
il se passe devant
allant sans but

In spite of a cryptic note on Leonardo da Vinci immediately preceding it, there seem no grounds for assuming that the 'ermitage' of the next poem refers, even in a flight of Beckettian fancy, to the St Petersburg gallery of the same name. Poem thirty-one (no variants):

sitôt sorti de l'ermitage
ce fut le calme après l'orage

'À l'instant de s'entendre dire' returns to the ontological preoccupations of 'rien nul'. The *malin génie* of the life-force, overhearing the poet's oath 'ne plus en avoir pour longtemps', gloats knowingly over the *naïveté* he shows. In the first 'Sottisier' version we find '[x la nuit x] où il s'entendait dire' in place of the printed first line, 'pas plutôt qu'il s'entendait dire' and '[x le jour où il se laissa dire / qu'on ne pouvait plus rien x]' in the drafts:

à l'instant de s'entendre dire
ne plus en avoir pour longtemps
la vie à lui enfin sourire
se mit de toutes ses dents

By far the largest proportion of classical 'Sottisier' material, quotations and other jottings occurs in the last third of the notebook we are examining. The next poem, for instance, 'ne verra-t-il jamais', is hemmed in on both sides by quotations from the prologue of the *Summoner's Tale*, Heine's 'Die Heimkehr' and 'Ein Wintermarchen', an Italian commentary on Dante, Parnell's remark (to Morley in 1890) – which Beckett's four decades of personal experience at the time of writing could no doubt corroborate – that 'Ireland [was] a very good place to live out of', as well as tantalising unattributed fragments such as – once more in the spirit of 'rien nul' – 'ex nihil omne fit', 'on le pronostiqua mort' and, most piquantly, the sorry reflection that 'penury is all'. But perhaps it is Jacques Moran's inquiry in *Molloy*, 'What if the mass for the dead were read over the living?'[19], that comes closest to the impish tone of 'la nuit venue où l'âme allait', into which 'ne verra-t-il jamais' evolves. Note again, in the plethoric 'voilà-t-il pas', Beckett's preference for negative particles. Printed text:

la nuit venue où l'âme allait
enfin lui être réclamée
voilà-t-il pas qu'incontinent
il la rendit une heure avant

The escape 'une heure avant' here is a refinement on the first 'Sottisier' draft, where no means of evasion present themselves:

[x (ne) finira-t-il jamais
la nuit
où l'âme lui
sera réclamée x]

to which compare 'ne verra-t-il jamais', numbered item thirty-three:

ne verra-t-il jamais
finir la nuit
où l'âme lui
sera réclamée

Completing the numbered sequence, 'pas davantage' is a frankly autobiographical poem. No variants:

pas davantage
de souvenirs qu'à l'âge

d'avril un jour
d'un jour

Turning next to the three outstanding published poems, we find 'son ombre une nuit' on the next page:

son ombre une nuit
lui reparut
s'allongea pâlit
se dissolut

as considerably condensed from an eight-line draft version:

[x dans la nuit
lui reparut
s'allongea pâlit
dans la nuit se dissolut

son ombre ^[une] [x dans la x] nuit
lui reparut
s'allongea pâlit
se dissolut x][20]

The two other pieces, 'à bout de songes un bouquin' and 'le nain nonagénaire', are more problematic. Their displacement and reinstatement in the Minuit *Poèmes* and omission from the Calder *Collected Poems* have already been remarked upon; but their print history is by no means their most confused aspect. Without access to the drafts, 'le nain nonagénaire' must strike the reader as elliptic. Dwarfs may have been on our author's mind since the litter-bearing pair with which he peopled *For to End Yet Again*, composed only three years previously. 'Le nain nonagénaire':

le nain nonagénaire
dans un dernier murmure
de grâce au moins la bière
grandeur nature[21]

In the drafts Beckett begins by drawing up a list of significant elements, 'nain / bière / cercueil / lit de mort / avant d'exprimer / agonie', before proceeding to a first-person death-bed address from the dwarf:

que l'on m'enterre
dit le vieux nain
à l'agonie
[¿ a la tort fin ?]
de l'agonie
que l'on m'enterre

si l'on veut bien
dans une grande bière
avant que [¿ l'éxxxxxxxx ?]
au moins la bière
xxx grandeur nature

The agony and burial-reference both disappear then, leaving us with one of those shadowy figures on the fringes of the Beckett pantheon, much like Obidil and Yerk in *Molloy*, or the mysterious Quin in *Watt* and *Malone Dies*.

What, though, can the uninformed reader hope to make of 'à bout de songes un bouquin'? As printed:

à bout de songes un bouquin
au gîte à dire adieu astreint
de chasse lasse fit exprès
d'oublier le chandelier

The 'Sottisier' goes some way towards providing a skeleton key in the shape of a quotation from La Fontaine's 'Le Lièvre et les Grenouilles':

Car que faire en un gîte
à moins que l'on n'y songe?

The fable presents an easily frightened hare, to whom the experience of his frightening the frogs in a pond comes as a revelation, as La Fontaine goes on:

Il n'est, je le vois bien, si poltron sur la terre
Qui ne puisse trouver un plus poltron que soi.[22]

The printed text replaces 'a déguerpir contraint' in line one of the first 'Sottisier' version with 'à dire adieu astreint', while in the numerous drafts the phrasing strays as far from the final version as the following example:

[x à bout de songes un bouquin
en hâte à finir son gîte astreint
fit diligence au point d'oublier
l'indispensable chandelier x]

(Alternatively, we might translate 'bouquin' as 'book' and interpret the poem as a self-referential parting gesture.)

Of the other 'Sottisier' material in the last pages of the notebook, besides the unpublished poems and sketches for poems already listed, mention must also be made of the numerous quotations from, among others, Schopenhauer (*Vom Leiden der Welt* and *Über die vierfache*

Wurzel des Satzes vom zureichenden Grunde – from both of which quotations are given in the *Whoroscope* notebook of forty years before), *King Lear*, Kierkegaard and Pope. Beckett's lifelong fondness for the word 'pensum', and its metaphorical overtones of a 'life disease' to be expiated in death ('Life penal colony', as one unsourced quote telegraphically opines), can now be traced to Schopenhauer's *Vom Leiden der Welt*, as presumably (from the same quote) can the word '*defunctus*' with which Beckett ended the *Proust* monograph of 1931. Of the Shakespeare quotes, Edgar's 'The lamentable change is from the best, / The worst returns to laughter' from *Lear* can be matched to the diptych 'ce qu'ont les yeux' and 'ce qu'a de pis'; of the others, Pope's 'damned to fame' (*Dunciad*) and his *bon mot* on 'the last and greatest art, the art to blot' are of interest, as is a gloss on 'die-back', a 'disease of orange trees xxxxxxxx in which tree dies from top downward' – as Swift, the source acknowledged, once feared that he himself would do. A full page is devoted to a dramatic monologue, dated '28.12.80', beginning 'That head', snatches of Schubert and Schumann *Lieder* are remembered, a classical tag randomly mangled ('nulla dies sine lacryma', 'look ^[in thine] xxxxxxxxx arse xxxx & write'), and a striking English three-line poem (dated 'June 81') thrown out at random:

ashes burning more than all
the burning all
to ashes

Apart from a list of personal memoranda inside the back cover, the final entry is a spectral valediction from Mallarmé's 'Brise Marine':

. . . la clarté déserte de ma lampe
sur le vide que la blancheur défend.

The 'clarté déserte' of the lamp provides as apt a metaphor as any for the light the 'Sottisier' and draft poems we have looked at shed on their published counterparts. So many of these poems have dramatised the painful struggle forward, physical and verbal, of the speaker out of darkness towards the light, no less than the failure with which it is invariably met, as to lend an aching grandeur to the equation, here, of the lamp-light by which the poet finds himself working with the impossible purity of the blank page barring the way of the poem that he must write, 'la blancheur que le vide papier défend'. In 'rentrer' the light was turned off for the moment of poetic illumination to take place –

éteindre voir
la nuit voir

– in the same way that we as readers frequently find the meanings of these poems available to us only on the principled refusal to be satisfied with the 'clarté déserte' of the finished item, driven instead to the draft *disjecti membra poetæ*, where, in the murk of textual uncertainty, the real work has been done. What more perfect image, then, of the relation in which these drafts stand to their finished versions than that with which the sequence, in the Minuit printing, now ends: a forgotten candlestick left burning in an empty house from which its occupant has fled?

à bout de songes un bouquin
au gîte a dire adieu astreint
de chasse lasse fit exprès
d'oublier le chandelier

Notes

1. In a letter of 16 April 1994 Gerry Dukes informs me of a letter of Jérôme Lindon to him in which the grouping of 'le nain nonagénaire' and 'à bout de songes' with the *Poèmes* rather than the *mirlitonnades* in the 1978 printing is acknowledged as an error.
2. The following conventions will be used in the quotations of manuscript material:

   [x x], legible erasure
   xxxxxxxxxxxx, illegible erasure
   [¿ ?], doubtful reading
   ^[ ], superscript
   <[ ], marginalium

3. The published poems not preserved in draft form (but all in the abovementioned list) are 'ce qu'ont les yeux', 'ce qu'a de pis', 'vieil aller', 'fous qui disiez', 'morte parmi', 'sitôt sorti de l'ermitage', 'à l'instant de s'entendre dire', 'la nuit venue où l'âme allait' and 'pas davantage'.
4. Hugh MacDiarmid, 'To One Who Urges More Adventurous Flights'.
5. Cf. Kevin Perryman's translation in *Babel* (p. 29):

   back
   to night
   place to sleep
   light on

   light off see
   night see
   stuck to the pane
   the face

6. The 'Sottisier' quotations are from Job V, Voltaire's *Le Désastre de Lisbonne* and Pope's *Essay on Man*.

7. Perryman's translation (*Babel*, p. 29):

> listen to this
> addition
> words
> and words
> wordlessly
> steps
> and steps
> one by
> one

8. Cf. Mrs Lambert's lentil-sorting in *Malone Dies*, p. 42:

> She sat down, emptied out the lentils on the table, and began to sort them. So that soon there were two heaps on the table, one big heap getting smaller and one small heap getting bigger. But suddenly with a furious gesture she swept the two together, annihilating thus in less than a second the work of two or three minutes.

Following *Malone meurt*, pp. 72–3:

> Elle s'assit, vida les lentilles sur la table et se mit à les trier. De sorte qu'il y eut bientôt deux tas sur la table, un grand qui allait diminuant et un petit qui allait grandissant. Mais soudain d'un geste rageur elle les confondit tous les deux, anéantissant ainsi, en moins d'une seconde, le travail de deux ou trois minutes.

9. Perryman's 'crack at it', as Christopher Ricks describes it (in *Beckett's Dying Words*, p. 48):

> just think if all this
> one day all this
> one fine day
> just think
> if one day
> one fine day all this
> stopped
> just think

10. In an abandoned play of early 1956 (UoR MS 1227/7/16/2), one Ernest, 'un mouchoir sur le visage, un seau à champagne [*sc.* a spittoon] accroché au cou', is fixed throughout to a mechanical cross.
11. Going on to copy her epitaph from Browning's *Epilogue to Asolando*:

> One who never turned her back but / marched breast forward / never doubted clouds wd. break / never dreamed though right were / worsted wrong wd. triumph / held we fall to rise, are baffled to / fight better, sleep to wake

12. Between 'vieil aller' and 'fous qui disiez' in the 'Sottisier' we find a seventeen-line English poem, 'one dead of night', remarkably prescient of *Stirrings Still*.
13. Perryman's liberal translation (*Babel*, p. 31):

fools who said
never again man
quick
play it again Sam

14. Entire poem diagonally crossed out. 'aller xxxxxxxx avant' in line one horizontally scored through.
15. Among the more unusual pieces of 'Sottisier' material occurring at this point, and recalling the more scabrous entries of the 1930s *Whoroscope* notebook, is Johnson's definition of 'pessary': 'an oblong form of / medicine, made to thrust up / into the uterus upon some / extraordinary occasion'!
16. 'par une faille dans l'inexistence' (no variants):

    par une faille dans l'inexistence
    s'infibrent des miasmes d'oxygène
    dans le silence du pseudo-silence
    de la pénombre par bonheur à peine

    The oxygen and eye themes also feature in the numerous drafts for the abandoned 'à quelques centimètres'.
17. 'ou' circled.
18. Perryman's translation (*Babel*, p. 29):

    the worst
    is dead ahead
    until you
    laugh instead

19. Samuel Beckett, *Molloy*, p. 179; after French *Molloy* (Paris: Éditions de Minuit, 1951), p. 259: 'Si l'on disait la messe des morts pour les vivants?'
20. Entire poem crossed out diagonally; 'dans là' in line five scored through horizontally.
21. Perryman's translation (*Babel*, p. 31):

    the dwarf in his 90th year
    with his very last breath
    grant me at least a bier
    that will fit in death

22. Jean de La Fontaine, *Œuvres Complètes I*, pp. 63–4.

Bibliography

Beckett, Samuel, *Malone Dies* (London: Calder and Boyars, 1958).
Beckett, Samuel, *Malone meurt* (Paris: Éditions de Minuit, 1951).
Beckett, Samuel, *Molloy* (London: John Calder, 1959).
Beckett, Samuel, *Proust and Three Dialogues with Georges Duthuit* (London: Calder and Boyars, 1965).
La Fontaine, Jean de, *Œuvres Complètes I: Fables, Contes et Nouvelles*, ed. René Groos and Jacques Schiffrin (Paris: Gallimard, 1954).
MacDiarmid, Hugh, 'To One Who Urges More Adventurous Flights', in

Michael Grieve and W. R. Aitken (eds), *The Complete Poems of Hugh MacDiarmid* (Harmondsworth: Penguin, 1985), p. 57.

Perryman, Kevin, 'Samuel Beckett, Translated by Kevin Perryman', *Babel*, 6 (1990), pp. 28–31.

Ricks, Christopher, *Beckett's Dying Words* (Oxford: Clarendon Press, 1993).

5.

Pour finir encore: A Manuscript Study

Mary Bryden

One day in the 1930s, Samuel Beckett wrote down in the small, red, battered book now known as the *Whoroscope* notebook (and preserved in the Beckett Collection at University of Reading Library[1]) what seemed to be a definition of the art of translation. It ran as follows: 'Translation: not so loose as paraphrase, nor so close as metaphrase', and after it Beckett wrote in brackets 'Dryden'. It formed part of a number of quotations Beckett copied down in that notebook, taken down from his reading of Samuel Johnson's *The Lives of the English Poets*. Beckett was, of course, deeply interested in Johnson at that time, just as Johnson was deeply interested in Dryden, to whom he devotes more space than to any of the other twenty-four poets covered in the volume. In his analysis, Johnson recognises the dilemmas familiar to any translator: 'When languages are formed upon different principles, it is impossible that the same modes of expression should always be elegant in both. [. . .] Where correspondence cannot be obtained, it is necessary to be content with something equivalent.' And, then, to back this up with the authority of Dryden, he adds: '"Translation, therefore," says Dryden, "is not so loose as paraphrase, nor so close as metaphrase,"' where metaphrase refers to a word-for-word, line-for-line translation, while 'paraphrase', to use Dryden's words, is 'translation with latitude'.[2] This, then, is the sentence that struck Beckett sufficiently to prompt him to copy it down.

Johnson was, however, himself employing a little poetic licence. In presenting the quotation in the way he does, he finds it convenient to imply that the golden mean between paraphrase and metaphrase constitutes a kind of *definition* of translation. Dryden does not in fact use those precise words. He states in his preface to his translation of Virgil that 'The way I have taken is not so strait as metaphrase, nor so loose as paraphrase: some things too I have omitted, and sometimes have added of my own'.[3] In other words, although others may care to extend its applicability, his statement is merely an observation of his own working practice with regard to that text, not of some universally applicable credo. In other words, he talks of the way *he* has taken, and not, as Johnson renders it, of the way upon which any translator must embark.

The reason for drawing attention to this manipulation of Dryden by Johnson is to point out that Dryden's *actual* description is probably closer to Beckett's translating practice than would be the description *imputed* to Dryden. To follow Beckett through different stages of translation drafts is to follow somebody who is meticulously careful, infinitely accommodating of the original, and yet who is able to let go of it if he absolutely must. However, to reach the stage where such decisions can be taken requires enormous energy and motivation. Dryden and Beckett – both word-hypochondriacs – found translating physically draining, and made no secret of it. Dryden begins the preface to his translation of the *Sylvae* by stating: 'For this last half year I have been troubled with the disease [. . .] of translation; the cold prose fits of it, which are always the most tedious with me, were spent in the *History of the League*: the hot, which succeeded them, in this volume of Verse Miscellanies.'[4] Beckett, too, as James Knowlson's recent biography makes clear, could find translation utterly wearying. 'How sick and tired I am of translation,' he wrote to his friend Thomas MacGreevy in 1957, 'and what a losing battle it is always. Wish I had the courage to wash my hands of it all.'[5]

Beckett's case does differ from that of Dryden, however, in that Beckett is translating himself. At least, in a sense he is translating himself. He is translating – either into French or into English – a text generated by a self that existed some months or years previously. As Beckett remarks in the first of his *Texts for Nothing*, 'Yes, I was my father and I was my son.' He concludes the text with the statement 'And this evening again it seems to be working, I'm in my arms, I'm holding myself in my arms, without much tenderness, but faithfully, faithfully'.[6]

That notion of self-embrace, and faithfulness to himself, is applicable to Beckett's self-translation. This is not a slavish faithfulness. Beckett does not hold himself on a semantic leash. The root of the word 'translation' has to do with conveying or transferring from one place to another. In what Gerry Dukes has termed 'Beckett's deracinated condition', something uprooted can actually benefit from breathing a different air in a different soil.[7]

In any case, Beckett's fidelity to himself cannot be judged on the evidence of lexical items alone. When Beckett said to his friend André Bernold that 'J'ai toujours écrit pour une voix' ('I've always written for a voice'), he was not simply discussing his works for stage, radio and television.[8] He was referring to all of his work, including novels, prose and poetry: all of these emerge from words, rhythms, sounds and silences that Beckett had heard before transcribing them.

The task of translating into another language the auditory memories and echoes of a text clearly caused Beckett enormous difficulty. Indeed, in 1957 he wrote to Thomas MacGreevy, speaking of his translation of the play *Fin de partie* into English: 'I find it dreadful in English, all the sharpness gone, and the rhythms.'[9] Yet, despite his reservations, Beckett's sensitivity to rhythm constantly redeems his efforts. Few people listening to the speech rhythms of, for instance, Barry McGovern as Clov in *Endgame* would suspect that the play was not written originally in English.

Certainly the title, *Endgame*, is sharper and starker than the original. This is not always the case. Titles are to some extent special cases. They are attention-grabbing; they have nothing to hide behind. Moreover, in order to accommodate publishers, the target language title should preferably be at the very least suggestive of the source language title. The prose text *Company* simply becomes *Compagnie* in French, just as, among the plays, [Fr] *Catastrophe* becomes [Eng] *Catastrophe*, and *Not I* becomes *Pas Moi*.

In the case of the prose text *Pour finir encore*, the title proves more resistant to transformation, as the manuscripts of all four successive drafts of the translation into English demonstrate.[10] In the French original, the title is an echo of, or a prelude to, the first three words of the text: 'Pour finir encore crâne seul dans le noir.'[11] Beckett's first handwritten translation draft bears no title at all. The reason for this quickly becomes clear, for the first sentence – which will, as it were, generate the title – proves to be immediately productive of dilemma. Beckett begins by writing 'For to end yet again', but suppresses that opening in favour of 'To have done again'. By the second draft, now typewritten, Beckett opts for a third version: 'To end yet again'. This typewritten version, heavily corrected by hand, nevertheless leaves the opening intact. On the strength of that, Beckett writes in by hand afterwards the title 'TO END YET AGAIN'. He has further thoughts, however, at the outset of the following draft, and types the title *For to End Yet Again*, altering the opening words accordingly. This title will remain through to the published version.[12] Over the course of the drafts, therefore, Beckett can be seen to have come full circle, returning to the formula 'for to end yet again' that he used at the very beginning of the translating process. It is a slightly odd, archaic-sounding title in English, but Beckett clearly concluded that it was the best he could achieve.

For to End Yet Again is in any case a text that opens itself only guardedly, revealing a timeless, nameless landscape of dust, greyness and ruin.

The final typewritten draft of the French original occupies 126 typed lines; the length is only slightly reduced in the English translation (121 lines). The text consists of a slowly evolving series of images – a skull, a falling fragment of dust, two white dwarves carrying a litter, halting and then moving off again, ruined elevations, a little body, still but staring, its brilliant blue eyes the only touch of colour in a bleached landscape. These visions sometimes seem to succeed one another by virtue of their own impetus, sometimes to be rewound and edited by a surveying consciousness. It is a curiously hypnotic text, with no paragraphs, and no punctuation other than full stops. It is like an extended prose poem, with a slowly reeling soundtrack of words in often ambiguous collocation.

For Beckett the translation probably represented an absorbing but frustrating enterprise. The first handwritten draft of the translation exhibits a mixture of fluency and uncertainty. Some words recommend themselves on the spot, and survive all redrafts, suggesting that they had already crystallised in Beckett's mind before he set pen to paper. An example of this is his transformation of 'lieu clos' into the phrase 'pent up', thus shifting the emphasis from the space to the being enclosed within that space. A later example is the long white stretcher being manoeuvred by the dwarves. It is covered by a white sheet and, in one manifestation, bears a pillow, to mark the place of the head. A human burden – dead or ailing – is therefore imaginatively present in its own absence. In the original French, the stretcher is referred to as both 'la civière' and 'le brancard à fumier'. In the English translation, however, the object is consistently translated as a 'litter', or 'dunglitter'. Beckett's decisiveness in this instance is probably attributable to his finding pleasing the double meaning of 'litter' (human transport and human detritus), particularly given a context in which dust and ruins are so pervasive.

Other parts of the translation were less straightforwardly arrived at. Where an alternative seems to Beckett immediately preferable, he simply deletes the existing word and replaces it with the new one. This is best seen on the first typewritten version, the most heavily corrected of all. This particular version incorporates no fewer than three stages of correction, the first in a fine black pen, the second in a thicker black pen, and the third in a black ballpoint pen. This can be seen, for example, in the sixth sentence of the piece. In the original French, this reads, 'Se remet donc ainsi à se faire encore pour finir encore le crâne lieu dernier au lieu de s'éteindre'. The first manuscript version simplifies this somewhat, by removing the title phrase 'pour finir encore', perhaps to place more emphasis upon a central opposition between kindling and extinguishing. This version runs, 'Thus then the skull last remaining place starts to kindle again instead of going out'. The first typewritten version, already modified, initially runs, 'So then the skull starts to glimmer again instead of going out'. This is corrected by fine pen to 'Thus then the skull starts to gleam again instead of going out'. In a third version, a heavy pen restores the word 'glimmer', by means of a tick, signifying 'stet', leaving the sentence as 'Thus then the skull starts to glimmer again instead of going out'. This pen has a substitution waiting on the sidelines, however. Beckett is toying with the idea of replacing 'instead of' with 'in lieu', but he pulls back from definitive removal, and keeps 'instead of' on the field. In a fourth and final stage, a black ballpoint amends 'starts' to 'makes', leaving 'Thus then the skull makes to glimmer again instead/in lieu of going out'. By the time of the following draft, 'in lieu' has won the contest with 'instead', and survives to the published version.

Occasionally, if Beckett judges a whole section to have gone badly astray, he will firmly delete several lines and reformulate them immediately afterwards. This is the case, for instance, at the bottom of the second page in the handwritten version, where five and a half lines are deleted. Where he feels a slight dissatisfaction with a passage, but is unsure of how to amend it, he will sometimes underline the relevant words, to remind himself to consider them later. A good example of this is on the second page of the handwritten version, and concerns the passage related to the movement of the dwarves. In many of Beckett's later prose texts that bear some resemblance to *For to End Yet Again* – for instance, *Imagination morte imaginez* and *All Strange Away* – there is a preoccupation with geometrical positioning. (Given his father's profession of quantity surveying, Beckett's first exposure to geodesy was presumably at his side.) In all of these texts there is a kind of urgency attached to situating bodies in space, in relation to each other, to the light or to other proximate features of the landscape. In pursuit of this exactitude, Beckett will often give the precise calibrations or measurements involved. This raises the issue of cross-cultural equivalents. In the relevant passage of the French original, one of the dwarf brancardiers is said to be slanting to the north, or to some other cardinal point, while the other faces 'vers l'antipode' (i.e. in a diametrically opposite position). Then, in the projection of the viewer, the aspiration is expressed: 'Que l'un s'arrête et autour de ce pivot que l'autre fasse faire à la civière deux cents grades.'

This is translated in the handwritten first draft: 'Let one stop dead and the other about this pivot swing the litter through an arc of one hundred and eighty degrees.' The latter part of the sentence – that dealing with the measurement – is underlined, to stimulate further reflection. Beckett has not recalibrated the angle in transforming 'deux cents grades' into 'one hundred and eighty degrees'. Rather, between French and English, he has made the transition from the metric system to the sexagesimal system, more commonly used in English-speaking contexts.[13] Since a grade is equal to a hundredth of a quadrant, then two hundred grades equals half the circumference of a circle. Therefore, a grade is equal to nine-tenths of a degree, and a semicircle is equivalent to either two hundred grades or one hundred and eighty degrees. As far as the mathematics is concerned, Beckett's translation is correct, as would be expected. Yet Beckett probably hesitated over the conversion, since 'grade' has a multiplicity of other meanings in English. On the other hand, 'one hundred and eighty degrees' is a little too cumbersomely precise even for Beckett's finely tuned mathematical enthusiasms. Further pondering causes Beckett to write at the top of that page 'cause the litter to inscribe a semicircle'. Although the verb will vary in later versions – changing from 'inscribe' to 'swing' and finally to 'slew' – the 'semicircle' solution (clearly perceived as the best compromise) persists through to the published text.

Beckett's translation drafts reveal that, normally, he worked sequentially. That is to say, he opted for an initial draft, before altering, adding or omitting. Rarely does he allow two alternatives to hang unresolved in the air. Occasionally, however, this does occur, when Beckett finds himself unable to decide between two words whose candidatures are equally pressing. One notable example of this is the translation of the phrase 'lieu dernier'. 'Dernier' is a key word in Beckett's writing, which is always approaching the last, but never getting further than the penultimate. It occurs often in this text, in which extinction is always just out of reach. Beckett seems to feel in his initial translation that 'last' is too insignificant or peremptory a word to allow of the lingering-despite-itself that he wants to suggest. He therefore adopts the formula of 'last remaining place'. 'Remaining' is probably also attractive to him because of the association of 'remains' with 'ruins' and 'dust', and perhaps also because of the slight oxymoronic flavour obtained by combining the ingredients of 'last' (i.e. almost gone) and 'remaining' (not gone). In the first typescript, however, Beckett seems to develop a distaste for the blend. While 'last' is retained, 'remaining' acquires brackets. It is still in play, but is demoted. Subsequently, it is crossed out altogether, and Beckett's thin black pen installs the phrase 'last place left'. However, 'left' too will be a casualty; perhaps Beckett fears confusion with 'left' as opposed to 'right'. His final solution is 'last place of all', and this remains to co-resonate with its sister phrase 'last change of all'.

The translation Beckett is striving for – and achieves – is, like its original, characterised by a plain and austere style that is nevertheless dense, and intensely poetic. The chosen lexical items are sober and stark; few of them draw attention to themselves other than as constituents of a whole. These are bony words, bleached of colour, hard and reliable, hooking on to each other to obtain extension in space. It is noticeable that Beckett is careful to remove any glittery words, or words that seem incongruously archaic. Hence, the skull's 'gleam' is snuffed to a 'glimmer', and the litter said to be 'betwixt' the dwarves is subsequently said to be 'between' them. Similarly, the phrase 'à l'infini', initially rendered as the somewhat esoteric word 'bourne' ('bourne upon bourne'), is altered to 'verge upon verge'. As well as being a more common word, 'verge' suggests a beyond, a horizon, while 'bourne' focuses more upon limits, or boundaries. 'Bourne' also has the unfortunate property of being a homophone of 'born': the past participle of the verb denoting, in Beckettian terms, the original sin *par excellence*.

Mention of homophony recalls the primacy of sound in Beckett's writing. Many of Beckett's substitutions throughout these drafts appear to derive not only from a desire for simplicity, a desire to say more with less, but also from a sensitivity to rhythms and durations. Thus, 'undimmed' becomes 'bright', 'depresses the dust' becomes 'stirs the dust', and 'as chance will' becomes 'driftless'. In a longer phrase, 'tantôt à l'avant tantôt à l'arrière au gré des permutations' is rendered first clumsily as 'now fore now aft depending on permutations', and then, more gracefully, as 'now fore now aft as permutations will' (finally coming to rest in the – in my view less successful – 'now fore now aft as permutations list'). One sentence that was recurrently productive of difficulty was that which in the original French read: 'Mêlés à la poussière vont s'enlisant les débris du refuge dont bon nombre déjà n'affleurent plus qu'à peine'. This is a complex sentence by any standards, with its minglings, sinkings, enumerations and qualifications. At first, Beckett struggles to incorporate all the semantic elements: 'Sinking mingled with the dust many already only barely emergent the debris of the refuge'. The first typescript modification cannot be said to be an improvement: 'Sinking slowly mingled with the dust the ruins of the refuge many already only just emerging'. In a heavier pen, Beckett later considers, in a marginal note, replacing 'only just emerging' with the further undermined 'almost [later changed to 'all but'] gone'. In the penultimate typescript, the sentence is still in transition, being the most heavily corrected of all. In its corrected form (at top of page), it reads: 'Mingling with the dust slowly sinking some almost sunk the ruins of the refuge'. The final typescript adds one more meticulous qualification – the word 'quite' – to bring the text into accordance with its published version: 'Mingling with the dust slowly sinking some almost quite sunk the ruins of the refuge'. The lengthy process has resulted in the incorporation, with maximum economy, of all the essential elements of the original French. Moreover, by means of the addition of the adverb 'slowly', Beckett has been able to acknowledge the gradual movement implicit in the verb 's'enliser': a slow engulfment, rather than the collapse that a verb such as 'sombrer' or 's'affaisser' would denote.

Studying these drafts closely brings home to the reader the extent of Beckett's commitment to his translations, as well as an understanding of why he could sometimes view them as deeply debilitating exercises. Beckett's concentration is on the one hand directed to the micro-level. One sentence in the final version of *For to End Yet Again* reads: 'First change of all in the end a fragment comes away and falls. With slow fall for so dense a body it lights like cork on water and scarce breaks the surface.' The strength and intensity of that image derives from nothing more substantial than the shedding of a tiny particle. Momentous inconsequence. But particles are heavy for Beckett, whether they be grammatical particles (conjunctions, prepositions, prefixes, suffixes) or imagistic ones. Like physical particles, they are the prime matter for the genesis of his text.

Beyond the micro-level, however, Beckett is also attentive to wider patterns and echoes within the text as a whole. Sometimes, whole sentences must be read aloud in order to appreciate the aural dynamic that Beckett was striving to create amid his semantic concerns. One subtle but important element of the landscape evoked in *Pour finir encore* is its slightly unreal or magical quality. Indeed, the word 'magique' occurs as early as the seventh sentence, as the hour of dawn is evoked: 'S'y leve enfin soudain ou peu à peu et magique s'y maintient un jour de plomb'. This becomes in the final version: 'There in the end all at once or by degrees there dawns and magic lingers a leaden dawn' (incidentally, both French and English magically achieving the same number of words in each sentence). Beckett chooses at first to revert to the magical referent later in the English translation. In doing so, he adds and develops rather than translates, since the French original, hinged upon the word 'malin', attributes keen sight, not second sight, to the putative viewer. The original runs: 'Bien malin l'oeil capable de le déceler désormais mêlé aux ruines mêlées à la poussière sous un ciel déserté par ses charognards'. Beckett at first renders this as: 'Wizard he whose eye shall discern him now mingled with the ruins mingled with the dust beneath a sky forsaken of its vultures'. The 'wizard eye' here is a clear echo of the earlier necromantic suggestion. At this point, however, something very interesting happens. Perhaps Beckett laid the text aside for a day or two and then came back to it. It was, after all, just before Christmas 1975 when he was working on this translation. Perhaps, conscious of the year's end approaching, he had other demands on his time. Certainly, James Knowlson has confirmed that Beckett cannot have been working uninterruptedly on the translation, since his diary does show various meetings and a medical appointment around this time. Whatever the reason, Beckett is suddenly put in mind, not of fantasyscapes and the magic eye of wizards, but of biblical images of deserts and bone-strewn landscapes.

Early in the text, the 'grey timeless air' of *For to End Yet Again* is established as being 'of those nor for God nor for his enemies'. Yet Beckett's vision of the dusty ruins under a forsaken sky suddenly chimes in his consciousness with allied panoramas invoked in the Old Testament. On the last page of the handwritten draft, near the phrase 'sky forsaken of its vultures', Beckett writes in the margin a biblical reference, 'Isa. vii. 16'. This verse, in the King James translation familiar to Beckett from his Protestant upbringing, reads: 'For before the child shall know to refuse the evil, and choose the good, the land that thou abhorrest shall be forsaken of both her kings'. The child referred to is the one mentioned two verses earlier in that well-known passage that so often forms part of Advent and Christmas liturgies: 'A virgin shall conceive, and bear a son, and shall call his name Immanuel'. These verses form part of the succession of so-called Emmanuel oracles delivered by the prophet Isaiah, and here addressed to King Ahaz, threatened by the invading forces of the Kings of Israel and Syria. The prophet's tragic monotone, which is alternately stern and tender, and elegantly sustained throughout the Book of Isaiah, is perhaps perceived most resonantly in the King James translation, and it is here that the word 'forsaken' appears.

What is interesting here is the fact that, even while deeply immersed in the minutiae of translation, Beckett was not immune to intertextual echoes – in this case, with the Bible. What is open to conjecture is whether Isaiah's visions of parched lands and fallen empires was always present, even at a subliminal level, within Beckett's perception of the piece, or whether they were elicited by the trigger-word 'forsaken'. The latter scenario is quite feasible, given that 'forsaken' is not a common verb in English, and that the verb used in the French original – 'déserté' – is not used in the most commonly used French biblical translations of the corresponding Isaiah passage, where the operative word would normally be 'dévasté' or 'abandonné'. If Beckett did visualise the devastated, dusty scene as in some way touched by the light of expectancy rather than that of apocalypse, then perhaps the notion of ending is a little more relegated or deferred than before.

What is certain, however, is that the sentence that emerges from

Beckett's brimming wastepaper bin is a noteworthy one. The final version (with the wizard dematerialised) reads: 'Eagle the eye that shall discern him now mingled with the ruins mingling with the dust beneath a sky forsaken of its scavengers'. If Beckett was at some level responding to, or remembering, the beauty of the Emmanuel oracles, then the resulting sureness of his translation, with its harmonious cadences suspended between the eagle at the outset and the scavengers at the close, does seem worthy of anything to be found within the King James translation.

The above example raises the possibility of a text acquiring additional 'meanings' during the process of translation. At other times, a reverse or retrospective hermeneutics may apply, for comparisons of tried and discarded versions of the translation can often, if not resolve ambiguities (for ambiguities are often to be welcomed), then at least suggest other ways of reading. An example of this is the third sentence of the piece, which in the French reads: 'Crâne donc pour finir seul dans le noir le vide sans cou ni traits seule la boîte lieu dernier dans le noir le vide'. The published English translation reads: 'For to end yet again skull alone in the dark the void no neck no face just the box last place of all in the dark the void'. The dominant images in both cases are: skull; dark; void (no neck or face); box. Yet what is the box? Is the skull in a box, ready to jump out, like Worm in *The Unnamable*, who speaks of 'this gnawing of termites in my Punch and Judy box'?[14] Or is it perhaps on top of the box, like Worm's head, who sometimes confuses himself with the jar he lives in?[15]

The draft translations, however, point to the interchangeability of the skull and the box. The skull *is* a kind of box: a box to keep the brain in, a container for the teeming mind. Hence, the first draft translates 'boîte' as 'pan': 'no neck no face just the pan'. Nevertheless, in the first typewritten draft, the word begins to worry Beckett. 'Brainpan' is straightforward enough. Indeed, Beckett was quite fond of the word, using it in *The Unnamable* as the site of possibility: 'a brainpan where anything may happen'.[16] The disadvantage of the word 'brainpan' is that it is perhaps too distractingly colloquial; on the other hand, 'pan' provokes unwelcome images of cooking. Crossing out 'pan', Beckett first replaces it with 'case', then reinstates 'pan', and then adds 'chamber'. Yet 'chamber' is more suggestive of space or hollowness than of casing or enclosure.

The dilemma persists in the next draft. Beckett has determined upon 'case', and types it within the body of the text. However, his irresolute pen deletes it in favour of 'brainbox'. Finally, the word 'brain' is crossed out, leaving the simple 'box' that the French original suggests. In French, 'la boîte' is possibly more readily associated with 'la boîte du crâne' than is 'box' with 'brainbox' in English. Nevertheless, *faute de mieux*, Beckett the drafter errs on the side of vaguening rather than precision.

It is thanks to Beckett's retention of so many drafts of his completed work that these glimpses of compositional dilemmas can be afforded to the reader. Moreover, their physical existence draws into question the complex relationship between 'original' and 'translation'. Implicitly or explicitly, such a question must repeatedly have posed itself to Beckett, particularly when, as was the case for instance with the translation of the 1946 novel *Mercier et Camier* (completed nearly thirty years later), many years had elapsed since the original text had been written.

To return to Dryden's paradigm, it is clear that, if the sample text-set of *Pour finir encore* is symptomatic of Beckett's translating practice elsewhere – and the rigour of its genesis is certainly replicated in many other manuscript examples – then neither of the terms 'metaphrase' and 'paraphrase' can be considered applicable. Neither can their accompanying adjectives – respectively, 'close' and 'loose' – for the former implies slavishness, while the latter implies a casualness at odds with the tension that these labour-intensive drafts exhibit. Yet to search for a third concept, synthesising elements of both, would be unproductive. The fact that Beckett often experienced the process of translation as stressful indicates that there is no easy accommodation between two imperatives: that of a completed source-language text, finely tuned in a particular linguistic and semantic context, and that of a potential target-language text which must acknowledge its predecessor, while still achieving an independent existence in a different cultural and chronological zone.

Perhaps, in the case of a writer so attuned to the auditory medium – to music, sound, silence and rhythm – the best that can be said is that Beckett's source-language and target-language texts are like musical impulses scored for different instruments, or in different keys. Patrick Bowles, who assisted Beckett in 1953 with the translation of *Molloy* into English, has recourse to the musical metaphor in describing the process:

> Every day we revised a few pages, pen in hand, but debating virtually every word. Occasionally Beckett would throw the cat among the chickens by saying, 'Give it a bit of rhythm.' That could mean re-casting an entire paragraph. One could not just inject a drumbeat into one phrase alone. It had to play its part in the paragraph. Every night, not much sleep, retyping the day's work.[17]

It was an exhausting process, but Bowles concludes: 'Without care, one loses touch with one's self.'[18]

Following the stages of Beckett's translations makes clear the extent of that care. Beckett once jotted down in his *Whoroscope* notebook the phrase 'a sentence that deserves to be translated into a dead language'. Like music, Beckett's translating activity is never deathly or automated. It is always organic, which is why he finds it so difficult to control. Johnson forces a compromise upon Dryden by stating that 'where correspondence cannot be obtained, it is necessary to be content with something equivalent'. The idea of 'equivalence' is difficult to reconcile with Beckett's translations, which do not simply 'equal', or 'come to the same thing as', their source-texts. By maintaining that translations are neither one thing nor another, Dryden allows the dynamism and unpredictability of the process to remain in play. So, too, does Beckett. His translations have elements of both recreation and re-creation (though this is careful play, not carnival). Beckett's *Pour finir encore* and *For to End Yet Again* are siblings, but with independent lives.

Notes

1. UoR MS 3000.
2. Samuel Johnson, *The Lives of the English Poets*, p. 309; John Dryden, *Essays of John Dryden*, Vol. 1, p. 237.
3. Dryden, *Essays of John Dryden*, Vol. 2, p. 227.
4. Dryden, *Essays of John Dryden*, Vol. 1, p. 251.
5. Quoted in James Knowlson, *Damned to Fame*, p. 438.
6. Samuel Beckett, *Collected Shorter Prose*, p. 74.
7. Gerry Dukes, 'The Word Become Spirit', p. 42.
8. Quoted in André Bernold, *L'Amitié de Beckett*, p. 107.
9. Quoted in Knowlson, *Damned to Fame*, p. 438.
10. See University of Reading Library MSS 1551/2–5.
11. Beckett, *Pour finir encore*, p. 9.
12. Beckett, *Collected Shorter Prose*, pp. 179–82.
13. Nevertheless, I recently came across a letter to *The Times* in 1968 – some years before *Pour finir encore* – in which the correspondent wrote: 'May I make a plea that the makers of theodolites cease producing circles marked in the sexagesimal system and use the metric system – that is, divide a right angle into 100 grades?' (*The Times*, 24 June 1968, p. 25).
14. Beckett, *Three Novels*, p. 342.
15. Ibid. p. 343.
16. Ibid. p. 363.
17. Patrick Bowles, 'How to Fail', pp. 24–5.
18. Ibid. p. 25.

Bibliography

Beckett, Samuel, *Collected Shorter Prose 1945–1980* (London: John Calder, 1984).

Beckett, Samuel, *Pour finir encore, et autres foirades* (Paris: Éditions de Minuit, 1976).

Beckett, Samuel, *Three Novels by Samuel Beckett* (London: John Calder, 1959).

Bernold, André, *L'Amitié de Beckett* (Paris: Hermann, 1992).

Bowles, Patrick, 'How to Fail: Notes on Talks with Samuel Beckett', *PN Review*, 20.4 (March–April 1994), pp. 24–38.

Dryden, John, *Essays of John Dryden*, ed. W. P. Ker, 2 vols (Oxford: Clarendon, 1926).

Dukes, Gerry, 'The Word Become Spirit', *The Irish Times*, 5 October 1996, p. 42.

Johnson, Samuel, *The Lives of the English Poets: The Works of Samuel Johnson*, Vol. 7 (London: W. Pickering, 1829).

Knowlson, James, *Damned to Fame: The Life of Samuel Beckett* (London: Bloomsbury, 1996).

6.

Dates and Difficulties in Beckett's *Whoroscope* Notebook

John Pilling

When Yeats spoke of 'the fascination of what's difficult' he had in mind 'theatre business, management of men'.[1] For students of Joyce and Beckett the phrase irresistibly summons up their notebooks, and in Beckett's case the most 'difficult' instance is his so-called *Whoroscope* notebook, so called because he has scored the title of his first separately published work (1930) deep into its front board. Its *front* board I said, but in saying so a difficulty immediately arises. One thinks of this board as the front one because of the 'title' on it; but the notebook has two front boards, having been written in from both ends towards the middle, albeit with more material in what (for convenience's sake) I shall continue to refer to as the 'front end' of this inverted pantomime-horse.

Something of the 'doubleness' of the *Whoroscope* notebook is graphically embodied in the only 'doodle' or graffito it contains: the skeletal figure apparently walking away from us on the back end-paper, but with head half-turned round looking back at us, an image upside-down for anyone using this notebook from the 'back'. This image is an early anticipation of 'Dante's damned' as remembered by Dan and Maddy Rooney in *All That Fall* (1957) who move 'arsy-versy', and the *Whoroscope* notebook figure is at once 'arsy' and 'versy' at both the literal and figurative levels. I presume this image must date from the 1930s, as everything at all datable in the notebook certainly does, and most probably from about the time of the composition of *Murphy*, between September 1935 and July 1936, around which dates much of the material found in the notebook clusters. But there is of course no firm evidence for this supposition; inference has taken over to remove a difficulty, which retains its 'fascination', irrespective of its intractability.

With the specifically *Murphy*-related material in the notebook – by which I mean the numbered items at the 'front' end, and the items headed 'FOR INTERPOLATION' at the other – we can fairly confidently invoke the known limit dates of the composition of the novel, with the numbered sections presumably taking precedence, given that you can hardly interpolate material into something that does not already substantially exist, even if it is not yet – as indeed the notion of interpolation indicates – actually complete. Prospective dates in this connection, then – or rather in these separated connections – are late summer/early autumn 1935 for the numbered items, and late winter/spring of 1936 for the items to be (as in fact most were *not*) interpolated, given Beckett's known difficulties of composition in early 1936 after a fairly fruitful four months at the end of 1935. In saying as much of the latter, however, one is bound to remain uneasily aware that Beckett may have set his sights on what was in due course to become *Murphy* as much as two or three years earlier, when it was beginning to dawn on him that no publisher (at home or abroad) would take on *Dream of Fair to Middling Women* (complete, with 'missing parts', by July 1932) and as he elected to compromise with a book of short stories, *More Pricks Than Kicks* (1934). The short form neither promised nor in the event gave Beckett any satisfaction; despite his very recognition of the demands made by 'ars longa',[2] it was the long form that remained his aim, which was one reason – perhaps the most important reason – why the short stories were 'all jigsaw',[3] mechanical exercises in interconnectedness all of them, such that they could almost be read (as indeed they have subsequently been read, though Beckett never thought of them as such) as a novel *manqué*.

The disconnected jottings of the *Whoroscope* notebook – necessarily disconnected, because it is not the job of the notebook to supply the continuity – were for the most part entered there with some connective purpose in mind. In saying as much I deliberately intend a contrast between them and the more obviously continuous entries in the *Dream* notebook which Beckett kept in 1931 and 1932, and which he may have begun even earlier, in 1930. The continuities or 'blocks' of the *Dream* notebook suffer atomisation in the frantic randomness of the 'novel' for which they supply so much raw material. The already atomised material of the *Whoroscope* notebook naturally cannot supply any fuel for the very different enterprise of *Murphy* unless some connective material – not the kind of stuff that finds its way into notebooks – can also be found outside the closed circle, or flurry of monads. The differential character of the *Whoroscope* notebook (as against the *Dream* notebook) suggests, to this reader at least, a change of tack on Beckett's part, perhaps the first such change to take into account what would later become his habit of never repeating the form, however doomed to repetition the content might be. At the very least, in 1935 – having effectively 'moved' to London and having been exposed to much more 'real' life than *Dream* could ever have accommodated – the image of a

Beckett moving forward, naturally enough with eyes and a head stubbornly turned half-round to look back at the past, seems to make a kind of sense beyond any of the bedevilling, however fascinating, business of date 'identifications' we can never resolve into a packagable 'neatness'.

This line of thinking can be furthered by emphasising that the *Whoroscope* notebook contains only two actual dates, although to say as much is to be reminded that the *Dream* notebook contains none at all. The two dates in question are themselves differential in character, however: one (4/12/35) is to an article by Dean Inge in the London *Evening Standard* entitled 'Enemies of Life', which we can presume Beckett kept as a pull-out (the article seeks to combat suicidal impulses by offering reasons for going on living) long after the newspaper was wrapping up fish dinners. (He seems to have done something similar with the newspaper, the *Daily Sketch*, in which he first encountered the photograph of the two chimpanzees playing chess, or with the German illustrated magazine in which it reappeared, as mentioned in a letter to George Reavey, 'months' after Beckett had first seen it.[4] And it seems probable that it was the same kind of instinct which prompted Beckett to stick two newspaper clippings in French into the notebook proper.) The Inge date, the first of the two dates in the *Whoroscope* notebook, may not be much more than an aide-mémoire, although it may also have been a kind of benchmark from which to measure progress forwards, an important concern if Beckett was harbouring any suicidal impulses of the sort that surface in *Dream*, notably with Nemo,[5] though Belacqua rather ominously locates the 'modus Vivendi' at 'the dead point'[6] and only just conquers the problem of being left '[m]arooned on the bridge and far from shelter' in the final tableau of the novel.[7] The second of the two dates – Germany 2/10/36 – seems to stem rather from a need to record some progress already achieved, as if movement away from misery in Dublin in the direction of something quite other might be a good in itself. In the event, however, the German trip, undertaken at least in part in the hope of 'whispering the turmoil down' (as 'Assumption' (1929) describes the condition)[8], proved a vain endeavour. Beckett had only succeeded in moving towards another set of miserable circumstances, as he was obliged to admit ruefully in a letter to Mary Manning Howe of 13 December 1936 from Berlin: 'It has turned out indeed to be a journey *from*, not *to*, as I knew it was, before I began it.'[9]

Any specific date presupposes an implied continuity which necessitates specification in the first place, and the fact that the only two dates here are in a successive relationship chronologically speaking seems to point unavoidably to the most mundanely commonsensical of insights, namely that the bulk of the entries at the 'front' end of the notebook were made over a relatively restricted period of time, and in the order in which they appear. This is effectively confirmed by the fact that there are entries made during the six months in Germany which can be matched up with equivalent material in the extensive diary entries that Beckett kept during this time, although there are naturally no smooth sequences in the notebook, and inevitably one or two sudden disruptions which may indicate an intermittent or prolonged suspension of notebook-jotting. When, as here, the material must *post*-date the version of *Murphy* first sent to publishers in July 1936, the issue seems hardly to matter much. However, when – at the point just before the well-known Mauthner entries, to be found midway into the notebook – Beckett brackets material from Céline ahead of them, and after them (a few pages later) leaves unidentified two entries which must have been taken directly from Jean-Paul Sartre's first publication, *L'Imagination* (1936), the dating game comes engagingly alive. Beckett could not have read Céline's *Bagatelles pour un massacre* before 28 December 1937, the date of its publication in Paris. Having (perhaps not very surprisingly) failed to find the much better-known *Voyage au bout de la nuit* in the Dublin bookshops in the months after its Paris publication in late 1932,[10] any interest Beckett retained in Céline could obviously only be prosecuted on the Continent. Late 1937 found him, by good fortune if not necessarily much forward planning, back in Paris after six months of German *Angst* and then more than six months of distress in Dublin. How much less likely it was – given Céline's fame and indeed his increasing notoriety – that Beckett could ever have come across in Dublin *L'Imagination*, a book with very limited distribution by a philosopher of a (Husserl-inspired) phenomenological bent, later of course to be world famous, but in the mid-1930s known only to the *cognoscenti* of the Left Bank and the Latin Quarter.

Nothing better illustrates Beckett's catholicity of interests in the *Whoroscope* notebook than the pages in which he moves from Céline's *Bagatelles* (on this evidence trifles indeed) through Mauthner's *Beiträge* (a much more substantial obstacle), and then on to Sartre and at about the same time the philosophy of Immanuel Kant (arguably an even more demanding figure than Mauthner). The trajectory reflects a Beckettian tendency throughout the *Whoroscope* notebook to treat ideas – especially ideas developed in an elaborate and systematic manner – as of more potential importance than mere literary snippets, useful as these might be in the production of a novel priding itself on being a contribution to literature, rather than simply a commodity in a crowded marketplace. No doubt Beckett saw, as others had done, the curve of Céline's career from *Voyage* and *Mort à crédit* to pamphleteering and anti-Semitic rhetoric as something from which the higher reaches of philosophy might supply relief, if not necessarily a lasting remedy. In a world lurching irreversibly towards war, and war with Germany, Beckett turned towards the greatest of Enlightenment philosophers, and towards his dauntingly colourless and difficult German prose.

The Kant entries (each one given a Roman volume number and an Arabic page number) are to be found interspersed among the predominantly 'block' entries of Mauthner – the Mauthner/Kant chemistry helping Beckett to create the poem 'ainsi a-t'on beau', probably written in the summer of 1938 – and are from volume 11 of the *Complete Works* of Kant as published in Berlin in the early 1920s by the firm of Bruno Cassirer. Beckett told MacGreevy in a letter of 5 January 1938 (two days before the stabbing incident in the Avenue d'Orléans) that 'the entire works' of Kant had just arrived from Munich, and in the months that followed he obviously took on the challenge of a multi-volume set printed in Gothic lettering with something of the commitment he typically brought to other projects of a similarly demanding nature (the life of Johnson, for example, the primary research focus of the April–October return to Dublin in 1937). These notebook entries are not, however, taken directly from the works of Kant, but rather from the classic 'Life and Work' study of Kant by the great philosopher Ernst Cassirer, which occupies the eleventh and last volume of the set. In the difficult early months of 1938 in Paris – Beckett was obliged to return to the hospital for regular check-ups, he was short of money and in need of finding an apartment that would lessen the expense of hotels, and he was moving cautiously back into the Joyce circle though reluctant to become too dependent on it for support and/or inspiration – Beckett turned first to Kant, famous for his exemplary devotion to a routine and ordered lifestyle, and for having seen no reason to disturb it by leaving his native Königsberg. The contrast between Kant and himself must have provoked a wry smile on the part of Beckett; the gulf between Kant's life of settled purpose and his own career of chaotic randomness could hardly have been greater. So 'antinomial' was this encounter between two very unkindred spirits that it is difficult to reconstruct what Beckett thought he might achieve by it, although the implicit narrative told by the notebook is a turning away (perhaps in distaste) from Céline – who was nevertheless to remain a powerful influence stylistically and expressively – towards much more abstruse, but perhaps much more consolingly abstract, matters of permanent philosophic interest, unconditioned by the hard political realities of a troubled time.

The Céline-Mauthner-Sartre-Kant-Cassirer pages of the *Whoroscope* notebook cannot, of their very nature, tell the inner history of Beckett's psyche in late 1937/early 1938, although they tell more perhaps than one might expect from such impersonal material. They may or may not imply that, amidst what inevitably looks like randomness to us, there are other continuities masked from view as of now, and possibly forever. The 'difficult' thing in an area like this is when you move off-road, off the map, or – to shift to a much older cliché – when you try to change horses in mid-stream. Not even a given, demonstrated continuity guarantees that there will be others, or indeed any other. The notebook that presumes an external ordering factor which it cannot include – a novel to write, or a need to begin another creative enterprise – is always incommensurable with and within itself, hence its capacity to frustrate, even as it fascinates.

Addenda: Extracts from the *Whoroscope* Notebook (UoR MS 3000)

Significant entries from the notebook are given in bold, followed by a brief commentary. The Mauthner material is found between [verso 91] and [recto 116].

Verso 91

boîte à sperme

Derived from Louis-Ferdinand Céline, *Bagatelles pour un massacre* (Paris: Denoël and Steele, 1937), p. 106. Deirdre Bair (*Samuel Beckett: A Biography*, pp. 275–6) states that Beckett read Céline's earlier diatribe *Mea Culpa* (published by Denoël and Steele on 28 December 1936) on returning to Paris from Dublin in late 1937, citing it as information received from Peggy Guggenheim. But in a letter of 15 June 1937 to George Reavey from 6 Clare St, Dublin (Harry Ransom Humanities Research Center) Beckett thanks Reavey for sending *Mea Culpa*, which suggests that Peggy Guggenheim may have confused the two Céline titles.

Céphalo Bill
Toutvabienovich

Céline, p. 108. There is no evidence that Beckett read beyond this point in *Bagatelles pour un massacre*.

Verso 97

Kant's exact description of Westminster Bridge (having never set foot outside Prussia) – vol. XI, p. 45

In the passage corresponding to the German original in James Haden's translation of Ernst Cassirer, *Kant's Life and Thought*, this occurs on p. 46. It is on Westminster Bridge that Arsene meets, or claims he has met, Mr Ash in *Watt* (written 1942–1945; published 1953).

"Gibt mir Materie, ich will eine Welt daraus bauen"
'Give me matter, and I will build a world' (Haden trans., p. 46).

Recto 103
das fruchtbare Bathos der Erfahrung
Haden trans., p. 162: 'the fertile lowland of experience'. The phrase reappears in the 'Addenda' to *Watt*. The next item in the notebook is a kind of aide-mémoire: **Bathos = deep (Gr.) !**

Verso 117
omnis determinatio est negatio
Haden trans., p. 211: 'negation is the determining factor/delineation of everything' or 'the limit (or end, or boundary) of everything is negation'. This Latin phrase is also found in the 'Science and Laboratory' notebook (UoR), dating from after 30 October 1936. Beckett would have first encountered this Spinozan dictum in W. R. Inge, *Christian Mysticism* (London: Methuen, 1899, and many times reprinted), p. 121, footnote 1.

ens originarium, ens summum, ens entium
Haden trans., pp. 211–12: 'originary being, highest being, being of beings'.

His rare imperatives were hypothetical (cf. Kant XI, 161)
Haden trans., pp. 234, 245–6, 248.

short stories antinomial
Cassirer speaks (Haden trans., p. 249) of 'the antinomy between freedom and causality'. An 'antinomy' is a logically impossible conclusion derived from an apparently correct proof, but in Kant it means a contradiction resolved by one statement applying to things as they appear to us (*phenomena*) and the other statement applying to things as they are in themselves (*noumena*). Beckett's critical attitude towards the short-story form is apparent in a number of letters of 1933 to Thomas MacGreevy previous to the publication in 1934 of *More Pricks Than Kicks*, which Beckett thought of as 'stories'.

Recto 118
Socrates' [erasure]
TI EOTI (Kant XI 294)
Transformed by Aristotle into
TO TI nv EIVAI (Do; 295)
Haden trans., p. 276: 'the problem of the concept is transformed into the problem of teleology'. Beckett's letter-card to Joyce supplying him with three Greek items for possible use in *Finnegans Wake* is reproduced in facsimile in Patricia Hutchins, *James Joyce's World*, p. 169.

Verso 123
Leibniz to Locke:
"Nihil in intellectu quod non prius fuerit in sensu, <u>nisi ipse intellectus</u>."
Beckett has taken this famous notion – the phrase translates as 'Nothing can be in the intellect that was not first in the senses, except the intellect itself', and occurs in a form mangled by the parrot in *Malone Dies* – from Jean-Paul Sartre, *L'Imagination*, Paris: Alcan, 1936 (Paris: PUF edition, 1948, 16, 18), a book which he probably purchased in Paris in late 1937/early 1938, and which he kept in his personal library until his death. An Italian version of the phrase occurs in the 1929 essay 'Dante... Bruno. Vico.. Joyce' (*Disjecta*, p. 24), where it is dubbed 'the Scholastics' axiom', and there is a passage from Mauthner, Vol. 2, p. 477, quoted in the notebook, which adapts it to apply to the strengths and weaknesses of Kant's thinking.

noème, noèse
Sartre (*L'Imagination*, p. 51) derives both terms from Husserl; the first refers to the object of thought, the second to the act of thought.

the <u>geology</u> of conscience – Cambrian experience, Cainozoic judgments, etc . . .
Sartre (*L'Imagination*, pp. 141, 144ff) speaks of a 'géometrie' in Husserl; Beckett is using 'conscience' in the French sense, to mean sensibility.

The two actual dates in the notebook are:

Verso 51
The wise man . . . will not marry the sister of a bleeder (Dean Inge: E.S. 4/12/35)
This is from the article 'Enemies of Life' by 'The Very Rev W R Inge D D' on p. 7 of the London *Evening Standard* of the date given. There is of course a female 'bleeder' in *Watt*.

Recto 66
Germany 2/10/36-
This is found opposite **Kraft durch FREUDE** on verso 67, a phrase also found in German diary 1, entry for 24 November 1936, and in a letter to Thomas MacGreevy of 28 November 1936.

Between recto 106 and verso 109 of the notebook Beckett copies out a long passage from volume 2, pp. 644–5 of Fritz Mauthner's *Beiträge zu einer Kritik der Sprache* (Leipzig: Felix Meiner, 1923), which on 107 contains the word 'Eiszeiten' (i.e. 'ice-ages'), and the next short entry (no page number is given, but it is taken from p. 648 of Mauthner's second volume) reads: **a generation of oaks.** In the French poem of (June/July?) 1938 'ainsi a-t-on beau', lines six to nine read:

> les périodes glaciaires n'apportant rien de neuf
> la grande chaleur du treizième de leur ère
> sur Lisbonne fumante Kant froidement penché
> rêver en generations de chênes et oublier son père

A peculiar connection between the first line of the third of the French poems ('être là sans mâchoires sans dents') and a repeated phrase in the four typewritten pages of Mauthner material at TCD (MS 10971/5) – 'bissen sich der Scholastiker daran die Zähne aus . . . ein Theologe mit ausgebissenen Zähne' (from Mauthner, Vol. 2, p. 474) – raises the intriguing possibility that in his poem Beckett is paying oblique homage to Mauthner's critique of metaphors and false analogies. The German phrases literally mean '[he/they] wore their *teeth* out' (my italics), but they are both understood (metaphorically) to mean '[he/they] got nowhere'.

Notes

1. W. B. Yeats, 'The Fascination of What's Difficult', p. 38.
2. Samuel Beckett, *Dream of Fair to Middling Women*, p. 168.
3. Beckett, letter to Thomas MacGreevy of 22 June 1933.
4. Beckett, letter to George Reavey of 13 November 1936.
5. Beckett, *Dream*, pp. 182–4.
6. Ibid. p. 27.
7. Ibid. p. 241.
8. Beckett, 'Assumption', p. 3.
9. Beckett, letter to Mary Manning Howe of 13 December 1936.
10. Beckett, letter to Thomas MacGreevy of 23 April 1933.

Bibliography

Bair, Deirdre, *Samuel Beckett: A Biography* (London: Jonathan Cape, 1978).

Beckett, Samuel, 'Assumption', in S. E. Gontarski (ed.), *Samuel Beckett: The Complete Short Prose, 1929–1989* (New York: Grove Press, 1995), pp. 3–7.

Beckett, Samuel, 'Dante... Bruno. Vico.. Joyce', in Ruby Cohn (ed.), *Disjecta: Miscellaneous Writings and a Dramatic Fragment* (New York: Grove Press, 1984), pp. 19–33.

Beckett, Samuel, *Dream of Fair to Middling Women*, ed. Eoin O'Brien and Edith Fournier (Dublin: Black Cat, 1992).

Beckett, Samuel, Letters to Mary Manning Howe, A. J. Leventhal, and George Reavey, Harry Ransom Humanities Research Center, University of Texas, Austin.

Beckett, Samuel, Letters to Thomas MacGreevy, Department of Books and Manuscripts, Trinity College Dublin.

Cassirer, Ernst, *Kant's Life and Thought*, trans. James Haden (New Haven: Yale University Press, 1981).

Hutchins, Patricia, *James Joyce's World* (London: Methuen, 1957).

Sartre, Jean-Paul, *L'Imagination* (Paris: Alcan, 1936).

Yeats, W. B., 'The Fascination of What's Difficult', in Richard J. Finneran (ed.), *The Collected Poems of W. B. Yeats* (New York: Scribner, 1996), p. 38.

7.

'the remains of trace': Intra- and Intertextual Transferences in Beckett's *Mirlitonnades* Manuscripts

Mark Nixon

In the first manuscript notebook of Samuel Beckett's *Watt*, we find the following passage:

> The dominant sensation of James' youth, and indeed as it turned out of his entire life, was one which he was later to find, if not expressed at least suggested, in the night piece on the Asiatic Shepard of Giacomo Leopardi and in other passages of the same unhappy writer . . . This discovery, which constituted the sole literary satisfaction of a long and patient life, was made during the brief period accorded by James to a consideration of the celebrated passages of the more celebrated works of the most celebrated authors; a period which, after deduction of its numerous intermissions, cannot have fallen much short of 18 calendar months.[1]

There is an autobiographical investment at work in this extract, in that the period of eighteen months mentioned here corresponds to Beckett's own time of study at Trinity College Dublin. Furthermore, the sensation of unhappiness found in Leopardi's work remained with Beckett – as it did with James – all his life; having copied out the poem 'A se stesso' in the 1930s, he would later recall his admiration for Leopardi's 'pessimism, not his patriotism' in a letter of 21 April 1958 to A. J. Leventhal.

Further autobiographical and cultural allusions within the *Watt* manuscripts appear in the fourth notebook, where Beckett includes references to the painters Kaspar David Friedrich, Hercules Seghers and Adam Elsheimer, with a similar indication that Watt's knowledge of these artists had been acquired through careful and dedicated study.[2] The references in this case can be traced back to Beckett's 'German Diaries' of 1936–7, from which much of the discussion in the notebook is drawn.

In both instances, the explicit intertextual allusions did not survive into the final version of *Watt*, even though traces, especially in the case of Leopardi's poem, remain. The excision of the references is already anticipated by the ironical treatment such learnedness receives in the notebooks.

Beckett's decision to remove a large proportion of the overt allusions in *Watt* is symptomatic of his attempts, from about 1936 onward, to move away from a compositional strategy heavily reliant on his reading. Thus, his early work, in particular *Dream of Fair to Middling Women*, but also *Murphy*, depended upon what Beckett in letters to MacGreevy called 'phrase-hunting'[3] or 'note-snatching'.[4] The fruits of Beckett's labours are, of course, visible in the large corpus of notebooks from the first half of the 1930s – the *Dream* and *Whoroscope* notebooks, as well as the various notes on philosophy, literary history, the visual arts, psychology and so forth. It is this material that has allowed critics to move beyond speculation when confronted with the challenge phrased in *Dream*: 'We stole that one. Guess where.'[5]

From 1938 onward, however, Beckett stopped taking notes from his reading (the last occurring in the *Whoroscope* notebook). The shift in his note-taking strategy is reflected in a reduced use of intertextual borrowings in his subsequent work, as well as an attempt to obscure some of those allusions that did remain.[6] Yet Beckett continued to draw on his reading, but of books he had read at an earlier point, at times also using his 1930s notebooks as his source, which is evident in the two examples from the *Watt* manuscript material. Indeed, the published version of the novel signposts the change in Beckett's compositional approach by deliberately drawing attention, in the 'Addenda', to material of external origin *not* included in the text proper. Moreover, the 'Addenda' to *Watt* not only highlights the nature of material not incorporated in the final version, but also acknowledges the existence of what we could broadly term 'avant-textes' – drafts, source notebooks and so forth. Beckett had of course done this before; already in *Dream* the narrator, struggling to quote a line from Heinrich Heine, wonders, 'did I do well to leave my notes at home?'.[7] The post-war work similarly contains references to draft manuscript material, generating an inherent textual awareness of its own (inter)textuality. *How It Is* thus refers to 'dear scraps recorded somewhere',[8] and *All Strange Away*[9] explicitly alludes to the philosophy notes we now know as MS 10967 (held at Trinity College Library in Dublin).[10]

Having made his final notations in the *Whoroscope* notebook in late 1938, it was nearly fifty years before Beckett once again turned to the use of a notebook to jot down sentences and words from his reading. He did so in the small 'Sottisier' notebook, which he kept between 1976 and 1983 and which is now located in the Beckett Archive in Reading (UoR MS 2901). The notebook contains, besides reading notes from a variety of sources, drafts of the *mirlitonnades* and other poems, as well as notes (entitled 'The Voice' or 'Verbatim') toward what later became

Company. In what follows, I will examine the relationship between these reading notes and the texts that Beckett produced in these years, and offer some suggestions as to why Beckett returned to his old habit of 'note-snatching'.

The years 1976–83 are marked by a frenzy of writing approximating the one immediately after the war, but which followed on from a period in which Beckett struggled to find a way of going on. During these years Beckett was specifically engaged with several texts at once, as he was occupied with translating texts while also writing, or trying to write, new ones. Several pieces for theatre and television were written at this time, as was the so-called trilogy 'Nohow On' comprising *Company*, *Ill Seen Ill Said* and *Worstward Ho*. In addition, there are several fragments dating from this period, both aborted pieces and drafts that ultimately fed into other texts. And between 1976 and 1979 Beckett also wrote many poems, most of which were grouped and published as the *mirlitonnades*.

Beckett referred to the *mirlitonnades* in letters to Alan Schneider and Ruby Cohn as 'gloomy French doggerel[s]'[11] containing 'sinister stuff' (3 May 1977); they are short in length and written in French, although there are further pieces in English and French written between 1980 and 1983 that are thematically and formally related. As their name suggests, these *vers de mirliton* are light in manner, condensed witticisms that telescope the thematic concerns Beckett was addressing (mainly) in prose. Beckett had of course always tried his hand at such 'rimailles/rhymeries/versicules',[12] most notably in his rendition of Chamfort's Maxims a few years earlier. But such doggerels can also be found in early texts such as *Dream*, in the 'German Diaries', and in letters to friends. Thus, for example, Beckett sent a piece of light verse in French to Arland Ussher in 1938, noting that it took the form of Goethe and Schiller's 'Xenien' poems.[13]

By nature these pieces have a throw-away quality, and are often little more than sexual puns, but at times they are expressive of profound issues taxing Beckett – the fleeting nature of life, vain striving and the absence of God. Moreover, they were often composed at times of compositional struggle, allowing Beckett to keep his writing hand alive just as the doodles in manuscripts kept his hand on the page.

However, the *mirlitonnades* are nevertheless somewhat different from these earlier pieces of light verse, in that they were both more carefully crafted and revised, and, of course, ultimately published. In terms of draft material, there are three sources.[14] First of all, there are the scraps of paper on which he noted the poems, ranging from diary pages, café notepaper and metro tickets to parts of the packaging of a whisky bottle (UoR MS 2640). Secondly, we have the 'Sottisier' notebook, and thirdly Beckett's correspondence. Thus Beckett's letters contain a variety of material and references relevant to the genesis of the poems, as well as some variant versions. The relationship between these drafts is more complex than it might at first sight appear. We might assume that Beckett noted the *mirlitonnades* on the scraps of paper when he felt inspired, and then transferred any resulting final version to the 'Sottisier' notebook. Presumably, he wanted to keep the notebook as free from revisions as possible. However, Beckett's otherwise unusual tendency to date this material suggests otherwise: at times the versions written on scraps of paper post-date the 'Sottisier' entry. In some cases Beckett made further revisions to poems in the notebook, and then copied the final version back on to the original scrap of paper, as if to make sure that the material documents contained not only drafts but always the final form.

The *mirlitonnades* manuscript material is unique, or at least startling, in two respects: the scraps of paper found here attest to an immediacy of notation within an outburst of creative inspiration not evident elsewhere, and the specific nature of the scraps and their dating contextualises this moment of writing. On the one hand they testify to an alertness to external agency, in that they are written in response to things seen or experienced. On the other, they are concerned with capturing moods, emotional insights and the flotsam and jetsam of mental observations. Essentially, they cut to the core of Beckett's concern with *traces* at this time; thus texts such as *Company* or *Ill Seen Ill Said* grapple with things misremembered, ill-heard or faintly seen. At the same time, the poems and other texts written around this time foreground traces of literary and philosophical sources, thematising Winnie's complaint in *Happy Days* that 'one loses one's classics', even if 'a part remains'.[15] As if to avoid permanent loss, Beckett appears to have gone back to using a notebook as a repository for lines taken from his reading. If Beckett was returning to scenes of his childhood and youth in his prose of the late 1970s and early 1980s, he was simultaneously returning to books that had sustained his emotional outlook and creative endeavours in the 1930s: 'Only reading Dante again with memories of student reading.'[16]

The quotations in the 'Sottisier' notebook are, in accordance with the title given to the notebook, drawn from a wide variety of sources: lines from the Bible, quotations taken from Heine, Goethe – both, however, referenced via their setting by Schubert and Schumann – Pascal, Chaucer, Shakespeare, Schopenhauer, Parnell, as well as an Italian commentary on Dante (giving Belacqua a further appearance), to name but these. More often than not, the list of sources reveals that Beckett was returning to texts that he loved and knew well, compiling what in *Proust* he had referred to as a 'treasury of nutshell phrases'.[17] Thus we find Beckett noting down again Schopenhauer's line 'Das Leben ist ein Pensum zum Abarbeiten: in diesem Sinne ist defunctus ein schöner Ausdruck' ('Life is a pensum to be worked off: in this sense defunctus is a fine expression') in 1979, a phrase he had used nearly fifty years earlier in *Proust*.[18] Furthermore, Beckett's correspondence from 1975 to 1983 is littered with references to his reading. While he had obviously continued to read widely in the previous thirty years, the quotations in the 'Sottisier' notebook, as well as the references to his reading in his correspondence, reveal just how much these texts were at the forefront of his mind.

Although it is important not to overemphasise the point, there is a sense in which Beckett was not only returning to books he had read in the 1930s, but also drawing on them for new material in much the same way as he had done in that decade. The difference, however, is that Beckett in the late 1970s was no longer a young writer struggling with the anxiety of influence, but could enter into a more direct dialogue with the authors that he admired. The foregrounding of Beethoven and Yeats in the titles of *Ghost Trio* and *. . . but the clouds . . .*, written in 1976, bear witness to this. Furthermore, unlike in the 1930s, he was not reading with specific texts in mind, so that many of the quotations in the 'Sottisier' notebook were never used, just as many of the allusions contained, for example, in *Company* were not previously noted in the notebook.

Nevertheless, drawing on his reading would also have given Beckett some relief, particularly at a time when writing was becoming more and more difficult, as a remark made to Alan Schneider in a letter of February 1978 indicates: 'No new work. Prose begun at a standstill. Mind going very silent.'[19] Although he was referring here specifically to the writing of *Company*, during the late 1970s Beckett's writing was generally marked by interruption – he began texts, only to cast them aside for some period of time, or abandon them entirely. 'With me endless interruptions,' he told Jocelyn Herbert on 15 May 1977.

Yet at the same time, Beckett was drawing inspiration from extraneous material, as his reference to an abandoned text indicates. The piece was projected to be a play on the Fates, concentrating in particular on Atropos, the Fate of Death. Beckett had already been attracted to this figure in the 1930s, and references to Atropos and her scissors, severing the thread of life, can be found in the French poems 'Arène de Lutèce' and 'être là sans mâchoires'. Indeed, Beckett had probably first come across the figure of Atropos in Goethe's poem 'Harzreise im Winter', a poem that profoundly impressed him and that served as one of the inspirations to his own piece, 'The Vulture', of 1934. Beckett reanimated his interest in Atropos in April 1977, when the thread of life of his friends was being cut – Geoffrey Thompson's the previous year, Mary Hutchinson's and Geer van Velde's the previous month. As he told Alan Schneider: 'Attempts to get going on something new in vain. Just a few rhymes in French [*mirlitonnades*]. Wish I could do an Atropos all in black – with her scissors.'[20]

The dismissive reference to the French rhymes here should be read with caution, as Beckett tended to diminish the value of everything he was writing at the time, referring for example to *Ill Seen Ill Said* as 'mere prose' three years later.[21] Indeed, it was precisely in the form of a *mirlitonnade* that Beckett was able to express his sentiments about the random acts of Atropos. Eleven days after mentioning the projected play on the Fates, Beckett penned the poem 'noire soeur' while in Tangier, on the back of a scrap of cardboard:

noire soeur
qui es aux enfers
à tort tranchant
et à travers
qu'est-ce que tu attends[22]

The poem, quickly finalised after going through only two draft versions, contains a similar tone of resistance to the powers as Goethe's 'Harzreise' had done, or the German poet's poem 'Prometheus', one of Beckett's favourite pieces.[23] It appears as if Beckett then transferred the poem immediately into the 'Sottisier' notebook, as there are no variations between the two. What is interesting here, however, is that in the following entry in the 'Sottisier' notebook Beckett jots down several general attributes of the Fates:

Clotho (youngest) – birth – distaff
Lachesis – life – spindle
Atropos – death – scissors
dressed in black
Ministers of Pluto, sitting
at foot of his throne
a clew of thread (yarn)
Proserpine[24]

The connection between 'noire soeur' and the Fates is made more obvious by the reference, in the first draft of the poem, to their position as 'Ministers of Pluto, sitting at his throne'. It is possible that Beckett decided to note down the background material to the *mirlitonnade* poem in the hope that it would eventually form the basis of the play on the Fates, but ultimately nothing was ever written.

The German connection at the heart of Beckett's use of Atropos is evident in further entries in the 'Sottisier' notebook.

> . . . was soll es nützen
> Stets das alte Lied zu leiern? (Heine: Die Heimkehr)
> ----
> "Singende Flammen"
> (D's Inf. Heine: Deutschland: Ein Wintermärchen)[25]
>
> Nur wer die Sehnsucht kennt, weiss was ich leider [*sic*] (W.M. Mignon. Schubert. Wolf.)
> ----
> Ich grolle nicht u. wenn das Herz auch bricht. (Heine. Schumann. Dichterliebe)[26]

Once again, these four entries refer back to the 1930s in the same way as the general note-taking strategy of the notebook itself does. They show Beckett returning to old favourite texts ('Mignon's Song' from Goethe's *Wilhelm Meister*) and music (Schubert and Schumann), reminding us that Beckett's early knowledge of German poetry came via Schubert's *Lieder*. Heine was a relatively new but important discovery (at some point during the 1970s), and Beckett told Charles Juliet in November 1977 that he was in particular attracted to the late poems because they read like lamentations.[27] Indeed, Beckett's reading note from Heine's poem 'Deutschland', with its reference to a terrible hell from which not even God can provide rescue, can be brought to bear upon the material surrounding Atropos.

Noted down in either April or May 1981, these reading – or perhaps rather listening – notes reflect Beckett's use of German *Lieder* in his dramatic work around this time. Already in 1979, in an annotated copy of *Eh Joe* in German given to Rick Cluchey, Beckett had written in the margin 'W. M. Harfenspieler',[28] revealing his renewed interest in Goethe's *Wilhelm Meister* and the *Lieder* contained therein. And in February 1982 Beckett began to work on the TV piece *Nacht und Träume*, drawing on Schubert for the tone and setting. Moreover, John Pilling is surely right in remarking that the two English *mirlitonnades*, 'one dead of night'[29] and 'head on hands',[30] anticipate the thematic concerns of the TV play.

The cross-fertilisation of extraneous material between the 'Sottisier' notebook, the *mirlitonnades* and a more substantial piece of writing becomes more evident when we turn to Beckett's use of a cluster of quotations from Shakespeare's *King Lear*. Towards the end of March 1981,

Beckett noted four lines from the play into his notebook, three of which play on the distinction between 'worse' and 'worst':

> "The lamentable change is from the best,
> The worst returns to laughter – "
> ----
> "Who is't can say, I am the worst."
> ----
> "– The worst is not so long as one can say, This is the worst"[31]

Beckett had already measured the range of bad to worse in the *mirlitonnade* 'ce qu'a de pis', recorded in the notebook in March 1977:

> ce qu'a de pis
> le coeur connu
> la tête pu
> de pis se dire
> fais-le
> ressusciter
> le pis revient
> en pire[32]

Similarly, a further *mirlitonnade* dated November 1977 also seems to be based on the first of the Lear quotations recorded in the 'Sottisier' notebook:

> en face
> le pire
> jusqu'à
> ce qu'il fasse rire[33]

Although there is no textual evidence to suggest that Beckett had *King Lear* in mind when he wrote these two *mirlitonnades*, as they predate the entry in the 'Sottisier' notebook by nearly four years, it appears as if Beckett had been reading Shakespeare in that period. Closer in time to the 'Sottisier' entries is Beckett's use of *King Lear* in the translation of *Mal vu mal dit*, *Ill Seen Ill Said*. In the typescript of the translation, dating from late December 1980 or early January 1981, Beckett replaced the words 'weary eyes' with the phrase 'vile jelly' from Shakespeare's play.[34]

Rather aptly, the original title for *Mal vu mal dit* was 'Traces', which was only abandoned during the proof stages. The prose piece does indeed play on traces, of things said or perceived, minute fragments of memory – and of Beckett's reading. Indeed, if we follow the *King Lear* traces further, or rather return to the 'Sottisier' notebook, we find Beckett reformulating the movement from bad to worse, or from something already worse to something becoming more worse, in two short lines:

bail bail till better
founder[35]

This short piece, which plays on Shakespeare's distinction that 'The worst is not; so long as we can say, "This is the worst"', must have been of some importance to Beckett, as he cited the two lines in letters to Ruby Cohn (20 April 1981) and Jocelyn Herbert (1 May 1981) during the following weeks.[36] Essentially, they represent the overall movement of Beckett's writing at this time, and form, at least in part, the germination of the last of the three texts comprising 'Nohow On', *Worstward Ho*.[37]

Anticipating the 'fail again fail better' motif of *Worstward Ho*, the failure in question is specifically one of expression, in that the word 'worst' loses its worstness, so to speak, the moment it is measured in writing or utterance. Already in *Ill Seen Ill Said* the narrative seeks the right word, which is subsequently defined as being the 'wrong word'. This idea is encapsulated in Beckett's working title for *Worstward Ho*, 'Better Worse', which he began working on in August 1981, four months after initially noting the King Lear quotations.[38] The movement towards the worst word, a movement that never finds an end, is generated by an internal rhythm of going on, whereby every worst word necessitates a worse word, in keeping with Shakespeare's lines.

This verbal movement, whereby words die only to be resurrected, is played out in the draft versions of one of Beckett's *mirlitonnades*, number twenty-seven following the order of the Minuit edition. In the early drafts of this poem, written in July 1977, Beckett explored the relationship between words and life, and the idea (familiar from Beckett's late prose) that the end of words is somehow connected to the end of life. Unable to decide on the precise relationship between the two – of life dying of words, or words dying of life – Beckett noted various versions on the back of a piece of a whisky bottle box, before settling on the following version:

mots mourant
de male vie
un dernier moment
tenez-nous compagnie[39]

The draft versions show a slow gravitation towards a textual, and ultimately existential ending. It is, ultimately, a trajectory into silence, yet one that is not without comfort – words are, after all, 'company'.

Beckett proceeded to copy the four lines, as he usually did with most of the *mirlitonnades*, into the 'Sottisier' notebook.[40] However, a few days later (on 27 July 1977), he proceeded to cross out this version, and noted down in the notebook a new version with slight but profound changes:[41]

mots survivants
de la vie
encore un moment
tenez-nous compagnie

Why Beckett chose to insert the rather more hopeful 'mots survivants' and 'encore un moment' in this revised version is unclear (but it certainly did not have anything to do with Johnson's definition of 'pessary' on the same page). Yet the example encapsulates, in microcosm, the tension between beginning and ending inherent in Beckett's late work, and replicates the spiralling, revivifying cycle of *Worstward Ho*.

The 'worstward' yet still onward movement of the late prose is explored in other *mirlitonnades*, and frequently it revolves around the concept of traces. It is, for example, invested in Beckett's repeated use of the image of footsteps, which he compared to the process of writing in that both leave traces. The poem 'écoute-les' succinctly illustrates this:

écoute-les
s'ajouter
les mots
aux mots
sans mot
les pas
aux pas
un à
un[42]

The struggle to continue writing expressed in this piece is reflected by a statement Beckett made in a letter to Mary Manning Howe dated 21 March 1971, where he writes that he finds it 'increasingly difficult to put one word in front of another'.

During the productive period of writing between 1976 and 1983, Beckett's reading, as well as the writing of the *mirlitonnades*, helped to generate a more substantial exploration of the confluence between the existential and textual spheres in the late prose. The web of 'traces blurs signs' forms a subtext that we would more readily expect to find in works such as *Dream*.[43] Individual intertextual references resurface in a variety of disguises, or, as *From an Abandoned Work* states, they return as 'all the variants of the one'.[44]

Beckett's interest in the nature of traces was, of course, not limited to the latter stages of his writing career, and references to textual, personal and cultural traces crop up in a variety of earlier works. Thus, in the third notebook to *Watt*, Beckett spent considerable time outlining notions of lineage, both of family and of servants, documenting in particular (with reference to the line of servants in the house) 'all those of whom all trace is not lost, though their names be forgotten'.[45] In what is surely a precursor to Beckett's preoccupation with the act of 'witnessing', the survival of traces is again the subject of a further passage in the *Watt* manuscript material in which the narrator is unable to recollect whether the spectacle of the dog feeding ritual had ever been seen on any continent at any time:

> But what does this prove? For traces cannot endure forever, but the time comes, for every trace, when it must disappear and leave no trace behind, to tell where it had been. For as things vanish, so must traces vanish, and the traces of traces as the traces of things.[46]

In the search for the 'worst word', in the movement towards silence or nothingness enacted by the late prose, Beckett's compositional method is mediated precisely through the 'remains of trace[s]'.[47] Teetering on the brink of this silence, Beckett's late texts reach towards the 'bounds of boundless void',[48] seeking to write, in the words of the poet Paul Celan, ever-smaller 'enclosures around the limitlessly wordless'.[49]

I am grateful to the Estate of Samuel Beckett for permission to cite from unpublished manuscript material.

Notes

1. Samuel Beckett, *Watt* notebook 1, p. 61.
2. Beckett, *Watt* notebook 3, pp. 179–81. See David Hayman's discussion of these references.
3. Beckett, letter to Thomas MacGreevy, 25 January 1931.
4. Ibid. [11?] August 1931.
5. Beckett, *Dream of Fair to Middling Women*, p. 191.
6. See Mark Nixon, 'Guess where'. Already in the early 1930s Beckett at times made efforts to obscure the manner in which his writing depended on his reading, as is evident from the outline to *Murphy* in the *Whoroscope* notebook: 'keep whole Dantesque analogy out of sight', UoR MS 3000, 2r.
7. Beckett, *Dream*, p. 72.
8. Beckett, *How It Is*, p. 28.
9. Beckett , *All Strange Away*, in *The Complete Short Prose*, p. 175.

10. See also Beckett's response to Schneider's query regarding the 'Old Greek' in *Endgame*: 'I can't find my notes on the pre-Socratics', Maurice Harmon, *No Author Better Served*, p. 23.
11. Harmon, *No Author Better Served*, p. 355.
12. Beckett, 'Sottisier' notebook, inside cover.
13. Beckett, letter to Arland Ussher, 20 December 1938.
14. Two studies of the *mirlitonnades* manuscript material are indispensable: Wheatley's 'Beckett's *Mirlitonnades*: A Manuscript Study' and Cerrato's *Génesis de la poética de Samuel Beckett*. My discussion is indebted to both of these examinations.
15. Beckett, *Happy Days*, in *The Complete Dramatic Works*, p. 164.
16. Beckett , letter to Jocelyn Herbert, 30 June 1975.
17. Beckett , *Proust and Three Dialogues with Georges Duthuit*, p. 29.
18. Ibid. p. 93; 'Sottisier' notebook, 13r.
19. Harmon, *No Author Better Served*, p. 355.
20. Ibid. p. 355.
21. Beckett, letter of 20 November 1980; Harmon, *No Author Better Served*, p. 393.
22. Beckett, UoR MS 2460, 21 April 1977.
23. For a more detailed discussion of the importance of Goethe to Beckett, see Nixon, 'Scraps of German'.
24. Beckett, 'Sottisier' notebook, 5v, [21?] April 1977. Beckett's own dating is somewhat problematic here. He is probably drawing on *Lemprière's Classical Dictionary*, but it is unlikely that he had it to hand while in Morocco.
25. Beckett, 'Sottisier' notebook, 10v.
26. Ibid. 15r.
27. Charles Juliet, *Conversations with Samuel Beckett and Bram van Velde*, p. 162.
28. Beckett, UoR MS 2626.
29. John Pilling, *A Samuel Beckett Chronology*, p. 204.
30. Ibid. p. 215.
31. Beckett, 'Sottisier' notebook, 14v, [23?] March 1981.
32. Ibid. 5r, 31 March 1977.
33. Ibid. 9v, 12 November 1977.
34. The typescript of *Ill Seen Ill Said* is in the Carlton Lake Collection in the Harry Ransom Center in Austin.
35. Beckett, 'Sottisier' notebook, 11 April 1981.
36. Beckett would also often quote Shakespeare's original lines to friends; see conversation with Atik – 'They're very important' – of 24 August 1983, p. 105, and letter to Herbert, 12 December 1987.
37. Van Hulle in several essays provides further and more detailed discussions of the search for the last word(s) in Beckett last works; see for example his 'Les becquets de Beckett: vers une édition génétique des dernières œuvres bilingues'.
38. See Beckett's reference to 'Better worse fading memory' in a letter to Cohn dated 22 February 1982.
39. Beckett, UoR MS 2460.
40. Beckett , 'Sottisier' notebook, 8r.

41. Beckett also copied this new version back on to the scrap of paper that he had used for the first drafts, and dated it 'Tanger août 77'.
42. Beckett, 'Sottisier' notebook, 2v.
43. Beckett, 'Ping', in *The Complete Short Prose*, p. 193.
44. Beckett, *From an Abandoned Work*, in *The Complete Short Prose*, p. 162. Derrida of course thematised the endless referential chain of words or traces in *Difference* (and elsewhere), defining the textual trace as 'not a presence rather the simulacrum of a presence that dislocates, displaces, and refers beyond itself'. Derrida defines the importance of the trace in the fact that it is not merely positioned in a linear or chronological setting, but more importantly follows the web-like, interwoven nature of language itself. In 'Positions', Derrida compares verbal traces to the notion of textile weaving, a concept equally found in Joyce as well as in Beckett (cf. his letter to Kaun of July 1937, reprinted in *Disjecta*).
45. Beckett, *Watt* notebook 3, p. 63.
46. Ibid. p. 151.
47. Beckett, *Ill Seen Ill Said*, p. 52.
48. Beckett, *Nohow On*, p. 116.
49. Celan took the line from Rainer Maria Rilke to describe his own poetry; quoted in John Felstiner, p. 97.

Bibliography

Atik, Anne, *How It Was: A Memoir of Samuel Beckett* (London: Faber and Faber, 2001).

Beckett, Samuel, *All Strange Away*, in S. E. Gontarski (ed.), *The Complete Short Prose, 1929–1989* (New York: Grove Press, 1995), pp. 169–81.

Beckett, Samuel, *Company* (London: Picador, 1982).

Beckett, Samuel, *Complete Poems in English and French* (New York: Grove Press, 1977).

Beckett, Samuel, *The Complete Short Prose, 1929–1989*, ed. S. E. Gontarski (New York: Grove Press, 1995).

Beckett, Samuel, *Disjecta: Miscellaneous Writings and a Dramatic Fragment*, ed. Ruby Cohn (London: John Calder, 1983).

Beckett, Samuel, *Dream of Fair to Middling Women*, ed. Eoin O'Brien and Edith Fournier (Dublin: Black Cat, 1992).

Beckett, Samuel, *Eh Joe* (Frankfurt am Main: Suhrkamp, 1968, with Beckett's MS annotations [1979]), photocopy, Beckett International Foundation, University of Reading, MS 2626.

Beckett, Samuel, *From an Abandoned Work*, in S. E. Gontarski (ed.), *The Complete Short Prose, 1929–1989* (New York: Grove Press, 1995), pp. 155–64.

Beckett, Samuel, 'German Diaries' [6 notebooks], Beckett International Foundation, University of Reading [no MS number ascribed].

Beckett, Samuel, *Happy Days*, in *The Complete Dramatic Works* (London: Faber and Faber, 1986), pp. 135–68.

Beckett, Samuel, *How It Is* (London: John Calder, 1977).

Beckett, Samuel, *Ill Seen Ill Said* (London: John Calder, 1982).

Beckett, Samuel, *Ill Seen Ill Said*, TS, Harry Ransom Humanities Research Center, The University of Texas at Austin.

Beckett, Samuel, Letters to Ruby Cohn, Beckett International Foundation, University of Reading.

Beckett, Samuel, Letters to Jocelyn Herbert, Beckett International Foundation, University of Reading.

Beckett, Samuel, Letters to A. J. Leventhal, Harry Ransom Humanities Research Center, The University of Texas at Austin.

Beckett, Samuel, Letters to Thomas MacGreevy, Trinity College Dublin, MS 10402.

Beckett, Samuel, Letters to Mary Manning Howe, Harry Ransom Humanities Research Center, The University of Texas at Austin.

Beckett, Samuel, Letters to Arland Ussher, Harry Ransom Humanities Research Center, The University of Texas at Austin.

Beckett, Samuel, *Mirlitonnades*, Beckett International Foundation, University of Reading, MS 2460.

Beckett, Samuel, *Nohow On: Company, Ill Seen Ill Said, Worstward Ho* (New York: Grove Press, 1996).

Beckett, Samuel, 'Ping', in S. E. Gontarski (ed.), *The Complete Short Prose, 1929–1989* (New York: Grove Press, 1995), pp. 193–6.

Beckett, Samuel, *Proust and Three Dialogues with Georges Duthuit* (London: John Calder, 1965).

Beckett, Samuel, 'Sottisier' notebook, Beckett International Foundation, University of Reading, MS 2901.

Beckett, Samuel, TS of Leopardi's 'A se stesso', Trinity College Dublin, MS 10971/9.

Beckett, Samuel, *Watt* (London: John Calder, 1976).

Beckett, Samuel, *Watt* notebooks, Harry Ransom Humanities Research Center, The University of Texas at Austin.

Beckett, Samuel, *Whoroscope* notebook, Beckett International Foundation, University of Reading, MS 3000.

Cerrato, Laura, *Génesis de la poética de Samuel Beckett: apuntes para una teoría de la despalabra* (Buenos Aires: Fondo de Cultura Económica, 1999).

Felstiner, John, *Paul Celan: Poet, Survivor, Jew* (New Haven: Yale University Press, 2001).

Harmon, Maurice (ed.), *No Author Better Served: The Correspondence of Samuel Beckett and Alan Schneider* (Cambridge, MA: Harvard University Press, 1998).

Hayman, David, 'Beckett's *Watt*: The Art-Historical Trace: An Archeological Inquest', *Journal of Beckett Studies*, 13.2 (spring 2004), pp. 95–109.

Hulle, Dirk Van, 'Les becquets de Beckett: vers une édition génétique des dernières œuvres bilingues', *Samuel Beckett Today/Aujourd'hui*, 17 (2006), pp. 405–18.

Juliet, Charles, *Conversations with Samuel Beckett and Bram van Velde*, trans. Janey Tucker (Leiden: Academic Press Leiden, 1995).

Nixon, Mark, '"Guess where": From Reading to Writing in Beckett', *Genetic Joyce Studies*, 6 (spring 2006), <http://www.geneticjoycestudies.org/GJS6/GJS6Nixon.htm> (accessed 8 May 2012).

Nixon, Mark, '"Scraps of German": Samuel Beckett Reading German Literature', *Samuel Beckett Today/Aujourd'hui*, 16 (2006), pp. 259–82.

Pilling, John, *A Samuel Beckett Chronology* (Basingstoke: Palgrave Macmillan, 2006).

Wheatley, David, 'Beckett's *Mirlitonnades*: A Manuscript Study', *Journal of Beckett Studies*, 4.2 (spring 1995), pp. 47–75.

8.

The Stamp of the Father in *Molloy*

Phil Baker

Jacques Moran's unfortunate son Jacques Moran Junior keeps a stamp collection, under the predictably close supervision of his father, and father and son come into conflict over one of the stamps.

> Do you know what he was doing? Transferring to the album of duplicates, from his good collection properly so-called, certain rare and valuable stamps which he was in the habit of gloating over daily and could not bring himself to leave, even for a few days. Show me your new Timor, the five reis orange, I said. He hesitated. Show it to me! I cried.[1]

In a novel written to a less private aesthetic a fictitious stamp might have been sufficient, but the Timor 5 Reis Orange is a real stamp, issued by the Portuguese colony of Timor in 1895. Its primary significance lies in the word 'timor', Latin for 'fear', which is appropriate to the way that Moran the tyrant father terrorises his son: 'I was sometimes inclined to go too far when I reprimanded my son, who was consequently a little afraid of me.'[2] Moran beats Junior ('those clouts he so dreaded'[3]) and confiscates his possessions, all by virtue of his authority as a father within a hierarchical chain of father figures extending down from Youdi.

Three stamps are cited in *Molloy*. Moran finds the other two during a search of his son's collection:

> I put down the tray and looked for a few stamps at random, the Togo one mark carmine with the pretty boat, the Nyassa 1901 ten reis, and several others. I was very fond of the Nyassa. It was green and showed a giraffe grazing off the top of a palm tree. They were all there. That proved nothing. It only proved that those particular stamps were there.[4]

The visual details given for the Nyassa and Togo are accurate, but the Timor differs in that its picture is not described. This missing detail is concordant with the larger aesthetic of lacunae in Beckett's work, where absence is frequently an emphasis or aesthetic effect: things are conspicuous by their absence. When Moran outlines his knowledge of Molloy he proposes to 'draw attention . . . to the most striking lacunae'.[5]

The two incidental stamps that are described, bearing a boat and a giraffe, not only 'prove nothing' but signify nothing either. In contrast, the Timor stamp not only signifies fear, but above the word is an undescribed picture, the image of a thoroughly upright-looking man with a moustache.

Moran, the incarnation of upright pomposity, describes his own moustache as an integral part of his identity: 'It suited me, without a moustache I was inconceivable.'[6]

By his own account of the *doppelganger* he resembles, Moran is a little more ferrety-looking than the stamp, and has an 'abortive' moustache.[7] Although he fails to live up entirely to its masculine image, this stamp constitutes an underlying icon within Moran's half of *Molloy*.

The book is structured to an almost unprecedented degree by parallels and symmetries, and the Moran stamp corresponds to a stamp of a different kind that Molloy has: 'perhaps I knew nothing of Mother Molloy, or Mollose, save in so far as such a son might bear, like a scurf of placenta, her stamp'.[8] Just as the two halves of the novel are concerned with a yearning son-mother relationship and a tyrannical father-son relationship, so Molloy has the figurative stamp of his mother and bears her name, while Jacques Moran Junior has the literal stamp of his father ('I had given it to him myself'[9]) and bears his name. The Moran stamp can be seen as a concrete emblem of the book's double Oedipal structure, with its positive maternal and negative paternal relationships.

S. E. Gontarski gives a resumé: 'Both halves of the novel, then, develop aspects of the Oedipal paradigm, the Molloy section with maternal, the Moran section with paternal, emphasis.'[10] The first half is under the sign of the mother and the second half is under the sign of the father. It is tempting to see the stamp simply as an approximate picture of Moran, but it is both less and more than this. Moran's stamp, which he has given to his son and which he believes is valuable, is a kind of totem within the patriarchal theme of *Molloy*'s second half: it is an instance of the archetypal male face with its motif moustache that recurs throughout Moran's narrative. This moustache motif is absent from Molloy's half, and this exception to the trilogy's general pattern of repetition underlines the thematic design.

The moustache motif is introduced in isolation during Moran's discussion with Father Ambrose (Sunday without Communion is like 'the kiss without a moustache'[11]), and including Moran himself there are five variations on the same model. The face on the stamp is the first (non-) appearance of the type, followed by Moran's self-descriptions;[12] his double;[13] a description of Gaber ('He came and bent over me. He had a walrus moustache, chestnut in colour'[14]); and finally the menacing bowler-hatted farmer that Moran encounters in the rain: 'the water was dripping from his bushy moustache'.[15]

We see the paternal moustache elsewhere in middle Beckett. In 'The Expelled', the narrator's Rankian rebirth from the stable is hosted by the cabman and his wife, who stand as surrogate parents, and the narrator's first description of the cabman is 'All I saw was his moustache'.[16] Like the stamp, this is a glimpse of the paternal imago in Beckett. The imago, an internal object representation of parents or other key figures, is strictly speaking unconscious, but the word is often used simply to mean a prototypical image; Beckett makes ambiguous use of it in a 1930s poem, 'Malacoda', with reference to his dead father: 'mind the imago it is he'.[17]

One of the obvious things to be said about Beckett's moustache motif is that his father had a moustache, but we need to remember that this was true of most respectable men of his generation. Céline, second only to Joyce for Beckett before the war, writes of the father in *Death on Credit*: 'He had nothing in his favour but his school diploma, his moustache, and his principles'; 'I'd never seen him so moved . . . His whole moustache was trembling . . . "That's splendid my boy!"'[18] There is a striking similarity between Beckett's moustached and bowler-hatted father (the first photograph in the Deirdre Bair biography) and the father in Max Ernst's 1923 painting *Pietà, or Revolution by Night*. Ernst's painting features a moustached and bowlered father cradling his son, and the subversion of a knowingly Oedipal theme is signalled by the classical Greek head of the son and the figure of Freud to the right of the couple.[19] Ernst's picture and Beckett's moustache motif both play with the iconic stereotype of the early-twentieth-century father.

In the patriarchal chain the God-like Youdi is at the top and Jacques Moran Junior (or perhaps Baby Jack, his teddy bear) is at the bottom. Moran speaks down to Moran Junior in precisely the same way that Youdi speaks down to Moran: 'a simple prophetic present on the model of those employed by Youdi'.[20] Despite being the boy's biological father, he also addresses Junior in the literally 'patronising' mode appropriate to a Catholic priest like Father Ambrose (who also stands *in loco patris* to Moran Senior): 'Have you shat, my child . . .'[21]

The journey that Moran and his son embark on at the command of higher authority has elements of Abraham and Isaac, and Moran comments 'It was not for nothing I had studied the Old Testament'.[22] Abraham and Isaac are an archetypal image of patriarchy, and Lacan discusses them in his aborted 1963 seminar on the Names-of-the-Father (*les noms-du-père*), using the painting by Caravaggio as his illustration.[23] Within the chain Moran fears Youdi just as Moran Junior fears Moran, with Gaber as the intermediate link:

> Is he angry? I said . . . I'm asking you if he is angry, I cried. Angry said Gaber, don't make me laugh, he keeps rubbing his hands from morning to night, I can hear them in the outer room. That means nothing, I said. And chuckling to himself, said Gaber. He must be angry with me, I said . . . Has he changed? I cried. Changed, said Gaber, no he hasn't changed, he's getting old, that's all, like the world.[24]

Before the end of the book Moran's authority falls to pieces. Two pages earlier Moran has had 'childish hopes'[25] that his son would take pity on him, or that Molloy himself would become a friend, 'and like a father to me . . . so that Youdi would not be angry with me and would not punish me!'.[26] Moran's dependence on his son and Molloy is almost Saturnalian in its reversal, and his authority over Moran Junior crumbles into

> the scandal . . . of my son's defying me, and going left when I told him right, or right when I told him left, or straight on when I told him right or left as he had been doing of late, more and more frequently.[27]

Patriarchal authority and rationality fall together in *Molloy*, which ends by disappearing in the Cretan Paradox of Moran's vanishing report: his narrative opens 'It is midnight. The rain is beating on the windows'[28] and ends 'Then I went back into the house and wrote, It is midnight.

The rain is beating on the windows. It was not midnight. It was not raining.'[29] This theme of falling authority is also suggested in Moran's comment that his 'familiars' include the dragon tree of Tenerife, which 'perished at the age of 5000 years, struck by lightning. It was an example of longevity.'[30] The celebrated longevity of the dragon tree chimes with Youdi 'getting old', and its lightning nemesis accompanies the Moran theme of seniority and downfall.

It is the Oedipal scenario that gives the 'Timor' polarity its full context in the novel. It was 'with her alone, I – no, I can't say it. That is to say I could say it, but I won't say it, yes, I could say it easily, because it wouldn't be true.'[31] Molloy's denial enacts Freud's figure of *Verneinung* or 'negation', the subject of his 1925 paper of the same name, where the subject neatly raises and disowns the repressed idea at the same time. Freud: '"You ask who the person in this dream can be [says the patient]. It's *not* my mother." We emend this to "So it *is* his mother".'[32] Henceforth, '"I've got a new obsessive idea" he says, "and it occurred to me at once that it might mean so and so. But no; that can't be true, or it couldn't have occurred to me."'[33]

This is precisely the logic that Molloy has employed. 'What he is repudiating,' comments Freud, 'on grounds picked up from his treatment, is, of course, the correct meaning of the obsessive idea.'[34] There is little point in 'diagnosing' Molloy, but the most interesting part of Freud's comment must be 'on grounds picked up from his treatment': this is writing which shows exposure to psychoanalytic thought and its idiosyncratic logic. There is another emphasis by deletion, this time a kind of censorship, a little later in Molloy's narrative:

> Now men, I have rubbed up against a few men in my time, but women? Oh well, I may as well confess it now, yes, I once rubbed up against one. I don't mean my mother, I did more than rub up against her. And if you don't mind, we'll leave my mother out of all this.[35]

But leaving her out is not so easy. She reappears by slippage in the very next sentence, which begins 'But another who might have been my mother';[36] a parodic example of displacement and 'the return of the repressed'. Beckett is invoking the kernel myth of Freudian psychoanalysis here – the Oedipus complex – in a rampant parody that is part of his larger play with 'myth', citation and cliché. It fulfils Dylan Thomas's 1938 comment on *Murphy*, which Thomas pronounced to be 'Freudian blarney: Sodom and Begorrah'[37] – a flip comment but a prescient one, in view of the far greater amount of Freudian blarney to come in *Molloy*.

Molloy's obsessional quest for his mother is part of his essentially twentieth-century belief that this is the most significant relationship of his life: 'And if I'm ever reduced to looking for a meaning to my life, you never can tell, it's in that old mess I'll stick my nose to begin with, the mess of that poor old uniparous whore and myself.'[38] Molloy's belief that his relationship with his mother is the key to his life declares the maternal theme of his half. In contrast, Jacques Moran Junior's mother, 'Ninette',[39] is erased from the patriarchal half: all we read of her is that she allegedly died in childbirth, and her name suggests something diminutive, negative or inconsequential; a female cipher. Molloy's understanding of his quest is concordant with Stephen Dedalus's discussion of maternity and paternity in *Ulysses*, where he argues that while 'a father . . . is a necessary evil', '*Amor Matris*, subjective and objective genitive, may be the only true thing in life'.[40] If this is the subject of Molloy's half of *Molloy*, then Moran's half deals with 'Timor Patris'.

The later Joyce plays just as equivocally as Beckett under the sign of 'adipose rex' and the 'eatupus complex',[41] and it is no surprise to find there are 'amor' compounds in the *Wake* such as 'once amore as babes'[42] and 'Mamor!'.[43] The other, 'patrified'[44] side of the polarity is represented with the 'feary father',[45] and the paternal 'timor' is already in the *Wake*, where it is associated with 'our awful dad, Timour of Tortur'.[46]

Fear is less playfully associated with the father elsewhere in Beckett, as in the high-diving reminiscence of *Company* ('He calls to you to jump. He calls, be a brave boy. The red round face. The thick moustache.').[47] Three decades earlier this received a less muted treatment in *Eleuthéria*, with Victor Krap's textbook Freudian nightmares:

> VICTOR *(In his sleep)* No – no – too high – rocks – my body – papa – be brave – good little boy – I am brave – a good little boy – good little boy. (*A silence. He tosses and turns. Louder*) Fathom – full fathom five – at low tide – low water – deep – deep – deep surge. *(A silence. Enter the glazier. He goes toward the bed)* There the eyes – a thousand ships – the towers – circumcised – fire – fire.[48]

A dream scramble of childhood fear, paternal echoes ('full fathom five') and 'deep'[s] of the depth-psychological kind valorised by *transition* magazine leads to castration anxiety in the form of circumcision and burned Marlovian towers.[49]

Moran Junior's relation to Moran contains another classical element of the negative Oedipal relation in his thwarted and impotent rage towards the father that Beckett fashions as an Oedipal tyrant, and in suffering the 'castration' of having things like his knife confiscated at the father's whim.

> He deserved his scout knife. Don't tell me you've left it behind, I said. Not likely, he said, with pride and satisfaction, tapping his pocket. Then give it to

> me, I said . . . Give me that knife! I cried. He gave it to me. What else could he do, alone with me in the night that tells no tales?
>
> . . . he must have thought that the rage which distorted his features and made him tremble would never leave him till the day he could vent it as it deserved. And not even then. Yes, he must have felt his soul the soul of a pocket Monte Cristo, with whose antics as adumbrated in the Schoolboys' Classics he was needless to say familiar. Then with a good clap on that impotent back I said, Off we go.[50]

Sheldon Brivic relates Joyce's Monte Cristo references in *Portrait of the Artist* back to Freud's Rat Man case, suggesting that 'Stephen becomes absorbed in the Count of Monte Cristo largely because of its intense enactment of Oedipal desires'; 'Monte Cristo's unjust suffering corresponds to childhood restraints; husband and usurpers, to father and authority figures'.[51]

The danger is in the neatness of identifications: it would be unwise to take Beckett's psychoanalytic material entirely at face value. The 'knowingness' of *Molloy*'s Oedipal material makes it ultimately a form of citation. We are not reading vital authorial symptoms but decayed signs, cryptic but nonetheless conventional. This knowingness is pervasive, so that – to take a banal example – if the banana in *Krapp's Last Tape* was a phallic symbol, then it would have to be 'a symbol of' a phallic symbol. It is in the nature of psychoanalysis itself, having to do with that which is definitively cryptographic, as well as painful, repressed and fugitive, that the irony in any such citation must be particularly unstable, along with any meaning: 'A hieroglyph is an especially elusive riddle if it's put in quotes'.[52]

The second major objection to a too simple psychoanalytic reading of Beckett's Oedipus is the attention to pure structure in Beckett's texts. Beckett seems to have had a lifelong fascination with the Oedipus complex: it forms the characteristically missing centre of his early work 'A Case in a Thousand', and he was the first person to notice the Oedipal structure of Robbe-Grillet's *Les Gommes*. But the Oedipus complex has considerable formal elegance, so what look like questions of gender and psychology in *Molloy* may equally be questions of pure polarity and structure, along the lines of Beckett's declared interest in 'the shape of ideas' rather than their content. Related to this is the extent to which the whole novel has a 'mania for symmetry'.[53] The trilogy is itself such an 'album of duplicates'[54] that almost everything in it has to be repeated. Rubin Rabinovitz's computer-assisted work on the trilogy has demonstrated the almost unparalleled extent of repetition, and there are still further repetitions that a computer would miss: Lousse's dog is called Teddy and Jacques Moran Junior has a (teddy) bear called Baby Jack, for example.

Some of these repetitions add to conventional meaning. Moran confiscates the stamp and says 'I had given it to him myself',[55] and when he confiscates the knife he also says 'I had given it to him myself';[56] clearly Moran giveth and Moran taketh away. The Oedipal structure is also pointed up by repetition: Moran's encounter with the fearsome farmer while supposedly going to the Turdy Madonna is an Oedipal structure that repeats Molloy's encounter with the policeman while going to visit his Madonna-associated mother. Other discreet repetitions with a thematic significance include Molloy's play with his sixteen sucking-stones[57] and Moran's pondering over his sixteen theological questions[58] – the one being regressive, oral and ultimately mother-oriented, and the other definitively patriarchal. Similarly, Moran's narrative begins on the Sabbath of the Judaeo-Christian God, which is the subject of a self-satisfied paragraph about religion and leisure,[59] while Molloy's sabbaths are more like witches' sabbaths: 'the within, all that inner space one never sees, the brain and heart and other caverns where thought and feeling dance their sabbath'.[60]

Ultimately this structural aesthetic of recirculating elements within a closed system exceeds thematic or psychological 'content', as in the name of Moran's dentist 'Mr. Py'[61]: Molloy has already considered the mysteries of twenty-two divided by seven ('then the true division begins, of twenty two by seven for example, and the pages fill with true ciphers at last'[62]). This is 'pi', although the word remains silent or unwritten in the text, just as the stamp remains faceless. Despite being silent it seems to determine Py's name, and the reason he is called Py and not Pi is evidently to link him again on a material level with the 'pyx' of Father Ambrose.[63] If this is a work like *Endgame*, of which Beckett said 'There are no accidents . . . Everything is based on analogy and repetition',[64] then it should be significant that the five Moran-types (five including the stamp) balance five Molloys: 'there were three, no, four Molloys. He that inhabited me, my caricature of same, Gaber's and the man of flesh and blood somewhere awaiting me . . . [and] a fifth Molloy, that of Youdi'.[65]

In addition to its role in *Molloy*'s double Oedipal structure, the Timor stamp also has more local significance. A moustached man called Jacques Moran and the son he intimidates, also called Jacques Moran, have in their common possession a 'Timor' stamp bearing the picture of a moustached man. Moran Senior authorises Moran Junior to take on their journey not his collection proper but his album of duplicates, since he has two albums, the large and the small.[66] By this point not only the more generally relevant notion of 'duplicates' but also the pair of albums, 'the large and the small', carry a strong suggestion of 'a chip off the old block', which has an obvious thematic relevance. This is one of Beckett's *mise en abymes* where a fragment is enactive of its larger situation. Closely related to this is the high degree of reflexivity in Beckett's novel, which contains key terms for reading it within locally appropriate observations, such as 'mania for symmetry',[67] 'striking lacunae'[68] and 'album of duplicates'.[69]

I have suggested that in its elusive way this stamp constitutes a kind of underlying Moran totem within the patriarchal theme of *Molloy*'s second half, and that it offers a sight of the paternal imago in the Beckett world, an imago which we have seen is central to the structure of the second half of *Molloy*. The question arising counter to this is whether it can really be said to be there at all, or the extent to which an occulted signifier can hold a place in the signifying chain: just as 'pi' was silent but kept its place in relation to Mr Py, I believe the stamp is 'there', by which I mean that Beckett was aware of the relevant image and had it in mind during composition, both because the other two stamps are described correctly and because of its salience to the 'moustached man' pattern.

In its visual relevance and non-appearance, the Timor stamp lies between the numerous painting citations in the early fiction and the picture with its face turned to the wall in *Endgame*. Unlike the sealed enigma of that picture, the latent illustration of the Timor stamp is a more finite mystery. Within the novel's 'striking lacunae' and pattern of reflexivity, Moran's doubled cry of 'Show me . . . Show it to me!'[70] points up the invisibility of the stamp, and this textually 'unconscious' invisibility matches that of the Obidil that Moran longed to see and never did, 'either face to face or darkly'.[71] He never describes the Obidil: the only mention it receives is when he tells the reader that he has refrained from mentioning it. Within the reflexive pattern, 'But why describe him?'[72] is also significant. The moustached Moran-type face is undescribed when it first appears on the stamp, and has 'But why describe him?' when it last appears on the farmer, completing a kind of circle; both also cost Moran a florin.[73]

The Moran stamp contributes to the characterisation of Moran in the 'Shem and Shaun'-style polarity between Moran and Molloy, in which the egotistical Moran is satirised as the petit bourgeois, anal-retentive and paranoid half of the dyad. Beckett's ethical vision is directed against the 'can-ers, knowers and doers' (to adapt Beckett's words from 1956: 'I think anyone nowadays who pays the slightest attention to his own experience finds it the experience of a nonknower, a noncaner').[74] This is particularly clear in *Molloy*, where there is an ethical preference for the character of Molloy himself, as against Moran. Before his dissolution, when they are scattered, Moran is the proud possessor of a huge bunch of keys. 'I have a huge bunch of keys, it weighs over a pound. Not a door, not a drawer in my house but the key to it goes with me, wherever I go.'[75]

Moran is in control, and his decision about the stamps is in keeping with this: 'To make assurance doubly sure, I said, we shall put the albums in the safe, until our return.'[76] Moran is a tremendous comic creation, and to associate him with the definitively petit bourgeois and anal-retentive pursuit of stamp collecting is just as much a part of his characterisation as his stress on punctuality,[77] his interest in double-entry book-keeping[78] and his walking 'with delicate steps, almost mincing, congratulating myself as usual on the resilience of my Wilton',[79] as well as what has been nicely called his 'Micawberish relish for the advertisement of principle'.[80] Some critics have suggested that Moran's cigar, fountain pen and propelling pencil are phallic symbols. This may be true as far as it goes, but the fountain pen and propelling pencil neatly side by side in his pocket are equally the accessories of a precise, punctilious character. It is representative of this characterisation within the Molloy-Moran polarity that Moran's stamp of the father should be a supposedly valuable postage stamp with a king's head on it, while Molloy's stamp of the mother should take the form of a 'scurf of placenta'.[81]

It is also richly in character for Moran to pride himself on having a 'bargain' with the stamp ('it had cost me a florin. A bargain, at the time'[82]). Moran's absurdly petit bourgeois self-satisfaction in having a little 'bargain' is being ridiculed here, as we can see if we compare it with the equally trifling competence of Saposcat's father in *Malone Dies*, who sells himself a fountain pen for his son from his own stationer's shop: 'One day Mr. Saposcat sold himself a fountain pen, at a discount'[83] (and once again father and son share the same name: 'The man's name is Saposcat. Like his father's'[84]). Seen in this light the stamp is not only the stamp of fear but also the stamp as bargain; a Pooterish footnote to a ridiculous character.

Oedipalised satire on patriarchy is clearly present in Moran's half of *Molloy*, and its 'disintegrations of the father',[85] but it is relatively good natured, without the bitterness it assumes in *Endgame*. Moran's dissolution fully exemplifies the Lacanian pun on '*Les noms du père*' and '*Les non-dupes errent*'. '*Les non-dupes errent*' was the title Lacan gave to his unpublished Seminar XXI of 1973–4: 'It is the wise guys who are really lost', a homonymy entirely in accord with Beckett's ethic and the contradictions of Moran's character.

Notes

1. Samuel Beckett, *Trilogy*, p. 109.
2. Ibid. p. 96.
3. Ibid. p. 124.
4. Ibid. p. 121.
5. Ibid. p. 113.
6. Ibid. p. 119.
7. Ibid. p. 151.
8. Ibid. p. 113.
9. Ibid. p. 109.
10. S. E. Gontarski, 'Molloy and the Reiterated Novel', p. 62.
11. Beckett, *Trilogy*, p. 100.
12. Ibid. p. 119; p. 151.
13. Ibid. p. 151.
14. Ibid. p. 165.
15. Ibid. p. 173.
16. Beckett, *Collected Shorter Prose*, p. 27.
17. Beckett, 'Malacoda', p. 26. I am concerned here with the imago as it emerges in the texts, irrespective of 'real' biographical concerns.
18. Louis-Ferdinand Céline, *Death on Credit*, p. 53; p. 135. For Beckett's opinion of Céline, as reported by Peggy Guggenheim, see Deirdre Bair, *Samuel Beckett: A Biography*, p. 275.
19. For the Freudian and personal background to the picture see Malcolm Gee, *Ernst: Pietà or Revolution by Night*.
20. Beckett, *Trilogy*, p. 109.
21. Ibid. p. 119.
22. Ibid. p. 119.
23. See Jacques Lacan, 'Introduction to the Names-of-the-Father Seminar'.
24. Beckett, *Trilogy*, p. 164.
25. Ibid. p. 162.
26. Ibid. p. 162.
27. Ibid. p. 161.
28. Ibid. p. 92.
29. Ibid. p. 176.
30. Ibid. p. 150.
31. Ibid. p. 19.
32. Sigmund Freud, 'Negation', p. 235.
33. Ibid. p. 235.
34. Ibid. p. 235.
35. Beckett, *Trilogy*, p. 21.
36. Ibid. p. 21.
37. Dylan Thomas, Review of *Murphy*, p. 455.
38. Beckett, *Trilogy*, p. 19.
39. Ibid. p. 174.
40. James Joyce, *Ulysses*, p. 266.
41. Joyce, *Finnegans Wake*, p. 499, line 16; p. 128, line 36.
42. Ibid. p. 336, line 16.
43. Ibid. p. 499, line 11.

44. Ibid. p. 87, line 11.
45. Ibid. p. 628, line 2.
46. Ibid. p. 136, line 21.
47. Beckett, *Company*, pp. 23–4.
48. Beckett, *Eleuthéria*, p. 125. There is another play on patriarchal fear in the radio drama. 'Fear' itself is 'man' in Gaelic ('fir' in plural), and in *All That Fall* 'fir' (the men's WC) and 'Grimm' (the philologist) allow the homophonic introduction of 'fear' and 'grim' into the radio play, within a local context of masculinity and sexual difference. Mr Rooney seems to have frightened a girl child into jumping from a train, so in this case the fear-man equation is salient. See *Collected Shorter Plays*, p. 35.
49. Beckett's Marlowe reference is to *Doctor Faustus* act 5, scene 1: 'Was this the face that launched a thousand ships, / And burnt the topless towers of Ilium?'
50. Beckett, *Trilogy*, pp. 131–2.
51. Sheldon Brivic, 'Joyce in Progress', p. 312; and *Joyce Between Freud and Jung*, p. 37.
52. Carter Ratcliff, 'Modern Life', p. 12.
53. Beckett, *Trilogy*, p. 84.
54. Ibid. p. 109.
55. Ibid. p. 109.
56. Ibid. p. 131.
57. Ibid. pp. 71–4.
58. Ibid. pp. 167–9.
59. Ibid. pp. 92–3.
60. Ibid. p. 10.
61. Ibid. p. 104.
62. Ibid. p. 64.
63. Ibid. p. 101.
64. Cited in Ruby Cohn, *Back to Beckett*, p. 152. If this were literally true it would be a kind of hermeneutic cranks' charter. One effect of Beckett's thoroughgoing textual repetition is to confound our commonsensical (and psychoanalytic) belief that anything that is repeated is significant, as repetition pure and simple generates potentially thematic material.
65. Beckett, *Trilogy*, p. 115.
66. Ibid. p. 109.
67. Ibid. p. 84.
68. Ibid. p. 113.
69. Ibid. p. 109.
70. Ibid. p. 109.
71. Ibid. p. 162.
72. Ibid. p. 173.
73. 'His chubby cheeks were streaming, the water was dripping from his bushy moustache. But why describe him?' (Beckett, *Trilogy*, p. 173). Having already written that the stamp cost him a florin when he bought it for his son (p. 109), he emphasises the florin again in his encounter with the farmer, whom he is frightened of and effectively 'buys off', as if with a toll or sacrifice. He introduces the episode: 'I reached home with my fifteen shillings intact. No, I spent two. This is how' (p. 173). He then tells the story of the

encounter, and closes it again with the florin: 'I took a florin from my pocket and gave it to him. For your poor box, I said. And I added, because of the dark, a florin for your poor box . . . That was how I spent a florin' (p. 104).

74. Interview with Israel Shenker in the *New York Times*, 5 May 1956.
75. Beckett, *Trilogy*, p. 126.
76. Ibid. p. 110.
77. Ibid. p. 98.
78. Ibid. p. 161.
79. Ibid. p. 109.
80. Michael Sheringham, *Beckett: Molloy*, p. 67.
81. Reworking the text into English (with Patrick Bowles) evidently gave Beckett opportunities to add to the parallels and correspondences, and Molloy's placental stamp of his mother is one of the additions. The French Molloy only carries her 'traces, comme des lambeaux de coiffe' (*Molloy* (Paris: Éditions de Minuit, 1988), p. 152).
82. Beckett, *Trilogy*, p. 109.
83. Ibid. p. 211.
84. Ibid. p. 187.
85. Ibid. p. 158.

Bibliography

Bair, Deirdre, *Samuel Beckett: A Biography* (London: Jonathan Cape, 1978).

Beckett, Samuel, *All That Fall*, in *Collected Shorter Plays* (London: Faber and Faber, 1984), pp. 9–40.

Beckett, Samuel, *Collected Shorter Plays* (London: Faber and Faber, 1984).

Beckett, Samuel, *Collected Shorter Prose 1945–1980* (London: John Calder, 1986).

Beckett, Samuel, *Company* (London: Picador, 1982).

Beckett, Samuel, *Eleuthéria* (New York: Foxrock, 1995).

Beckett, Samuel, 'Malacoda', in *Collected Poems 1930–1978* (London: John Calder, 1984), p. 26.

Beckett, Samuel, *Molloy* (Paris: Éditions de Minuit, [1951] 1988).

Beckett, Samuel, *Trilogy: Molloy, Malone Dies, The Unnamable* (London: John Calder, 1959).

Brivic, Sheldon, *Joyce Between Freud and Jung* (Port Washington, NY: Kennikat Press, 1980).

Brivic, Sheldon, 'Joyce in Progress: A Freudian View', *James Joyce Quarterly*, 13.3 (1976), pp. 306–27.

Céline, Louis-Ferdinand, *Death on Credit* (London: John Calder, 1989).

Cohn, Ruby, *Back to Beckett* (Princeton: Princeton University Press, 1973).

Freud, Sigmund, 'Negation', in *The Standard Edition of the Complete Psychological Works of Sigmund Freud, Volume XIX: The Ego and the Id and Other Works*, ed. and trans. James Strachey (London: Hogarth Press, 1961), pp. 235–9.

Gee, Malcolm, *Ernst: Pietà or Revolution by Night* (London: Tate Gallery, 1986).

Gontarski, S. E., 'Molloy and the Reiterated Novel', in *As No Other Dare*

Fail: For Samuel Beckett on his 80th Birthday by his Friends and Admirers (London: John Calder, 1986; New York: Riverrun Press, 1986), pp. 57–65.

Joyce, James, *Finnegans Wake* (London: Faber and Faber, 1939).

Joyce, James, *Ulysses* (London: The Bodley Head, 1960).

Lacan, Jacques, 'Introduction to the Names-of-the-Father Seminar' (*Le seminaire des noms-du-père*), 20 November 1963; translation by Jeffrey Mehlman published in *October*, 40 (spring 1987), pp. 81–95.

Ratcliff, Carter, 'Modern Life: Close Encounters with Unidentified Flying Zeitgeists', *Artforum International*, 24.9 (May 1986), p. 12.

Shenker, Israel, 'An Interview with Beckett', the *New York Times*, 5 May 1956; reprinted in Lawrence Graver and Raymond Federman (eds), *Samuel Beckett: The Critical Heritage* (London: Routledge and Kegan Paul, 1979), pp. 146–9.

Sheringham, Michael, *Beckett: Molloy* (London: Grant and Cutler, 1985).

Thomas, Dylan, Review of *Murphy*, *New English Weekly*, 17 March 1938, pp. 454–5.

9.

A Note on Benozzo Gozzoli

James Knowlson

In Samuel Beckett's story 'What a Misfortune', after the wedding of Belacqua Shuah to Thelma bboggs, the guests are all assembled in the drawing-room of Otto Olaf bboggs's house for the wedding reception, anxiously awaiting the arrival of the bride and groom, before they are allowed to tuck into the buffet lunch. 'To say that the drawing-room was thronged would be to put it mildly. It was stiff with guests,' writes Beckett. The throng and the 'whorled' disposition of the procession, 'loosely coiled in the midst waiting to move off', reminds Walter Draffin, who is shortly to propose the health of the happy couple, of 'a Benozzo fresco'. In his 'high-smelling voice', Walter passes on this comparison of the crowd with the fresco to the Alba, who replies 'with indescribable bitterness': 'Ass and all'.

This is one of the many passages in *More Pricks Than Kicks*, *Dream of Fair to Middling Women* and *Murphy* that are inspired by Beckett's early encounters with art. On the previous page of 'What a Misfortune', for instance, the gestures of the bride during the marriage ceremony have been compared to sculptures in the Musée Rodin or to figures in 'a Dürer cartoon'. Elsewhere there are allusions to paintings by (among others) the Master of Tired Eyes, Cranach, Perugino and Uccello. The problem with the Benozzo reference has not been in identifying the allusion as referring to frescoes painted by Benozzo Gozzoli in the chapel of the Palazzo Medici-Riccardi in Florence in 1459–60 but in seeing how the frescoes in question have been used by Beckett.[1] For only a close analysis can make proper sense of the passage in 'What a Misfortune' or explain the point of the Alba's witty, elliptical retort. The parallel also raises a number of other questions about the allusiveness of Beckett's early writing that are worth exploring by means of this example.

Beckett's easy familiarity with the Benozzo frescoes makes it apparent first of all that the Medici-Riccardi chapel must be added to the places that we can be certain he saw while he was visiting Florence during the summer of 1927. The frescoes on the walls of the chapel of the Medici Palace are divided between the two rooms of the chapel. The painter of the multiple frescoes was indeed Benozzo Gozzoli (c. 1421–97), assistant at one time to Cosimo de'Medici's favourite painter, Fra Angelico, and commissioned by the Medicis to decorate the chapel. The scenes depicted in the hall are those of the 'Journey of the Magi' travelling in busy convoy from Jerusalem to Bethlehem. The procession stretches across the east, south and west walls of the main chapel room: the Procession of the Youngest King is shown on the east wall, the Middle King on the south wall, and the Oldest King on the west wall. In the apse are scenes of angels flying, singing, worshipping and weaving festoons of flowers, and on two narrow strips of wall above the entrances to the two small sacristies are paintings that portray the 'Vigil of the Shepherds'. Through his fictional creation, Walter Draffin, Beckett chooses to focus in this passage on three aspects of Gozzoli's frescoes which have little to do with their religious meaning or with their significance as a tribute to the Medici family, various members of which are portrayed in the group of noblemen who follow one of the kings. 'There was something so bright and meaty about the assembly' is the first element to provoke Walter's highly self-conscious analogy with the Florentine fresco.[2] 'Bright and meaty' suggests an intensity of light and colour and a profusion of figures and incidents, and there are plenty of such features in Gozzoli's frescoes. The Youngest and Oldest Kings on facing walls are followed by a densely crowded retinue of noblemen, all dressed in tunics profusely decorated with gilt and wearing red and blue hats or headdresses. The prancing horses of the kings and the noblemen wear harnesses with brightly gilded adornments. And there are miniature scenes involving dogs, deer, camels, hawks, cheetahs and monkeys.

But the most striking aspect of the frescoes that Beckett clearly remembered from his visit to Florence only a few years before is the extraordinary 'coiling' of the procession that winds its way for vast distances over the hills and rocks, meandering through extremely narrow ravines, sometimes almost turning back upon itself. This second feature of the Gozzoli frescoes is applied in the Beckett story to the crowd at the wedding reception as 'something so whorled in its disposition' with the procession 'loosely coiled in the midst waiting to move off'. The parallel is then extended in a following paragraph in which Beckett combines the two elements of 'congestion' and 'coiling' so that

> In its present headless condition [it is headless, of course, in the sense that the bride and groom have yet to arrive] the procession could not uncoil itself out through the door as arranged, and it was obvious that until the procession uncoiled itself there could be no relief for the congestion of casual ladies and gentlemen of which it was, so to speak, the mainspring. But let the truant pair

> appear and take their station and lo the press, as though by magic, would tick off merrily to its stand-up lunch. In the meantime, what a waste of good saliva![3]

When Walter passes on his erudite artistic analogy to the Alba, she promptly pricks his balloon with her sharp rejoinder 'Ass and all'. But this is not just a routine put-down. It has a double meaning that would be comprehended only by someone with an intimate knowledge of the Gozzoli frescoes. For, on the wall over the entrance to the right-hand sacristy, in one of the two scenes of the 'Vigil of the Shepherds', is a large painting of an ass with huge ears prominently displayed in the centre just above the door, staring directly at the viewer. The ass is not merely playing a waiting role in the event of the nativity but is also anticipating its part in the entry by Christ into Jerusalem, a scene that Beckett was to evoke verbally many years later in his 1956 play for BBC radio, *All That Fall*.

As so often in his early prose, Beckett is demonstrating here – and very flamboyantly – his own considerable erudition and cleverness. The Gozzoli frescoes were in fact probably the inspiration for this entire passage rather than any real-life incident that recalled the paintings, although the latter possibility – a wedding that he had attended earlier in the year in which the story was written – cannot, of course, be ruled out. Yet as occurs elsewhere in the prose of *More Pricks Than Kicks*, the author at times mocks himself as well as his creations: Walter arrives at his comparison only 'slowly and surely', and the acid rejoinder from the Alba can be read in a self-deprecatory sense. The knowledge that lies behind this barb and the self-conscious 'look at me: I am clever enough to laugh at myself', however, makes such moments more complex and multi-levelled than they might at first appear.

Later in the story, too, Walter Draffin makes another, this time deliberately banal allusion to one of Italy's monuments, just as there had been earlier allusions to other architectural and cultural features of the city of Florence: the Piazza della Signoria; 'the sinister Uffizi'; the Palazzo Vecchio; and the monument to Cellini on the Ponte Vecchio. In this case the city evoked is Pisa. We cannot be certain that Beckett actually visited Pisa when he was in Italy in 1927, although in view of its relative proximity to Florence and the fact that he went much further afield to Venice, it seems very likely. He would not, however, have needed to have done so to make his unusual comparison:

> The tilted kepi of the attendant, its green band and gilt harp and the clang beneath in black and white of his riotous hair and brow, so ravished Walter that he merely had to close his eyes to be back in Pisa. The powers of

> evocation of this Italianate Irishman were simply immense, and if his Dream of Fair to Middling Women, held up in the limae labor stage for the past ten or fifteen years, ever reaches the public, and Walter says it is bound to, we ought all to be sure to get it and have a look at it anyway.[4]

Apart from the amusing piece of self-advertisement of a book that by that stage seemed unlikely ever to appear in print, the evocation is presented with gentle irony and self-mockery. And the distance from the observed object (the 'tilted kepi') to the remembered monument (the Leaning Tower of Pisa) is indeed considerable, justifying the expression of surprise at the observer's 'immense' powers of evocation.

But again the allusion may be more complex than at first appears. Those familiar with the work of Benozzo Gozzoli will be aware that some of his most famous frescoes of twenty-four Old Testament scenes were painted over a period of sixteen years in the Campo Santo cemetery in Pisa, where he had a house, died and was assigned his own tomb. The evocation of the Leaning Tower may then provide Beckett's (decidedly ambivalent) summation of his reactions to the entire set of Gozzoli analogies, enjoying the complexity of his own creative processes, revelling in the power of his visual memory and its resultant imagery, and yet undercutting its strange nature and its tortuousness.

However exhibitionistic the Gozzoli examples may be, they reveal how Beckett can make artistic allusions and motifs work to add resonance and density to the texture of his writing. Even without recognising the detailed allusions to the Benozzo frescoes, the reader can register the dominant imagery of shape and colour. Yet the scene of the bboggses' wedding reception is an excellent example of how specialised and recondite Beckett's allusions can become, and how capable they are of puzzling several different generations of readers. For, as so often with the early stories and novels, Beckett makes demands that, not surprisingly, frightened off a number of potential publishers, fearful of how alienated the readers would be by such dense allusiveness, making *Dream of Fair to Middling Women*, which Beckett cannibalised for *More Pricks Than Kicks*, appear totally unpublishable. On its publication in May 1934, *More Pricks Than Kicks* itself was, hardly surprisingly, criticised by many of its reviewers for its cleverness and its allusiveness. 'Every sentence is tortured out of its natural shape in the hope of impressing the reader with the author's cleverness,'[5] wrote *John O'London's Weekly*. The *Time and Tide* reviewer judged that 'his allusiveness is often merely smart . . . it is too clever a book to be first-rate'.[6] Edwin Muir, on the other hand, writing in *The Listener*, was not at all put off by this aspect of the book and found it 'somewhat like extremely good and calculated and quite impossible talk; it wanders round the subject and delights us with it wanderings'.[7] *The Times* reviewer, too, though finding the stories very uneven, discerned 'a definite, fresh talent at work in it' and ends with a Beckett quotation that is apposite to our theme:

> His book sometimes invites us to compare Mr. Beckett with one of his characters, an author, who thought out a very pretty joke but could find no one subtle enough to appreciate it: 'The only thing he did not like about it was its slight recondity . . . Well, he must just put it into his book.'[8]

Notes

1. See C. J. Ackerley and S. E. Gontarski, *The Grove Companion to Samuel Beckett*, p. 48, for a short entry correctly identifying the allusion. The Benozzo frescoes are not mentioned earlier in McMillan's excellent essay 'Samuel Beckett and the Visual Arts'. Gozzoli is referred to in a list of painters that Beckett alluded to in his prose writings in Vivian Mercier's *Beckett/Beckett*, but there is no discussion of the allusions to his frescoes in *More Pricks Than Kicks*, nor is the allusion mentioned in Anthony Farrow's *Early Beckett* or Lois Oppenheim's *The Painted Word.*
2. Samuel Beckett, 'What a Misfortune', *More Pricks Than Kicks*, p. 151.
3. Ibid. pp. 151–2.
4. Ibid. p. 153.
5. *John O'London's Weekly*, 9 June 1934.
6. Richard Sunne, *Time and Tide*, 26 May 1934.
7. Edwin Muir, *The Listener*, 4 July 1934.
8. *The Times*, 26 July 1934.

Bibliography

Ackerley, C. J., and S. E. Gontarski, *The Grove Companion to Samuel Beckett* (New York: Grove Press, 2004).

Beckett, Samuel, *More Pricks Than Kicks* (London: Calder and Boyars, [1934] 1970).

Farrow, Anthony, *Early Beckett: Art and Allusion in* More Pricks Than Kicks *and* Murphy (New York: Whitson, 1991).

McMillan, Dougald, 'Samuel Beckett and the Visual Arts: The Embarrassment of Allegory', in Ruby Cohn (ed.), *Samuel Beckett: A Collection of Criticism* (New York: McGraw-Hill, 1975), pp. 121–35.

Mercier, Vivian, *Beckett/Beckett* (New York: Oxford University Press, 1977).

Oppenheim, Lois, *The Painted Word: Samuel Beckett's Dialogue with Art* (Ann Arbor: University of Michigan Press, 2000).

Fair Papers:
Theories and Translations

10.

From the Lowlands to the Twin Peaks of 'Assumption'

J. D. O'Hara

We dance round in a ring and suppose,
But the Secret sits in the middle and knows.

Robert Frost

Samuel Beckett's brief 'Assumption', his first conventionally published piece, was published in 1929 and has escaped critical explanations until recently. Those explanations have demonstrated the value of the previous silence.

Basically, its bits of narrative imply a young man's experience from a bad time in a social world discomposed into fragments of unintelligent judgements perceived by a dangerously stressed superior unable to improve them. He becomes mentally stressed even apart from them. But then a woman from that society intrudes into his private bedroom world. The social world disappears. Her effect upon him, puzzlingly evoked, leads to his death. She grieves.

Unsurprisingly, that first condition of the man's existence is a brief and partial expression of the author's own. Its scattered mentions of real details evoke little. That life is better shown by testimony from the author, as he summarised his youth for James Knowlson:

> Beckett . . . went into a period of growing introspection, depression, and withdrawal. This probably resulted from a combination of factors: first, the natural tendency he had had from childhood to sit back, observe, and listen, noting the oddities of what others said and the idiosyncrasies or follies of their behavior; second, his keen awareness of his own intelligence and sensitivity. These characteristics were ultimately to contribute to Beckett's success as a writer. But during his time as a student, they seem to have led only to an unhappy separation from all but a few close friends . . . He was still strictly teetotal and a nonsmoker. He confessed later to feelings of superiority and contempt, which led to a depression that came to seem, to use the word he used himself, 'morbid'.[1]

Born in 1906, Beckett cannot be expected to have had so coherent a sense of his condition while writing 'Assumption'. Nor had he yet learned enough about Freud's new descriptions of mental life, despite his man's use of 'applied psychology'.[2] But he had read several poorly written stories by Balzac that used sources taken from Emanuel Swedenborg's grandiose claims about life and the afterlife and structuring the lives of one or two French characters.

Basically, Swedenborg claimed that every human is composed of two lives. The obvious one is embodied literally in his flesh and blood. The second is that of a seraph, a spiritual self trapped in that body that can escape only when the body dies. A sensitive person, such as the story's man, struggles with these two identities in the section beginning 'In the silence of his room'.[3] But Swedenborg would not approve these identities.

A 'wild rebellious surge',[4] caged and longing for realisation in sound and 'fused with the cosmic discord'[5] – the previous social comments are equally made here, quite exaggerated. 'Its struggle for divinity was as real as his own.'[6] A comic image undercuts that verbiage: 'the meanest mongrel . . . in the gutter'[7] can bark freely, like those students, but some Power keeps the man from its 'conscious completion'[8] and forces him to 'forget his fine imperfection'.[9] The man wants his inner seraph to be let out, though its need to express is not spiritual.

Until it is released, 'that flesh-locked sea of silence achieved a miserable consummation in driblets of sound'.[10] That last phrase introduces much liquidity, as dams break and so on, but 'each falling leaf'[11] echoes the whispering of the social man. The man's retreat to his room has given Beckett a chance to pile up metaphorically his explanation of the split self that will appear soon. Instead of a next day in the social world we learn that 'he scarcely left his room, scarcely spoke'.[12]

But this section began 'In the silence of his room'.[13] Now, out of time, he is 'listening for the . . . torrent that must destroy him'.[14] That statement picks up the 'afraid' from the paragraph's beginning. 'His fine imperfection'[15] is not fine, and he is afraid of both alternatives. Rather than settling for either cause of a split self and disaster, Beckett takes that conventional advice to detectives, 'cherchez la femme'.

'At this moment the Woman came to him . . . He was listening in the dusk when she came, listening so intently that he did not hear her enter.'[16] This transition is rather skilfully achieved. All the jumble of metaphors and conditions of existence are erased. The seraph is silenced. The young man is back in his social existence, cornered by one of those intellectually vapid culture-manglers.

But unlike those, this one has a sex. She also makes him wince at the regularity of her clear, steady speech. He had been listening for that torrent. We can skip the details of his confrontation with flesh and blood animal reality, evading his own wordings. James Knowlson has identified her as a significant part of Beckett's real life, Peggy Sinclair.[17] The man senses, apparently contradictorily, that 'something had gone out from him . . . something of the desire to live, something of the unreasonable tenacity with which he shrank from dissolution'.[18] The man is no longer desiring this double conception of life, seduced by the woman's role in hers.

But she is a day visitor and turns on lights. At night, when she has left, the intensity of that longing for the seraph returns, and brings with it its escape to an existence now evoked by meaningless general words (god gets three capitals) and defined by ordinary reality through negation: 'birdless, cloudless, colourless skies'.[19] 'Then it happened.'[20] Let Balzac tell the story.

It ends his novel *Louis Lambert*. Lambert has returned to Blois after years of Swedenborg studying in Paris. His uncle tells a former friend seeking him that he had returned to prepare himself to 'jeter une si vigoureuse clameur'.[21] But he merely returned. Then he met a wealthy Jewish heiress. 'Aussitôt que Lambert aperçut mademoiselle de Villenoix, il devina l'ange sous cette forme. Les riches facultés de son âme, sa pente vers l'extase.'[22] It was love at first insight. 'Mon pauvre neveu devait épouser la plus riche héritière de Blois, mais la veille de son mariage il est devenu fou.'[23] Undismayed, Mlle de Villenoix took him under her care, in her home. 'Lambert mourut à l'âge de vingt-huit ans . . . entre les bras de son amie.'[24] Beckett's own age, in short.

One final mention of Balzac provides a good ending. In *Séraphita* the escaping seraph's last ideas reach no audience, 'ni par la parole, ni par le regard, ni par le geste'.[25] That chapter of the novel is titled 'L'Assomption'.

Notes

1. James Knowlson, *Damned to Fame*, p. 79.
2. Samuel Beckett, 'Assumption', p. 4.
3. Ibid. p. 4.
4. Ibid. p. 4.
5. Ibid. p. 4.
6. Ibid. p. 4.
7. Ibid. p. 4.
8. Ibid. p. 4.
9. Ibid. p. 4.

10. Ibid. p. 5.
11. Ibid. p. 5.
12. Ibid. p. 5.
13. Ibid. p. 4.
14. Ibid. p. 5.
15. Ibid. p. 4.
16. Ibid. p. 5.
17. Knowlson, *Damned to Fame*, p. 90 ff.; p. 119.
18. Beckett, 'Assumption', p. 6.
19. Ibid. p. 7.
20. Ibid. p. 7.
21. Honoré de Balzac, *Louis Lambert*, from *Études philosophiques*, p. 114.
22. Ibid. p. 132. The angel under the fleshly form is a basic Swedenborgian notion.
23. Ibid. p. 152.
24. Ibid. p. 173.
25. Balzac, *Séraphita*, from *Études philosophiques*, p. 128.

Bibliography

Balzac, Honoré de, *Études philosophiques, V: La Comédie humaine: Oeuvres Complètes*, Vol. 31 (Paris: Louis Conard, 1910).

Beckett, Samuel, 'Assumption', in S. E. Gontarski (ed.), *The Complete Short Prose, 1929–1989* (New York: Grove Press, 1995), pp. 3–7.

Frost, Robert, *The Poetry of Robert Frost*, ed. E. C. Lathem (New York: Holt, Rinehart and Winston, 1969).

Knowlson, James, *Damned to Fame: The Life of Samuel Beckett* (New York: Simon and Schuster, 1996).

11.

Refiguring, Revising and Reprinting *The Lost Ones*

S. E. Gontarski

When David Warrilow was performing the stage adaptation of Beckett's story *The Lost Ones* in Germany, a literary critic accosted him after the show to suggest that the dimensions of the cylinder, 'fifty metres round and eighteen high', could not be correct. That is, if the total surface area of the cylinder (or even the total wall or 'mural' surface) was indeed 80,000 square centimetres, as all book versions of the story, French and English, have it on at least the opening page, then the cylinder would, in fact, have to be minuscule. Conversely, if the cylinder's dimensions were correct, then the surface area was in error.

Warrilow replied that he would see Beckett himself the following day and pose the question of the cylinder's dimensions to him directly. Beckett then acknowledged 'that the figure eighteen was indeed a most regrettable error'.[1] Some time later when Warrilow was making a film version of the story, he checked with Beckett a second time, and Beckett reconfirmed the figure of sixteen metres for the cylinder's height, adding, 'After all, you can't play fast and loose with pi'.[2] But Warrilow apparently never thought to raise the next logical question, that of the surface area derived from either the figures originally published in the English texts or the adjusted figure of sixteen metres, which was in accord with the original French text. In either case 80,000 square centimetres of surface area is very far off the mark, that is, by at least two decimal places, for a cylinder of either eighteen or sixteen metres with a circumference of fifty metres.[3]

The only texts to print the cylinder's correct height, sixteen metres, are the French text, *Le Dépeupleur*, and, surprisingly, an American version printed *after* all English book versions had appeared, that in Grove Press's rapidly failing literary magazine *Evergreen Review*. The *Evergreen Review* edition, printed as a Dell paperback in the spring of 1973, presents the total surface area for this cylinder of sixteen metres high as 'twelve million' square centimetres, the mathematically correct figure. The French edition, on the other hand, while it has the size of the cylinder correct, presents its surface area as 'quatre-vingt mille centimètres carrés' (i.e. 80,000 square centimetres), the same as both American and British editions. If, however, one calculates the surface area, including the area of the ceiling and floor, of a cylinder sixteen by fifty metres, the total surface would be about twelve million square centimetres – eight million for the wall surface and two million each for the areas of ceiling and floor. Each of the figures in the cylinder has approximately one square metre of floor space: 'One body per square metre or two hundred bodies is all round numbers' (actually 205 by most calculations);[4] Beckett, or rather the narrator, confirms these figures in the third paragraph of the story: 'Inside a cylinder fifty metres round and sixteen high for the sake of harmony or a total surface of roughly twelve hundred square metres [or twelve million square centimetres, i.e. including ceiling and floor] of which eight hundred [square metres or eight million square centimetres] mural [i.e. wall area]'.[5] All book versions of the story, French and English, however, present the total surface area on the opening page as 80,000 square centimetres, a figure that is then contradicted several pages later. When critic Enoch Brater notes the discrepancy in the height of the cylinder between the French and English texts, he concludes, 'Though the author initially told his English publisher that [the figure 50 x 18] was a misprint, and that the fault was entirely his own, he let it stand.'[6] Beckett, however, corrected the figures for the *Evergreen Review* version, which is the last version published and, it seems, the only text with the correct figures, but this text has been ignored by publishers and scholars alike.

In addition, both British and American book versions of the story (the latter simply photo-offset from the British edition in which the errors above were introduced)[7] contain another publishing blunder: 'The short queue is not necessarily the most rapid and such a one starting fifth may well find himself first before such another starting tenth assuming of course they start together.'[8] The figures above are as they appear in both English language book editions, but they are clearly transposed so that the sentence actually contradicts itself. In the *Evergreen Review* edition, on the other hand, the figures make sense: 'The short queue is not necessarily the most rapid and such a one starting tenth may well find himself first before such another starting fifth assuming of course they start together.'[9] In *Le Dépeupleur*[10] the figures accord with those of the *Evergreen Review* edition.

The *Evergreen Review* edition, however, contains one aberration worth noting. It drops the number from the following: 'The more so as the [two] storms have this in common.'[11] With the insertion of the word 'two' in the sentence above, the *Evergreen Review* text is the most accurate text available for *The Lost Ones*, French or English. It is that text – with the original French and *Evergreen* figure of sixteen metres for the cylinder's height but a total surface area of twelve million square centimetres for the cylinder, the mathematically accurate figure that appears only in the *Evergreen Review* edition – that has been reprinted by Grove Press in *Samuel Beckett: The Complete Short Prose, 1929–1989* (1995). That 'revised' text also has the queue with ten people move faster than the queue with five people as it does in the *Evergreen Review* and in *Le Dépeupleur*, and retains the number of storms at 'two' as it is in all book versions.

Notes

1. 'From David Warrilow', p. 87.
2. Ibid. p. 88.
3. The surface area of the cylinder itself would be determined by multiplying height by circumference, 16 x 50, for an area of 800 metres. But the conversion from square metres to square centimetres is derived by the multiplication not by 100, but by 100 x 100, or 10,000. Thus 800 square metres is the equivalent of 8,000,000 square centimetres. Despite Beckett's comment, pi enters the equation only for the area of ceiling and floor.
4. Samuel Beckett, *The Lost Ones* (Calder and Grove editions), p. 13.
5. Ibid. p. 16.
6. Enoch Brater, *The Drama in the Text*, p. 104.
7. The British (London: Calder and Boyars, 1972) and American (New York: Grove Press, 1972) editions are identical down to the missing page number on the final page, what should be p. 63.
8. Beckett, *The Lost Ones* (Calder and Grove editions), pp. 47–8.
9. Beckett, *The Lost Ones* (*Evergreen Review* edition), p. 58.
10. Beckett, *Le Dépeupleur*, p. 42.
11. Beckett, *The Lost Ones* (*Evergreen Review* edition), p. 56.

Bibliography

Beckett, Samuel, *Le Dépeupleur* (Paris: Éditions de Minuit, 1970).

Beckett, Samuel, *The Lost Ones* (London: Calder and Boyars, 1972; New York: Grove Press, 1972).

Beckett, Samuel, *The Lost Ones*, *Evergreen Review*, 96 (spring 1973), pp. 41–64.

Beckett, Samuel, *The Lost Ones*, in S. E. Gontarski (ed.), *Samuel Beckett: The Complete Short Prose, 1929–1989* (New York: Grove Press, 1995), pp. 202–23.

Brater, Enoch, *The Drama in the Text: Beckett's Late Fiction* (Oxford: Oxford University Press, 1994).

'From David Warrilow', in *As No Other Dare Fail: For Samuel Beckett on his 80th Birthday by his Friends and Admirers* (London: John Calder, 1986; New York: Riverrun Press, 1986), pp. 87–8.

Beckett and Leopardi

Daniela Caselli

> The powers of evocation of this Italianate Irishman were simply immense.[1]

Writing to Thomas MacGreevy in July 1930, Beckett defends his unfashionable choice to read Schopenhauer by referring to Leopardi and Proust:

> I am reading Schopenhauer. Everyone laughs at that. Beaufret & Alfy etc. But I am not reading philosophy, nor caring whether he is right or wrong or a good or worthless metaphysician. An intellectual justification of unhappiness – the greatest that has ever been attempted – is worth the examination of one who is interested in Leopardi & Proust rather than Carducci & Barrès.[2]

Samuel Beckett's *Proust*-based reading of Leopardi has been noted by those who see in Beckett's *oeuvre* a 'happy hunting ground for comparatists'.[3] The quotations of Leopardi in *Proust* are, however, not the only occurrences within the Beckett canon; indeed, Leopardi's intermittent appearances help us understand how Beckett's intertextual modalities change in time.

The semio-cultural notion of intertextuality will be my theoretical framework here. Taking intertextuality as what 'designates the multitude of ways a text has of not being self-contained, of being traversed by otherness',[4] I shall limit this otherness to literary texts in order to use intertextuality as a tool for interpreting Leopardi's presence in Beckett, taking up Cesare Segre's distinction between 'intertextual' and 'interdiscursive'[5] in order to avoid either stepping back into neo-positivistic comparativism or slipping into the assumption of pan-intertextuality.[6] Seeing, after Segre, intertextuality as part of the wider phenomenon of interdiscursivity, I propose to draw practical – rather than ontological – boundaries between linguistic productions that can be anchored to a specific text and discourses that circulate freely within the linguistic system.

My aim in analysing Beckett's texts is, then, not to reconstruct his authorial intentions, but to explore what kind of Leopardi we find in Beckett. In other words, I shall not focus on how much Leopardi Beckett knew and read, but on how we can read Leopardi's presence in Beckett. This is not to circumvent the problem that current evidence on Beckett's access to Leopardi is still inconclusive, but to reflect on the changing value of literary quotations, allusions and parodies in Beckett. There are no surviving notebooks for the years 1928 to 1930, so that the textual occurrence of Leopardi in the early works (together with Kant, Proust, Bergson, Vico, Bruno and Schopenhauer) has no archival correlative.[7] And yet, the correspondence and Beckett's library holdings confirm Leopardi's significance. At the time of his death, there were two editions of Leopardi in Beckett's library: *I Canti*, edited by Ettore Fabietti, published in 1936 in Milan by the Casa per Edizioni Popolari, and his undated *Prose*, edited by Pietro Giordani, also published in Milan by the Istituto Editoriale Italiano, possibly suggesting a more sustained engagement than previously thought with the *Operette morali* and the *Zibaldone*.[8]

The first Leopardi occurrence is to be found in the early essay 'Dante... Bruno. Vico.. Joyce' (1929),[9] in which Leopardi covertly introduces Dante as a term of the comparison with Joyce. We read:

> To justify our title, we must move North, '*Sovra'l bel fiume d'Arno alla gran villa*' . . . Between '*colui per lo cui verso – il meonio cantor non è più solo*' and the 'still to-day insufficiently malestimated notesnatcher, Shem the Penman,' there exists considerable circumstancial similarity.[10]

The first quotation (in italics) belongs to the *Comedy*;[11] Dante, in the sixth bolgia of the *Inferno*, speaks to Catalano dei Malvolti and Loderingo degli Andalò. When the two hypocrites ask him about his identity, he introduces himself saying 'I' fui nato e cresciuto / sovra 'l bel fiume d'Arno a la gran villa, / e son col corpo ch'i' ho sempre avuto'.[12] Dante's self-description is used by Beckett to begin the last section of his essay, the one devoted to the comparison between Dante himself and Joyce. The second quotation does not refer to a text by Dante, but to a line and a half of Leopardi's 'Sopra il monumento di Dante che si preparava in Firenze' (1818),[13] a poem that describes Dante as the only author capable of reaching Homer's poetic height. Beckett uses this brief quotation to simultaneously introduce, describe and praise Dante, notably in order to juxtapose him to Joyce. While not acknowledged (as most of Beckett's quotations in this essay are not), these lines by Leopardi construct a pedestal for Joyce.

The historic and patriotic elements of Leopardi's early poem are obliterated here, but Leopardi's admiration for Dante remains clearly perceptible. In Leopardi the juxtaposition of Dante and Homer works as a guarantee of Dante's poetic excellence; in Beckett, the comparison between Dante and Joyce is mediated by Leopardi's lines, within which another comparison is embedded, to highlight Joyce's indisputable literary greatness. Beckett's comparative operation is a *mise en abyme* – a game of mirrors in which Joyce's authority is reinforced by the literary tradition that goes from Homer to Dante, via Leopardi.

This first bit of evidence of Beckett's long-term interest in Leopardi is followed by a more sustained intertextual relationship in *Proust* (1931). Although Leopardi's presence in this essay has been noticed before, I would like to analyse the different functions of the three quotations from Leopardi's poem 'A se stesso' (1833), how they work in context, and what this reference means if contextualised in this phase of Beckett's work.[14]

Quoting 'A se stesso',[15] Beckett chose one of the most overtly anti-idyllic poems of Leopardi;[16] he did so against contemporary critical opinions, which tended to reduce the radical quality of the poem through biographical readings and dismiss its ontological preoccupations, judged to be excessively philosophical for a poem.[17] In 'A se stesso' Leopardi tries to negate 'cari inganni' (cherished deceptions) and 'vane speranze' (vain hopes). The poem, composed of a series of negations, negative pronouns, adjectives and nouns with a special negative connotation in Leopardi's idiolect,[18] declares dead not only hope but also desire. This creates its paradoxical structure: while asserting the death of desire, the poem is the place where desire is recreated through the testimony of its absence. Writing the death of desire means opening a space for desire itself, which can be experienced solely in a negative way – as void, as lack.

In 'A se stesso' Leopardi expresses the paradox of living as the constant oscillation between desire and disappointment; he proposes the death of desire as the only solution against the suffocating mechanism in which we are trapped – and yet, this solution is also an impossible one. The dialectics of seeing the suppression of desire as the only solution to suffering, and of expressing this impossible solution through poetry (therefore recreating desire itself), cannot but be a paradoxical process without synthesis. Leopardi uses reason as an implacable analytic instrument probing into the structure of reality, which, revealing itself as contradictory and paradoxical, forces him to recognise the limits of reason itself, and therefore to reject the Aristotelian principle of non-contradiction.[19] Leopardi represents the crisis of Enlightenment in Italian literature; reason is still used as an instrument, but it has lost its redemptive power. Consequently, Leopardi uses poetry not as an irrational instrument, but as the only possible way to allude to the untranslatable experience of the chaotic nature of existence; only poetry can bear witness to the inescapable paradox of existence and at the same time resist it. Leopardi's art lies in this dialectical process, which does not accept totalising negation as much as it refuses absolute affirmation.[20] It cannot provide the reader with a reassuring synthesis, and therefore remains an incessant interrogation: in Beckett's words, we could say that 'la négation n'est pas possible. Pas plus que l'affirmation. Il est absurde de dire que c'est absurde. C'est encore porter un jugement de valeur. On ne peut pas protester, et on ne peut pas opiner.'[21]

These characteristics of Leopardi's poetry recall the preoccupations of the early Beckett, in whom we find a dialectical movement that testifies to the absence of desire and simultaneously recreates a paradoxical space for desire to exist and for writing to proceed; they both refuse the totalising power of an absolute negation, and for this reason neither of them can be labelled a nihilist, and even less so a pessimist – *The Unnamable*'s famous last sentence would be an appropriate description of Leopardi's art. When Beckett writes about 'résister aux deux grandes tentations, celle du réel et celle du mensonge'[22] he is trying to do something similar to Leopardi negating Aristotle; he is trying to build a paradoxical in-between space where it is possible to live and to write.

The three quotations of Leopardi in *Proust* have different functions in the economy of the text. The first quotation, 'e fango è il mondo', appears on the frontispiece.[23] The name of Leopardi appears after the quotation, making the attribution clear. But if the ownership of the line is apparent, its meaning remains detached from the rest of the poem, since the intertextual activation of the non-quoted part of the poem would have been extremely difficult for an English speaker at that time. Therefore, this quotation seems to have the general function of announcing the tone of the essay, which cannot be regarded only as a work of criticism on the French author; as many scholars have noted, *Proust* is not simply an interpretation of the *Recherche*, but a series of metacritical reflections, intertwined with quotations and references to many literary texts, through which Beckett is seeking to trace the coordinates of what will be his future literary career.

The second Leopardi quotation appears in this context: Leopardi is called a 'sage', and lines four and five of 'A se stesso' are quoted: 'In noi di cari inganni / non che la speme, il desiderio spento'. This second quotation marks 'a first pause' in the text, as Beckett puts it in his 1956 letter to Barney Rosset.[24] Although Leopardi's lines are graphically detached from the text, they are connected to the context in a different way from the first quotation. Leopardi is catalogued as one of the 'sages' who proposed the only impossible solution to living – the 'ablation of desire'. The disruption of illusions and even the negation of desire is the *phármakon* that Beckett accepts from Leopardi. Leopardi is thus not simply a way to highlight some aspects of Proust's work, but he is (together with Schopenhauer and Calderón) part of a literary tradition to which Beckett turns because of similar preoccupations. He is still quoting, or rather misquoting, from 'A se stesso' in 1954 when in a dejected letter to Maurice Nadeau he writes: 'I feel I am further than ever from being able to write. Non che la speme il desiderio é morto. Or almost.'[25]

The second quotation from Leopardi in *Proust* leads us down a more complex intertextual path. The philosophical importance of Leopardi in *Proust* is clearer here, as 'A se stesso' maps out the dilemma of desire on which the essay focuses. Leopardi is now an authority to whom Beckett refers, the quotation working as both homage to and summary of Leopardi's thought. The synthetic formulation of Leopardi's thought as 'ablation of desire', which is likely to be indebted to a Schopenhauerian perspective on his work,[26] becomes apparent in the third occurrence of 'A se stesso'. The line quoted is, again, 'Non che la speme il desiderio', but now it is within the corpus of the text, and left incomplete; the reader has to link it back to the previous quotation and realise that it is an intratextual rather than an intertextual reference. The lines are an economical device to refer to the ablation of desire.

Leopardi is not just quoted in the Beckett *oeuvre*, however. In *Dream of Fair to Middling Women* and *Molloy* we find different forms of intertextuality, such as allusion and parody. *Dream of Fair to Middling Women* (written in 1932 but published posthumously) is the first fictional expression of *Proust*'s metaliterary theories. The text can be called an anti-novel since it sets out to destroy the realistic presuppositions that had dominated nineteenth-century fiction and yet it remains trapped in the very structure it wants to dismantle. *Dream of Fair to Middling Women* is representative of Beckett's early phase; the theoretical presuppositions that will be crucial for his subsequent works are here demonstrated, and the text can still be summarised and conceptualised. We do not yet experience the deep destabilisation of our interpretive habits, which Beckett will later create.[27]

In *Dream*, Beckett's verbal virtuosity and literary recycling often fizzle out in multilingual puns while targeting mimetic assumptions, while the metanarrative complexity performed by Beckett's more mature art is here boomingly voiced by a narrator who plays the role of puppet-master. There are two intertextual references to Leopardi in this text.[28] On page eighteen we read:

> So utterly did she queer his pitch that he was moved to quote 'le soleil est mort' in petto, and his time of the lilies shifted over to the night hours, sitting vigilant among the rats, alla fioca lucerna leggendo Meredith.[29]

'Alla fioca lucerna leggendo' is a modification of line fifteen of 'Le Ricordanze', another poem by Leopardi, dated 1829. The absence of diacritics and lack of attribution cast the reader into a state of uncertainty. The allusion to Leopardi's 'Le Ricordanze' in *Dream* modifies Leopardi's 'alla fioca lucerna poetando' into 'alla fioca lucerna leggendo'. The context in which this half-line from 'Le Ricordanze' is originally situated reads:

> [. . .] e spesso all'ore tarde, assiso
> sul conscio letto, dolorosamente
> alla fioca lucerna poetando,
> lamentai co' silenzi e con la notte
> il fuggitivo spirto, ed a me stesso
> in sul languir cantai funereo canto.[30]

The Beckett text brings Leopardi's words into a new circuit of meaning, which may well be a 'trouble de mémoire', justifiable by the whole structure of *Dream*, where quotations, allusions, references to other texts and literary puns abound and often seem to come directly from the imaginary Beckett archive of memory.[31] Nevertheless, this modification has a clear function, since it completes the sense of the English sentence with a quotation in French, and it ends with an allusion in Italian. In Leopardi, the lyrical 'I' was in an active situation, composing poetry; Beckett's confused Belacqua is instead passive. The Beckett anti-hero, endowed with his own literary aspirations, cannot compose poetry, but can only read, and, moreover, read a serious author of the English nineteenth century such as Meredith. The context of *Dream* thus renders Leopardi's poem banal: after the Smeraldina has 'raped' Belacqua, he no longer enjoys the hours spent waiting for her; now that the 'desiderio' is 'spento', Bel's favourite moments are those spent reading by the light of the 'fioca lucerna'.

The decontextualisation of Leopardi's poem has a parodic effect due both to the contrast between the Italian and the English, and to that between the original context of Leopardi's poem and the trivial 'story' told by the narrating voice of *Dream*. The lyrical 'I' of 'Le Ricordanze' faces the simultaneous existence of his hopes and his disillusionment, realising the impotence of his memory and his inability to recreate a time when he could still believe in these illusions. Belacqua, almost lost in a story where 'we don't quite know where we are',[32] is a character manipulated by a puppet-master whom the reader is continually invited to distrust. The parodic effect lies in this intertextual contrast, capable of producing a decontextualisation that we gradually understand to be not only linguistic, but also thematic, formal and structural.

The quotations from Leopardi's 'A se stesso' in *Proust* and the allusion to 'Le Ricordanze' in *Dream* have profoundly different functions. In *Proust* Leopardi is part of a tragic genealogy to which the text claims to belong; in *Dream* his lines are the object of parody. Parody is the main instrument through which this anti-novel tries to elaborate an alternative to the literary canon; it is a metaliterary device that draws attention to the text as artifice. Leopardi, in other words, contributes to *Dream*'s intertextual strategies aimed at subtracting credibility from literature, but this goal is missed due to the rather rigid anti-model structure of this text, which prevents it from being as subversive as it seems to be claiming.

The second reference to Leopardi in *Dream* is comparably revealing. After receiving 'the Smeraldina's billet-doux', Belacqua is victim of a 'severe bout of hepatic colics [which] confined him to his room'; he moans in different languages until he gets to the point where

> he declined the darkest passages of Schopenhauer, Vigny, Leopardi, Espronceda, Inge, Hatiz, Saadi, Espronerda, Becquer and the other Epimethei. All day he told the beads of his spleen. *Or posa per sempre*, for example, he was liable to murmur, lifting and shifting the seat of the disturbance, *stanco mio cor. Assai palpitasti* . . . and as much of that gloomy composition as he could remember.[33]

The italics of the Italian slightly modify the line: what in Leopardi was 'poserai' becomes in Beckett 'posa', shifting the verbal tense. It might be a simple mistake on the part of Beckett, but it seems to me much more likely that the mistake has to be attributed to Belacqua, who clumsily murmurs 'as much . . . as he could remember', accompanying his declamation with theatrical gestures.[34]

Leopardi is not simply mentioned, but becomes instead part of the fictive world of the novel while at the same time being listed among a series of partly invented and partly modified names. Leopardi is quoted by a Belacqua in crisis while also being the object of the narrator's observations, who, with ironic distance, judges 'A se stesso' a 'gloomy composition'. The parodic effect is multiple: Leopardi is the device through which the narrator taunts and mocks Belacqua and his literary-depressive states; he is also the instrument through which Beckett puts some distance between himself and that 'former self' who wrote *Proust*, using Leopardi as a literary authority;[35] finally, Leopardi's 'A se stesso' is parodied through the narrator's reductive phrase 'gloomy composition'.

The half-line of 'A se stesso' refers not only to the whole of Leopardi's text, but also to the use Beckett made of it in *Proust*. Leopardi's tragic nucleus that had been so acutely identified in *Proust* cannot survive within the destructive will animating *Dream*. This specific quotation with its parodic effects is a case of intratextuality, a frequent practice in Beckett's works. Leopardi participates in the general mechanism of destruction pervading *Dream*; he is one of the instruments used by Beckett to challenge the power of the strange institution called literature, while participating in it.

If Leopardi and his tragic depth as previously recognised by Beckett do not survive at the structural level, the ontological problematics of the 'ablation of desire' still bothers Belacqua, just as it will bother Murphy and, to a different extent, Molloy. Belacqua aspires to move 'with the dead and the dead-born, and the unborn and the never-to-be-born, in a Limbo purged of desire'.[36] In 'A se stesso', as we have already seen in the case of *Proust*, the necessity of the death of desire is paradoxically stated; the locus of this negation is a poem, where the assertion of the death of desire becomes a testimony of its absence, and therefore an allusion to it, and an indirect recreation of desire itself. This tentative suppression of desire in Leopardi is a rational operation, deriving from the knowledge of the 'arido vero', while in Belacqua it survives as an unconscious state of alienation. Belacqua is 'at his simplest . . . trine'; the 'third' Belacqua, whom we are not authorised to assume to be 'the real Belacqua', is:

> the dark gulf, when the glare of the will and the hammer-strokes of the brain doomed outside to take flight from its quarry were expunged, the Limbo and the Wombtomb alive with the unanxious spirits of quiet celebration, where there was no conflict of flight and flow and Eros was as null as Anteros and Night had no daughters. He was bogged in indolence, without identity, impervious alike to its pull and goading.[37]

For Belacqua it seems to be possible to reach the 'ablation of desire', which is at any rate an abandonment of the self, not a 'wilful abolishing of the will',[38] since

> he was grotesque, wanting to 'troglodyse' himself, worse than grotesque. It was impossible to switch off the inward glare, willfully to suppress the bureaucratic mind. It was stupid to imagine that he could be organized as Limbo and wombtomb, worse than stupid.[39]

At this point it becomes clear how Leopardi in *Dream* is little more than a starting point for a personal elaboration of the notion of 'ablation of desire'. In Leopardi the poetic assertion of the death of desire is a conscious and a rational act, deriving from the inescapable disappointment following desire and illusion. In the early Beckett this paradoxical Leopardian negation of desire becomes a desire for alienation, which Belacqua can still reach unconsciously. On the other hand, Murphy will fail to reach Mr Endon's catatonic state, never achieving 'the Belacqua bliss'.[40] Leopardi's presence in this text is now intratextual; once tragic but now gloomy, Leopardi is partially rescued at thematic level, since the 'ablation of desire' remains one of the crucial concerns of this anti-novel.

The fourth Beckett text that alludes to Leopardi is *Molloy*, chronologically and structurally distant from the two previously analysed. *Molloy* belongs to a different phase in Beckett's art, a phase where anti-plot, extensive use of verbal and interlinguistic puns, and the massive presence of intertextual references disappear to give place to an 'a-novel' (no longer an anti-novel), where our interpreting habits are constantly destabilised.[41] *Molloy*'s intertextual references (much less generously sprinkled throughout the text) perform, like the rest of the text, their own undoing.

Half of line five from Leopardi's 'A se stesso' appears in the English partially self-translated version, where Molloy describes the burial of Lousse-Sophie's dog, which he has killed. It is inserted in an overtly sexual context:

> It was she dug the hole because I couldn't, though I was the gentleman, because of my leg . . . I had so to speak only one leg at my disposal, I was virtually one-legged, and I would have been happier, livelier, amputated at the groin. And if they had removed a few testicles into the bargain I wouldn't have objected. For from such testicles as mine, dangling at mid-thigh at the end of a meagre cord, there was nothing more to be squeezed, not a drop. So that non che la speme il desiderio, and I longed to see them gone, from the old stand where they bore false witness, for and against, in the lifelong charge against me.[42]

Leopardi appears in the sentence by stealth; the reader realises the extraneous nature of the half-line through the use of Italian, since there are neither italics nor quotation marks. The presence of the Italian language has in *Molloy* a very different value from its previous occurrences in a multilingual text such as *Dream*, since its strangeness will be much more acutely perceived. The reader must complete the half-line by Leopardi: 'è spento' will be the conclusion of this sentence, meant to describe Molloy's impotence and absence of desire. Leopardi's 'A se stesso', a poetic distillation of the incurious seeker's 'deux besoins', appears here lacking and amputated, mirroring the narrator's reality and desires. Molloy's 'leg' is not just his 'bad leg' but what makes him a gentleman (his 'manhood'); the desired amputation is, suggestively, to take place 'at the groin' – his 'few' testicles, which are 'nothing to write home about', should also go. It is hard to resist the temptation to utter 'speme', Joyceanly, aloud: it sounds remarkably like 'sperm', adding an aural dimension to the joke.[43] The existential 'lifelong charge against me', the mark of 'someone interested in' Leopardi, Proust and Schopenhauer, is incorporated, both seriously and obscenely, through a paradoxically mutilated Leopardi.

This reflexive allusion has a different function from that of *Dream*; whereas in *Dream* the parodic effect of the allusion invested Leopardi, Belacqua and his way of reading him, and the way Leopardi was read by a younger Beckett, in *Molloy* we have an almost exclusively intratextual reference to Beckett's previous use of Leopardi. The text referred to by this allusion is not just the 'A se stesso' by Leopardi, but also the partial 'A se stesso' quoted and alluded to in *Proust* and *Dream*. We are no longer dealing with Leopardi, but with the specific synthesis of Leopardi's poetry and thought that Beckett had made in the two previous texts. In order to complete the missing half-line of Leopardi's poem, the reader does not have to go to Leopardi's text, but only to the quotation in *Proust*. The contrast between Leopardi's text and Beckett's sexual context creates a parodic effect that is doubled by the choice of the particular Leopardian line already used by Beckett and representative of his interpretation of Leopardi's thought. The potential of 'A se stesso' is, we could say, squeezed to its last drop.

If the suppression of desire towards which Leopardi aspires seems to be cancelled by this intertextual parodic practice, Molloy is nevertheless still the 'incurious seeker':

> [F]or to know nothing is nothing, not to want to know anything likewise, but to be beyond knowing anything, to know you are beyond knowing anything, that is when peace enters in, to the soul of the incurious seeker.[44]

The aspiration to the 'ablation of desire' is now translated into Molloy's desire for a progressive loss of his body parts and mobility, which causes in him a 'paradoxical cheerfulness'.[45]

A progression can be observed in Beckett's intertextual modalities of appropriation of Leopardi; in 'Dante. . . Bruno. Vico.. Joyce', the brief quotation from Leopardi is used as a way to produce Joyce's authority by placing him in a literary genealogy going from Homer to Dante via Leopardi. In *Proust*, Leopardi punctuates the text's themes: quoted three times, he appears as a representative figure of a tragic literary tradition of which Beckett temporarily considers himself to be part. Leopardi is also the 'sage' who proposed the formula summarised by Beckett as the 'ablation of desire', which represented the goal towards which Belacqua,

Murphy and, at least partially, Watt and Molloy struggled. In *Dream*, Leopardi's 'Le Ricordanze' is dismissed as 'gloomy', taunting both Belacqua and the author of *Proust* but keeping alive the 'ablation of desire' in Belacqua's aspiration to estrangement. In *Molloy*, the distance between Leopardi and Beckett is even greater: the reference is intratextual more than intertextual, and the ontological dimension of Leopardi's desire translates into the comic wish to self-castrate.

Beckett's use of Leopardi can be viewed as part of the general trajectory followed by his art.[46] The oscillation, in Beckett's early works, between a profound fascination with the literary heritage and a stubborn determination to disrupt the same legacy is reflected by the different roles played by Leopardi in 'Dante. . . Bruno. Vico.. Joyce', *Proust* and *Dream of Fair to Middling Women*. The inclusion of a half-line by Leopardi in the English version of *Molloy* is part of a strategy that blurs the boundaries between literary references and Beckett's own writing, gradually erases quotations – although still partially playing with parody and allusion – and transforms intertextual references into intratextual ones.

Leopardi is kept alive in these Beckett texts through the initial formula of the 'ablation of desire', a nucleus that survives all parodic transformations and which works as a stimulus for subsequent elaborations of this early concern. Leopardi's paradoxical and interrogative art fascinated Beckett at the time when he was writing *Proust*, and provided him with a model of a tragic art made of repeated rhetorical questions, which Beckett gradually transformed into his art of 'rhetorical questions less the rhetoric'.[47]

Notes

1. Samuel Beckett, *More Pricks Than Kicks*, p. 143. This chapter is an updated version of my 'Beckett's Intertextual Modalities of Appropriation: The Case of Leopardi', *Journal of Beckett Studies*, 6.1 (autumn 1996), pp. 1–24; translated into Spanish and republished in *Beckettiana*, 7/8 (Buenos Aires: Facultad de Filosofia y Letras, Universidad de Buenos Aires, 1999), pp. 41–66.
2. Beckett to Thomas MacGreevy, c. 18 to 25 July 1930, in *The Letters of Samuel Beckett 1929–1940*, p. 33.
3. Ruby Cohn, 'A Note on Beckett, Dante and Geulincx', p. 93; Jean-Pierre Ferrini, 'Dante, Pétrarque, Leopardi, Beckett', pp. 53–66; Giuseppina Restivo, 'Caliban/Clov and Leopardi's Boys'; Elina Montes, 'Leopardi, Friedrich, Beckett', pp. 121–8; Andrea Cortellessa, '"E fango è il mondo" Beckett e Leopardi'; Davide Sannia, 'Cielo Grigio Cenere e nessun rumore'.
4. Barbara Johnson, 'Les fleurs du Mal Armé', p. 116.

5. See Cesare Segre, 'Intertestuale, interdiscorsivo'. See also Gian Biagio Conte, *Memoria dei poeti e sistema letterario*, and Daniela Caselli, *Beckett's Dantes*.
6. Michael Riffaterre, 'Interpretation and Undecidability', p. 227. For a detailed discussion of the problems raised by Riffaterre's theories, see my 'Rifunzionalizzare la nozione di intertestualità' and *Beckett's Dantes*.
7. See Lawrence E. Harvey, *Samuel Beckett: Poet and Critic*, p. 34; John Pilling, *Beckett Before Godot*, p. 11; Everett Frost, 'Preface', *Notes Diverse Holo*, pp. 21–2. See also Caselli, 'Thinking of "A Rhyme for Euganean"', pp. 209–33, and 'Beckett and Italy' (forthcoming). John C. Barnes asserts that Beckett studied Leopardi during his third year at Trinity College, but, since Beckett was an omnivorous reader, we cannot assume this is the only access he had to the Italian poet; see Barnes, 'La fortuna di Leopardi in Irlanda', p. 44. Barnes finds this information in an unpublished dissertation by Patrick Gilligan, 'Beckett and Dante: The First Phase', pp. 18–20. Trinity College has no record of acquisition dates prior to 1953.
8. Giacomo Leopardi, *I Canti*, ed. Ettore Fabietti (no marginalia), and *Prose, con uno studio di Pietro Giordani* (no marginalia); no date for the latter item, but a postcard is inserted, which indicates the date '9/7/35'. See Dirk Van Hulle and Mark Nixon, *Samuel Beckett's Library* (forthcoming). I would like to thank Dirk Van Hulle for providing me with this information.
9. Beckett, 'Dante... Bruno. Vico.. Joyce', pp. 19–33.
10. Ibid. p. 30.
11. Dante Alighieri, *The Divine Comedy: Inferno*, XXIII.94–5.
12. 'I was born and grew up on the fair stream of Arno, at the great town, and I am in the body that I have always had' (Alighieri, *Inferno*, p. 241).
13. 'D'aria e d'ingegno e di parlar diverso / per lo toscano suol cercando gia / l'ospite desioso / dove giaccia colui per lo cui verso / il meonio cantor non è più solo' (Leopardi, 'Sovra il monumento di Dante che si preparava in Firenze', p. 10, lines 18–22). Geoffrey L. Bickersteth rather cumbersomely translates: 'Differing from us in air and mind and tongue / Strangers thro' Tuscan territory fared, / Eager to find the grave / Of such a singer that no more among / The bards Maeonides stands forth alone' (Bickersteth (ed.), *The Poems of Leopardi*, p. 145).
14. Beckett, *Proust*, on the frontispiece, p. 7, and p. 46.
15. The text of the poem follows: 'Or poserai per sempre, / Stanco mio cor. Perì l'inganno estremo, / Ch'eterno io mi credei. Perì. Ben sento, / In noi di cari inganni, / Non che la speme, il desiderio è spento. / Posa per sempre. Assai / Palpitasti. Non val cosa nessuna / I moti tuoi, né di sospiri è degna / La terra. Amaro e noia / La vita, altro mai nulla; e fango è il mondo. / T'acqueta omai. Dispera / L'ultima volta. Al gener nostro il fato / Non donò che il morire. Omai disprezza / Te, la natura, il brutto / Poter che, ascoso, a comun danno impera, / E l'infinita vanità del tutto' (Leopardi, *Canti*, quoted); 'Now be for ever still, / Weary my heart. For the last cheat is dead, / I thought eternal. Dead. For us, I know / Not only the dear hope / Of being deluded gone, but the desire. / Rest still for ever. You / Have beaten long enough. And to no purpose / Were all your stirrings; earth not worth your sighs. / Boredom and bitterness / Is life, and the rest, nothing; the world is dirt. / Lie quiet now. Despair / For the last time. Fate granted to our kind /

Only to die. And now you may despise / Yourself, nature, the brute / Power which, hidden, ordains the common doom, / And all the immeasurable emptiness of things' (Leopardi, *Selected Prose and Poetry*, p. 281).

16. For an interpretation of Leopardi as anti-idyllic poet see Anna Dolfi, *Leopardi tra negazione e utopia*; see also her *Leopardi e il Novecento*.
17. In Italy, 'A se stesso' was not anthologised during those years.
18. For example, 'per sempre' (forever) has for Leopardi the power of an absolute impossibility of recovering time; compare his *Zibaldone di pensieri*, pp. 42–8, pp. 23–96.
19. Leopardi, facing the ontological paradox, writes: 'Contraddizione evidente e innegabile nell'ordine delle cose e nel modo della esistenza, contraddizione spaventevole; ma non per ciò men vera: misterio grande, da non potersi mai spiegare, se non negando (giusta il mio sistema) ogni verità o falsità assoluta, e rinunziando in certo modo anche al principio di cognizione, *non potest idem simul esse et non esse*' (*Zibaldone dei pensieri* 4129, p. 2253); 'Evident and undeniable contradiction in the order of things and in the mode of existence, frightening contradiction; but not less true because of this: great mystery, never to be explained, if not denying (if my system is correct) every absolute truth or falsity, and in some way renouncing to the principle of cognition, *non potest idem simul esse et non esse*' (translation mine).
20. 'La Dialectique est le mouvement par lequel la dépense est récupere dans la présence, elle est l'économie de la répétition. L'économie de la verité . . . Le tragique n'est pas l'impossibilité mais la nécessité de la répétition' (Jacques Derrida, 'Le Théâtre de la cruauté et la clôture de la représentation', pp. 362 and 364; English translation 'The Theatre of Cruelty and the Closure of Representation', pp. 246 and 248).
21. Charles Juliet, *Rencontre avec Samuel Beckett*, p. 49. Leopardi considers the possibility of reversing Leibniz's dictum into the principle 'tutto è male' ('everything is evil'), but rejects it because 'Non ardirei però estenderlo a dire che l'universo esistente il peggiore degli universi possibili, sostituendo così all'ottimismo il pessimismo. Chi può conoscere i limiti della possibilità?' (*Zibaldone dei pensieri*, 4174, p. 2297); 'I would not dare to extend it and to say that the existing universe is the worst of the possible universes, substituting pessimism for optimism. Who knows the limits of possibility?' (translation mine).
22. Beckett, 'Henri Hayden', p. 150.
23. 'The omission of the Leopardi epigraph (which gave such pleasure to Joyce because it could be turned into a multilingual mirror-image – 'immonde' for 'il mondo') in the 1965 reprint is much to be regretted' (Pilling, 'Beckett's *Proust*', p. 10.
24. Beckett to Barney Rosset, 30 August 1956: 'Suggested Readings: . . . Proust: Pages 1–7 i.e. to first pause and Leopardi again' (*The Letters of Samuel Beckett 1941–1956*, p. 646).
25. Beckett to Maurice Nadeau, 19 October 1954, *The Letters of Samuel Beckett 1941–1956*, p. 509.
26. John Pilling shows how the quotation of Calderón at the end of the essay comes directly from Schopenhauer, who quoted exactly the same lines in a similar context of *The World as Will and Representation*; see Pilling,

'Beckett's *Proust*', p. 12. For a detailed analysis of Schopenhauer's major role in *Proust* see Terence McQueeny, 'Beckett as Critic of Proust and Joyce' (unpublished doctoral dissertation). See also Matthew Feldman, *Beckett's Books*.

27. Carla Locatelli, *Unwording the World*.
28. The first one is on p. 18, the second on pp. 61–2.
29. Beckett, *Dream*, p. 18.
30. Leopardi, 'Le Ricordanze', lines 113–18.
31. Antoine Compagnon, *La seconde main ou le travail de la citation*.
32. Beckett, *Dream*, p. 9.
33. Beckett, *Dream*, pp. 61–2 (Beckett's italics).
34. While line one is 'Or poserai per sempre', line six is 'Posa per sempre. Assai / palpitasti'.
35. Beckett's letter to MacGreevy dated 21 September 1937 echoes: 'When I was ill I found that the only thing I could read was Schopenhauer' (*Letters 1929–1940*, p. 550; also quoted in Deirdre Bair, *Samuel Beckett: A Biography*, p. 260). The name Becquer suggests an authorial voice looking back on an earlier Beckett who considered himself part of a tradition of artists once regarded as tragic, now gloomy.
36. Beckett, *Dream*, p. 44.
37. Beckett, *Dream*, pp. 120, 121, 123.
38. Nicholas Zurbrugg, 'Beckett, *Proust* and *Dream of Fair to Middling Women*', p. 59.
39. Beckett, *Dream*, p. 123.
40. *Murphy*'s 'second zone' is described by Beckett as 'the Belacqua bliss', *Murphy*, p. 65.
41. Carla Locatelli, *Unwording the World*, p. 54.
42. Beckett, *Molloy* (London: Faber and Faber, 2009), pp. 33–4. Beckett translated *Molloy* with Patrick Bowles. There is no intertextual reference to Leopardi in the French text, which reads: 'Je ne disposais pour ainsi dire que d'une jambe, j'étais moralement unijambiste, et j'aurais été plus heureux, plus léger, amputé au niveau de l'aîne. Et ils m'auraient enlevé quelques testicules à la même occasion que je ne leur aurais rien dit. Car mes testicules à moi, ballotant à mi-cuisse au bout d'un maigre cordon, il n'y avait plus rien à en tirer, à telle enseigne que je n'avais plus envie d'en tirer quelque chose, mais j'avais plutôt envie de les voir disparaître, ces témoins charge décharge de ma longue mise en accusation' (*Molloy* (Paris: Éditions de Minuit, 1951), p. 52).
43. According to Bernold, Beckett was fond of repeating this verse in old age; see André Bernold, *L'amitié de Beckett 1979–1989*. Beckett writes to David Hayman on 22 July 1955:

    > Writing this I remember once quoting to Joyce Leopardi's E fango è il mondo, to which his instantaneous and sole reaction consisted in seizing on the association Il mondo – immonde. This is beside the point, but the anecdote might amuse you. And perhaps suggest to you an exagmination of how in Joyce the form of judgement more and more devoured its gist and the saying of all the saying of anything, in a way more consistent with Bruno's identification of contraries than with the intellectualism of Mallarmé. (*Letters 1941–1956*, p. 537)

44. Beckett, *Molloy*, p. 59.
45. Wolfgang Iser, 'Patterns of Negativity in Beckett's Prose', p. 134.
46. Judith E. Dearlove, 'Allusion to Archetype', p. 121.
47. Beckett, 'Intercessions by Denis Devlin', p. 91.

Bibliography

Alighieri, Dante, *The Divine Comedy: Inferno*, trans. Charles S. Singleton (Princeton: Princeton University Press, 1980).

Bair, Deirdre, *Samuel Beckett: A Biography* (London: Jonathan Cape, 1978).

Barnes, John C., 'La fortuna di Leopardi in Irlanda', in Musarra, Vanvolsen, Guglielmone, Lamberti et al. (eds), *Leopardi e la cultura europea*, Acts of the International Congress of Leuven University, 10–12 December 1987, Leuven University Press (Rome: Bulzoni, 1989).

Beckett, Samuel, 'Dante. . . Bruno. Vico.. Joyce', in Ruby Cohn (ed.), *Disjecta: Miscellaneous Writings and a Dramatic Fragment* (New York: Grove Press, 1984), pp. 19–33.

Beckett, Samuel, *Dream of Fair to Middling Women* (New York: Arcade, 1992).

Beckett, Samuel, 'Henri Hayden', in Ruby Cohn (ed.), *Disjecta: Miscellaneous Writings and a Dramatic Fragment* (New York: Grove Press, 1984), pp. 146–7.

Beckett, Samuel, 'Intercessions by Denis Devlin', in Ruby Cohn (ed.), *Disjecta: Miscellaneous Writings and a Dramatic Fragment* (New York: Grove Press, 1984), pp. 91–4.

Beckett, Samuel, *The Letters of Samuel Beckett 1929–1940*, ed. Martha Dow Fehsenfeld and Lois More Overbeck (Cambridge: Cambridge University Press, 2009).

Beckett, Samuel, *The Letters of Samuel Beckett 1941–1956*, ed. George Craig, Martha Dow Fehsenfeld, Dan Gunn and Lois More Overbeck (Cambridge: Cambridge University Press, 2011).

Beckett, Samuel, *Molloy*, ed. Shane Weller (London: Faber and Faber, 2009).

Beckett, Samuel, *Molloy* (Paris: Éditions de Minuit, 1951).

Beckett, Samuel, *More Pricks Than Kicks* (New York: Grove Weidenfeld, [1934] 1972).

Beckett, Samuel, *Murphy* (London: Picador, 1973).

Beckett, Samuel, *Proust* (New York: Grove Press, 1931).

Bernold, André, *L'amitié de Beckett 1979–1989* (Paris: Hermann Editeurs de Sciences et des Arts, 1992).

Caselli, Daniela, 'Beckett and Italy', in Anthony Uhlmann (ed.), *Beckett in Context* (Cambridge: Cambridge University Press, forthcoming).

Caselli, Daniela, *Beckett's Dantes: Intertextuality in the Fiction and Criticism* (Manchester: Manchester University Press, 2005).

Caselli, Daniela, 'Rifunzionalizzare la nozione di intertestualità: alcune proposte italiane', *Strumenti Critici*, nuova serie, anno IX, 75–92: 80 (1996).

Caselli, Daniela, 'Thinking of "A Rhyme for Euganean": Beckett in Italy', in Mark Nixon and Matthew Feldman (eds), *The International Reception of Samuel Beckett* (London: Continuum, 2009), pp. 209–33.

Cohn, Ruby, 'A Note on Beckett, Dante and Geulincx', *Comparative Literature*, 12 (1960), pp. 93–4.

Compagnon, Antoine, *La seconde main ou le travail de la citation* (Paris: Éditions du Seuil, 1979).

Conte, Gian Biagio, *Memoria dei poeti e sistema letterario: Catullo, Virgilio, Ovidio, Lucano* (Turin: Einaudi, 1974 and 1985).

Cortellessa, Andrea, '"E fango è il mondo" Beckett e Leopardi', in G. Alfano and A. Cortellessa (eds), *Tegole dal cielo la letteratura italiana nell'opera di Beckett* (Rome: Edup, 2006), pp. 111–21.

Dearlove, Judith E., 'Allusion to Archetype', *Journal of Beckett Studies*, 10 (1985), pp. 121–33.

Derrida, Jacques, 'Le Théâtre de la cruauté et la clôture de la représentation', in *L'écriture et la différence* (Paris: Éditions du Seuil, 1967).

Derrida, Jacques, 'The Theatre of Cruelty and the Closure of Representation', in *Writing and Difference* (London: Routledge and Kegan Paul, 1978).

Dolfi, Anna, *Leopardi e il Novecento: sul leopardismo dei poeti* (Florence: Le Lettere, 2009).

Dolfi, Anna, *Leopardi tra negazione e utopia: Indagini e ricerche sui 'Canti'* (Padova: Liviana, 1973).

Feldman, Matthew, *Beckett's Books: A Cultural History of Samuel Beckett's 'Interwar Notes'* (London: Continuum, 2006).

Ferrini, Jean-Pierre, 'Dante, Pétrarque, Leopardi, Beckett: Une divine perspective', *Samuel Beckett Today/Aujourd'hui*, 17 (2006), pp. 53–66.

Frost, Everett, 'Preface', in Matthijs Engelberts, Frost and Jane Maxwell (eds), *Notes Diverse Holo: Samuel Beckett Today/Aujourd'hui*, 16 (2006).

Gilligan, Patrick, 'Beckett and Dante: The First Phase', unpublished dissertation, University College Dublin, 1983.

Harvey, Lawrence E., *Samuel Beckett: Poet and Critic* (Princeton: Princeton University Press, 1970).

Iser, Wolfgang, 'Patterns of Negativity in Beckett's Prose', in Harold Bloom (ed.), *Samuel Beckett: Modern Critical Views* (New York: Chelsea House Publishers, 1985), pp. 125–36.

Johnson, Barbara, 'Les fleurs du Mal Armé: Some Reflexions on Intertextuality', in *A World of Difference* (Baltimore: Johns Hopkins University Press, 1987), pp. 116–33.

Juliet, Charles, *Rencontre avec Samuel Beckett* (Paris: Éditions Fata Morgana, 1986).

Leopardi, Giacomo, *I Canti*, ed. Ettore Fabietti (Milan: Casa per Edizioni Popolari, 1936).

Leopardi, Giacomo, *The Poems of Leopardi*, ed. Geoffrey L. Bickersteth (New York: Russell & Russell, 1973 [first edition Cambridge University Press, 1923]).

Leopardi, Giacomo, *Prose, con uno studio di Pietro Giordani* (Milan: Istituto Editoriale Italiano, n.d.).

Leopardi, Giacomo, 'Le Ricordanze', in *Canti, Poesie varie, traduzioni poetiche e versi puerili, Parnaso italiano*, Vol. IX, ed. Carlo Muscetta and Giuseppe Savoca (Turin: Einaudi, 1968), p. 102.

Leopardi, Giacomo, *Selected Prose and Poetry*, ed. and trans. Iris Origo and John Heath-Stubbs (London: Oxford University Press, 1966).

Leopardi, Giacomo, 'Sovra il monumento di Dante che si preparava in Firenze', in *Canti, Poesie varie, traduzioni poetiche e versi puerili*, *Parnaso italiano*, Vol. IX, ed. Carlo Muscetta and Giuseppe Savoca (Turin: Einaudi, 1968), pp. 9–16.

Leopardi, Giacomo, *Zibaldone di pensieri*, ed. G. Pacella (Milan: Garzanti, 1992).

Locatelli, Carla, *Unwording the World: Samuel Beckett's Prose Works after the Nobel Prize* (Philadelphia: University of Pennsylvania Press, 1990).

McQueeny, Terence, 'Beckett as Critic of Proust and Joyce', unpublished doctoral dissertation, University of North Carolina, 1977.

Montes, Elina R., 'Leopardi, Friedrich, Beckett: Los universos silenciosos', *Beckettiana*, 7/8 (1999), pp. 121–8.

Pilling, John, *Beckett Before Godot* (Cambridge: Cambridge University Press, 1997).

Pilling, John, 'Beckett's *Proust*', *Journal of Beckett Studies*, 4 (winter 1976), pp. 8–29.

Restivo, Giuseppina, 'Caliban/Clov and Leopardi's Boys: Beckett and Postmodernism', in Bruce Stewart (ed.), *Beckett and Beyond* (Gerrards Cross: Smythe, 1999).

Riffaterre, Michael,'Interpretation and Undecidability', *New Literary History*, 12 (1981), pp. 227–42.

Sannia, Davide, 'Cielo Grigio Cenere e nessun rumore: Beckett e l'opera morale leopardiana', unpublished dissertation, University of Bologna, 2012.

Segre, Cesare, 'Intertestuale, interdiscorsivo: Appunti per una fenomenologia delle fonti', in C. Di Girolamo and I. Paccagnella (eds), *La parola ritrovata: Fonti e analisi letteraria* (Palermo: Sellerio, 1982), pp. 15–28.

Van Hulle, Dirk, and Mark Nixon, *Samuel Beckett's Library* (Cambridge: Cambridge University Press, forthcoming).

Zurbrugg, Nicholas, 'Beckett, *Proust* and *Dream of Fair to Middling Women*', *Journal of Beckett Studies*, 9 (1984), pp. 43–64.

13.

Recovering Beckett's Italian Translations

Norma Bouchard

From early in his career, Samuel Beckett had a deep interest in Italian literature that would reveal itself in that thick web of intertextual allusions to Italian poets, narrators, dramatists, philosophers and artists that weaves through his entire corpus. Indeed, from Beckett's essay on Joyce (1929)[1] to his latest works one finds endless references to classics, such as Dante, Bruno, Ariosto, Machiavelli, Vico, Leopardi and Manzoni, as well as more contemporary authors, the latter ranging from Carducci and D'Annunzio to Pirandello. While Beckett's debt to classic authors of Italian literature has been well documented, especially with regard to Dante,[2] very little work exists on Beckett's translations of Italian literature,[3] and it is to this sphere of his activity that I will now turn.

As a liberal arts student at Trinity College between 1923 and 1926, Samuel Beckett became acquainted very early on with Italian literature since Italian was one of his two honours subjects.[4] His professors, the lecturers Thomas Rudmose-Brown and Walter Starkie, were well versed in a number of Italian authors and strongly influenced the young student's taste. In addition, during these same years at Trinity College, Beckett attended Italian lessons given by a private tutor, Bianca Esposito.[5] A teacher of excellent reputation, Bianca held private classes in a small brick building at 21 Ely Place. Biographical records reveal that class time was devoted not only to the practice of the language, but also to discussions of works that Beckett was studying at Trinity College. In the summer of 1927, Beckett travelled to Italy for the first time on a journey that was certainly motivated by a desire to improve his language skills, but also to satisfy a growing interest in Italian architecture, painting and sculpture. Beckett's interest in Italian literature would manifest itself just a few years later, in a group of translations from the Italian that were completed during his 'Paris years'.

This period of his life began in 1928 when Beckett, at the age of twenty-two, left the city of Dublin and moved to Paris to work as 'lecteur' for the prestigious *Ecole Normale Supérieure* until the end of September 1930. The 'Paris years' proved to be extremely fruitful to his intellectual and artistic development. Thanks to Tom MacGreevy, a fellow Irishman and Beckett's predecessor at the *Ecole Normale Supérieure*, Beckett was introduced not only to James Joyce's circle, but also to Eugene Jolas, the editor of the journal *transition*, as well as to Edward Titus and Samuel Putnam, editor and associate editor respectively of *This Quarter*. Since Titus and Putnam had been planning a European series, they were seeking translations of Italian, German, Spanish and Polish texts. Although the series was never completed, in the spring of 1930 the Italian issue of *This Quarter* went to print with a sample of works by Arturo Loria, Massimo Bontempelli, Gabriele D'Annunzio, Luigi Pirandello, G. A. Borgese, Aldo Palazzeschi, Leo Ferrero, Grazia Deledda, Umberto Saba, Paola Masino, Antonio Fogazzaro, Giovanni Comisso, Raffaello Franchi and Eugenio Montale. While the issue was intended to provide a panorama of Italian literature from the nineteenth century to the late 1920s, the editors also sought to establish a distinction between two generations of Italian writers. Thus, in the preface that opens the volume, 'A Miniature Anthology of Contemporary Italian Literature', Samuel Putnam duly acknowledges D'Annunzio as a crucial figure, but a figure whose influential role has ended because, in his words, 'to the newer generations . . . he has little if anything to say; he is now an historic, rather than a literary figure'.[6] Grazia Deledda and Antonio Fogazzaro do not fare much better and are dismissed as expressions of an '*ottocentismo*' that 'is now a thing of the past'.[7] By contrast, the preface dwells at length on a younger group of writers, the 'young after-the-War literature',[8] whose work is presented also in a second essay by Samuel Putnam, 'I Giovani (Notes on Contemporary Italian Literature)'.[9] Putnam introduces this group of writers as exemplary of a 'nascent new literature dating, roughly, from 1925';[10] among them one finds the three authors that Beckett translated: Raffaello Franchi, Eugenio Montale, and Giovanni Comisso. While Franchi's 'Landscape' and Comisso's 'The Home-Coming' are selections from the authors' larger works, notably Franchi's *Piazza natia* (1929) and Comisso's *Giorni di guerra* (1928–9), Montale's 'Delta' is translated in full.

A cursory glance at these texts reveals Beckett's unique ability to interpret and highlight those qualities of the originals that he would later amply demonstrate in self-translations[11] as well as translations of French[12] and Mexican poets, the latter commissioned to him by UNESCO in 1957.[13] In short, Beckett's translations undoubtedly testify to what Octavio Paz, in the course of a 1990 interview, described as his 'memorable' work as a craftsman of the word.[14] However, in addition to testifying to Beckett's ability, the interest of these Italian translations carries over to an exploration of the motives that led him to the selection of these three authors. These are motives that extend far beyond Beckett's friendship with the editors of *This Quarter*, not to mention commission and money-making opportunities. They suggest that Beckett was attracted to these writers because their works resonated with issues of time, memory and consciousness that were crucial at this stage of his development as a writer. All that said, from our present perspective on the twentieth-century Italian literary canon, Beckett's trio might, at the very least, appear somewhat surprising, especially if we consider the status of the Nobel Prize winner Montale (1975) as opposed to the increasingly peripheral space devoted to Comisso and Franchi's works by most recent histories of Italian literature.[15] Yet, it is important to recall that in the 1920s Franchi, Comisso and Montale were young, emerging authors. Born in the last decade of the nineteenth century, they had only recently published their first significant works.[16] The year 1925, in fact, saw the publication of both Comisso's *Il porto dell'amore* and Montale's *Ossi di seppia*. With regard to Franchi, even though he had published the collections of prose *Ruscellante* in 1916, followed by *Luce sulle case* in 1918, it was only with the publication of *Pocaterra* (1924) and *Le maschere* (1925) that he gained a good measure of recognition. More significant than these biographical analogies was the fact that Franchi, Montale and Comisso were collaborators on the Florentine review *Solaria*.[17] Founded in Florence in 1926 under the direction of Alberto Carocci, and active until 1936, when Fascist censorship precluded further publications, *Solaria* assembled a heterogeneous group of writers. This group comprised Northern intellectuals shaped in the democratic cultural milieu promoted by Piero Gobetti and younger authors, who had been receptive to the renewal of literature by the Florentine journal *La Ronda*. As a result of this encounter, the writers of *Solaria* developed a programme that opposed, in fundamental ways, the intellectual autarchy that characterised not only the Fascist policy after Mussolini's speech of 3 January 1925, but also the idealism of Benedetto Croce. Thus, *Solaria* came to conceive Italian literature as an integral part of the larger European cultural scene and the journal championed writers, such as Joyce, Proust, Valéry, Rilke, Eluard, Gogol, Dostoevskii and Kafka, who had not only placed issues of time, memory and the unconscious at the centre of their work, but had articulated the self's difficult quest for personal and social integration. With regard to national literature, the 'Solariani' promoted a refined prose and poetic experimentation. At the same time, however, they shared an aversion for the bombastic style of D'Annunzio while clearly favouring the authors of the Italian modernism, namely Italo Svevo, to whom the journal dedicated a special issue in March/April of 1929, but also Federico Tozzi and Umberto Saba.[18] With the works of the European authors mentioned above and of Italian writers Svevo, Tozzi and Saba, the contributors to *Solaria* shared a sense of disorientation and loss that led them to explore, in both content and style, the many problematic facets of the modern self. In the words of Neri, these facets ranged '[f]rom the analysis of consciousness to the study of the psyche, and therefore from *Joyceanism* to *Freudianism*, from narrative memoirs to the representation of existential uselessness and alienation'.[19]

Beckett's intellectual development during the 1920s paralleled that of Franchi, Comisso and Montale. After his move to Paris in 1928, he had met one of the writers championed by *Solaria*, James Joyce, who had asked him to trace the presence of Dante, Bruno and Vico in his 'Work in Progress'. The result was Beckett's first essay, the famed 'Dante... Bruno. Vico.. Joyce'.[20] Beckett's subsequent publications were the highly experimental short story 'Assumption'[21] and the poem 'Whoroscope'.[22] Both Beckett's 'Dante... Bruno. Vico.. Joyce' and the two creative works reveal that he shared with Montale, Franchi and Comisso a concern with time, memory and a perceiving consciousness often prey to uncertainties and confusion. Given these developments in Beckett's work, it is not surprising that he was drawn to these writers, as their works resonated with the same issues that he had placed at the centre of his intellectual activity. His choice of translations testifies to this, while his relative fidelity to the originals suggests Beckett's intent to further highlight the crisis of the modern self that is expressed in the Italian texts.

From Franchi's *Piazza natia*, Beckett selects a short piece of prose, titled 'Paesaggio', where a perceiving consciousness seeks to lose itself in the aesthetic contemplation of a country landscape that has been enveloped by mist:

> Questo paesaggio ... si stende in chiare colorazioni tolte all'arcobaleno e commosse come se apparissero attraverso una leggera nebbia rugiadosa. Così, per tutto il panorama, da campo a campo, da casolare a casolare, e da una scoscenditura di roccia all'altra, il colore tenue, chiaro, come nei freschi dell'Angelico, diffuso da un soffio lieve, s'espande entro un limite ove si chiude, senza che un segno lo incida, ma come se la terra ne suggesse al margine l'umida luce. Onde ci prende una voglia struggente di essere anche noi bevuti da questo sorso silenzioso per andare a godere la fresca radice dei colori.[23]

> The landscape ... has plundered the rainbow and dimmed its spoils and spread them forth in trembling captivity behind a dewy muslin of mist. So,

> poured like a balm over the land, above every field and cottage and shelf of rock, the light, restless in the air, tenuous and dim as in a fresco of Fra Angelico, dies, lapping a hidden brink, yielding its bright moisture to the thirst of the earth. Until our desire is a flame—to be sucked down likewise within that well of stillness, and stir with our lips the paler source of the plain's pale colours.[24]

However, in both Franchi's original and Beckett's translation, the moment of aesthetic contemplation is but a brief occurrence, an event that lasts the space of one night only, like the flower born out of the earth that the perceiving consciousness stoops forward to gather. Thus, the epiphanic moment of salvation reveals the existence of another reality that the 'dewy muslin of mist' and the 'balm over the land' cannot efface. In this sense, the choice of vocabulary used by Beckett in the first paragraph of his translation is quite significant, as, opting for a variation, he transforms Franchi's landscape into a ransacking force. Such departure from the original conjures up images of depredation and pillage that have the effect of evoking the trauma of reality that Franchi's text only implies through his representation of a perceiving consciousness's quest for a moment of transcendence.

The second translation authored by Beckett is from Giovanni Comisso's *Giorni di guerra*, an autobiographical account that covers events spanning from 1914 to 1918. Out of a very large work, Beckett significantly selects a description of a return to a memory-haunted house of childhood. This return is chronologically set right after a moment of historical crisis, namely the days that immediately follow the Italian defeat at Caporetto in October 1917. The excerpts begin with a soldier-narrator recounting the dream, or perhaps the thought, of his homecoming to his native city of Treviso, that occurred one night as he was in the trenches in Gorizia: 'Quando ero nella zona di Gorizia, in una notte calda con il colera già diffuso nel nostro accampamento, sognai o pensai, non so, di aver fatto ritorno a piedi alla mia città natale.'[25] Beckett highlights, for the reader, the ontological uncertainty of the soldier's vision by a skilful use of gerundive forms and expressions that eschew precise definitions: 'I remember', so Beckett writes, 'one war night in the Gorizia zone, during the cholera outbreak, lying in camp and dreaming—or imagining—that I had tramped all the way back to my native town.'[26] However, when the soldier's vision becomes reality, the homecoming turns into a tragic experience. Not only are troops surrounding the city walls, but the family of the soldier has left for Florence, while his former friends appear to have become mysteriously hostile:

> Dopo una lunga marcia, ansioso di rivedere la mia casa, mi ero trovato alle porte della città chiuse e sbarrate da soldati armati che non mi lasciavano

entrare. Attesi tutta una notte e solo all'alba venne aperto, ma invece di ritrovare parenti e amici felici di rivedermi, quelli erano assenti e questi, irritati contro di me, non mi volevano guardare in faccia.[27]

Beckett recreated Comisso's passage in a prose that transforms the flow of the original into a syncopated sentence structure, whereby feelings of hope, frustration, surprise and disillusionment follow each other in a rapid succession of images:

> I was standing at the city gates, tired out with my long hike and impatient to get home; but the gates were closed, and the sentries on guard would not let me pass. I waited there all night, until it was dawn at last and they opened the gates. I needn't have been in a hurry; my family was away and my friends appeared to be angry with me; not one of them would look at me.[28]

As Comisso's text indicates, the hostility of the narrators' friends is due to the Italian defeat at Caporetto in October 1917, when 280,000 Italian soldiers were made prisoners and close to 600,000 were killed. By and large, public opinion blamed the soldiers for the defeat and the bombastic D'Annunzio described them as cowards who had sinned against the 'motherland'.[29] However, in Comisso's text, the source of alienation has other causes besides historical experience since the homecoming becomes a difficult journey into the memory-haunted house of the past. We read that, for fear that the Austrians might advance and loot the abandoned house, the narrator hides his family's furnishings, and walls in the door that leads to the house. When the news that the Austrians have been pushed back arrives, the narrator leaves with his division. One morning, however, he enters into the room of his commander and realises that his fellow Italian soldiers have stolen a number of objects from his house, including a woollen blanket that was particularly dear to him. Nevertheless, the sight of the blanket appears to redeem the experience of having been subject to a theft by his fellow comrades as the blanket brings back to the narrator memories of his childhood. These memories, he trusts, will sustain him in the future, in the trenches of Monte Grappa, a place to which he will return:

> Il rosso della coperta attraeva beatamente. A guardarla mi sentivo indietro nel tempo: ragazzo e altrove. Era un piacere avere quelle cose di casa mia, in attesa di salire sul Grappa. Le avrei portate con me sempre.[30]

Once again, however, the solace afforded by memory is short-lived. The soldier's commander storms into his room to convince the narrator not to make trouble over a blanket and, by so doing, destroys the magic moment of recovery of the time lost. Beckett's translation expands upon the original, dwelling more at length on the recovery of the past that is facilitated by the sight of the blanket:

> I couldn't take my eyes off the red blanket. Looking at it, I felt myself slipping back into the past, into the other world of my childhood. Sitting there, waiting for the climb up the Grappa, and with all my treasures about me, I could almost imagine myself at home again. I would keep them with me always.[31]

Yet, by expanding upon the original, Beckett renders the entrance of the commander and the interruption of the moment of recovery even more dramatic, as the materiality of life now fully effaces the epiphany:

> There was a knock at the door. The C.O.'s shave was over. He had come to apologize for his orderly.
>
> 'Surely, you do not want to make trouble over a wretched blanket. He'll get sent to the trenches, and he has a wife and children. Can't you leave him to me? I'll give him something that'll teach him to keep his hands off what doesn't belong to him.'[32]

Beckett's translation of Montale's text not only confirms his attraction to writers who placed memory, time and the perceiving consciousness at the centre of their works, but reinforces the frailty of an epiphanic, privileged moment of integration. Because of the complexity of Montale's original and Beckett's translation, I will report both texts in full.

1 La vita che si rompe nei travasi
2 secreti a te ho legata:
3 quella che si dibatte in sé e par quasi
4 non ti sappia, presenza soffocata.

5 Quando il tempo s'ingorga alle sue dighe
6 la tua vicenda accordi alla sua immensa,
7 ed affiori, memoria, più palese
8 dall'oscura regione ove scendevi,
9 come ora, al dopopioggia, si riaddensa
10 il verde ai rami, ai muri il cinabrese.

11 Tutto ignoro di te fuor del messaggio
12 muto che mi sostenta sulla via:
13 se forma esisti o ubbia nella fumea
14 d'un sogno t'alimenta
15 la riviera che infebbra, torba, e scroscia
16 incontro alla marea.

17 Nulla di te nel vacillar dell'ore
18 bige o squarciate da un vampo di solfo

19 fuori che il fischio del rimorchiatore
20 che dalle brume approda al golfo.[33]

1 To thee
2 I have willed the life drained
3 in secret transfusions, the life chained
4 in a coil of restlessness, unaware, self-angry.

5 When time leans on his dykes
6 then thine
7 be his allconsciousness
8 and memory flower forth in a flame
9 from the dark sanctuary, and shine
10 more brightly, as now, the rain over, the dragon's blood
11 on the walls and the green against the branches.

12 Of thee
13 I know nothing, only
14 the tidings sustaining my going
15 and shall I find
16 thee shape or the fumes of a dream
17 drawing life
18 from the river's fever boiling darkly
19 against the tide.

20 Of thee nothing in the grey hours and the hours
21 torn by a flame of sulphur,
22 only
23 the whistle of the tug
24 whose prow has ridden forth into the bright gulf.[34]

Composed in 1926, 'Delta' is a poem that belongs to the section 'Meriggi e ombre'. Added by Montale to the 1928 edition of *Ossi di seppia*, this section includes, among others, the famed 'Fine dell'infanzia', 'Flussi', 'Arsenio' and 'Casa dei morti'. These are poems that express a sense of disorientation with regard to the world being represented and the perceiving consciousness. As a result, not only are these poems marked by what Bonora, in his *Lettura di Montale*, describes as 'folto descrittivismo' ('thick descriptive mode')[35] suggesting 'l'ingorgo di oggetti' ('the obstruction of objects'),[36] but they reveal a self in a state of tormented, painful confusion over personal and public history. The inner power of memory has become the 'memoria stancata' ('tired out memory') described in 'Fine dell'infanzia', while transcendence has given rise to the sentiment expressed in 'Casa sul mare' that 'per i più non sia salvezza' ('for most of us, there is no escape').

As an integral part of 'Meriggi e ombre', 'Delta' is no exception and foreshadows, as does the entire section to which it belongs, the darker vision of the collection *Occasioni*.[37] The poem, which takes its title from the point where the flow of the river meets the waves of the sea in a turbulent encounter, is a complex meditation on the passing of life, the rush of time, the effects of memory, and a mysterious 'Thou'. This 'Thou' draws energies from the forces of the feverish torrent of both water and life and sustains, with a speechless message, the journey of the 'I'. Such poetic concentration of what Glauco Cambon, in *Eugenio Montale's Poetry*, describes as the physical, the metaphysical and the psychological[38] gives rise to a poetic diction that is both highly denotative and so concentrated as to be semantically and phonetically very dense.

Formally, Beckett's translation is fairly close to the original. His version retains the same number of stanzas as Montale's original and remains faithful to its rhyme structure, even if the English language forces him to find different metres. Beckett also respects phonic associations. For example, he renders the harsh sounds of what is perhaps the poem's most difficult linguistic invention – 'la riviera che infebbra, torba, e scroscia'[39] – with 'river's fever boiling darkly', a line whose sounds recapture well the image of the raging and roaring of the water at the river's delta. Equally faithful to the original texts are Beckett's parallelisms of lines 12, 13 and 20 ('Of thee', 'I know nothing' and 'Of thee nothing') that respect lines 11 and 17 of the original: 'Tutto ignoro di te' and 'Nulla di te'. However, as he had done in the case of Franchi and Comisso's translations, Beckett opts for some variations that render the translated text more dramatic. Thus, in the first stanza, one of the attributes of life's unawareness, namely the stifled presence of the 'Thou', is eliminated as a cause, while the description of life as secret transfusion ('si rompe nei travasi secreti') and conflict ('si dibatte in sé') is transformed into a much more powerful image of life as a complete state of mystery, anger and enchainment resisting explanation:

To thee
I have willed the life drained
in secret transfusions, the life chained
in a coil of restlessness, unaware, self-angry.

The translation of the second stanza is also decidedly free from a semantic point of view. It describes the surging forth of memory that brings back, as after a rain, the cinnabar of the walls and the green of the trees' branches. While a literal translation of Montale's text would have rendered lines 7 and 8 as 'and you rise, memory, more manifest / from the dark region where you descended', Beckett opts for 'and memory flower forth in a flame / from the dark sanctuary'. By way of this semantic variation, which is borrowed from a mystical and religious terminology,

Beckett is emphasising here the inexplicable and unpredictable surfacing of memory.[40] This choice is a very felicitous one since, as was the case of texts by Franchi and Comisso, Montale's moment of epiphany is extremely frail. Such condition is well exemplified in the third and fourth stanzas. Here the 'te', or 'Thou', is not a saving presence, a 'fantasma che ti salva' ('a saving apparition') that will take the poet through the break in the chain, to reprise one of Montale's best-known poems,[41] but a mysterious, perhaps even delusional being: a 'forma' ('shape') or 'ubbia nella fumea d'un sogno' ('the fumes of a dream'). While it exists as a momentary respite after the deluge, like the colour green of the trees, the cinnabar on the walls and the whistle of a tug-boat, it also remains a silent promise, an absent presence.

Montale's difficult epistemology is not lost on Beckett, who emphasises the ontological complexity of the 'Thou' in lines where the repetition of 'Of thee', 'nothing' and 'only' expresses the limits of knowledge, or even the state of unknowing of the poetic subject. In Beckett's words:

> Of thee
> I know nothing, only
> the tidings sustaining my going
> and shall I find
> thee shape or the fumes of a dream
> drawing life
> from the river's fever boiling darkly
> against the tide.
>
> Of thee nothing in the grey hours and the hours
> torn by a flame of sulphur,
> only
> the whistle of the tug
> whose prow has ridden forth in the bright gulf.

On the topic of the 'Thou', or, rather, Beckett's 'thee', it is worth noting that, once again, Beckett departs from the original by placing greater emphasis on the silent addressee. In the original, the presence of 'Thou' has to be inferred from disjunctive pronouns (lines 2, 11, 17), direct object pronouns (lines 4, 14) and possessive pronouns (line 6). By contrast, Beckett renders the addressee very visible by including the 'thee' in the first lines of three out of his four stanzas. Laura Visconti has commented on this important variation and has suggested that by transforming what is essentially a monologic structure into a more dramatic text, one might locate 'the first, premonitory step towards the eclipse and the negation of the subject which Beckett was to reach in his own work several decades later'.[42] While I fully agree with Visconti's assessment,

I would also like to add that while Beckett's translation de-emphasises the subject, it also reduces the already minimal anthropomorphic signs of the addressee by further conflating the image of the 'Thou' with time, memory and the torrent of life. Thus, in the third stanza, the 'speechless message' of the original, or 'messaggio muto', becomes 'the tidings' that sustain the poetic persona. While the word 'tiding' refers of course to events and news, in the semantic context of 'Delta' it also conjures up the ebbing and flowing of the water. By so doing, Beckett maintains the 'Thou' in a state of 'opacity' that has often been lost not only to Montale's translators, but also to commentators of 'Delta' who have incorrectly associated the 'Thou' with a woman.[43]

As these selections suggest, then, Beckett's interest in Italian authors associated with the journal *Solaria* testifies to the common concerns with the exploration of time, memory and the self that characterise the post-war generation of writers while undeniably demonstrating how Italian literature of the period resonated with issues that also animated the larger European scene. However, Beckett's choice of specific texts by Franchi, Comisso and Montale also indicates a desire to emphasise the limits of the self's ability to achieve personal and social integration. This is a desire that is revealed in those passages where Beckett opts for a variation or a decidedly freer mode of translation in order to highlight moments of crisis in the modern subject. Given these developments in Beckett's earlier work, it comes as no surprise that, during his 'Paris years', he began to work frantically on Proust's novel and, by the end of September 1930, just before returning to Ireland, was able to deliver to the publishers Chatto and Windus the long critical essay titled *Proust* that had been commissioned to him after winning the prize for 'Whoroscope'. In what has often been defined as an idiosyncratic reading of Proust's *A la recherche du temps perdu*, Beckett did not focus on the epiphanic power of art and the potency of episodes of involuntary memory but, rather, on the inability of the self to rise above the contingencies of personal and social life.[44] In rather Montalian fashion, for Beckett, the self had become a turbulent receptacle of waters: 'the seat of a constant process of decantation, decantation from the vessel containing the fluid of future time . . . to the vessel containing the fluid of past time'.[45] More fundamentally still, this was also a self for whom escape and salvation were becoming increasingly problematic because, in Beckett's words, the 'Thou' of 'involuntary memory is an unruly magician and will not be importuned'.[46]

In conclusion, then, Beckett's Italian translations of the 1930s resonate with issues and concerns that were crucial to him at this juncture of his intellectual activity as poet, short-story writer and critical essayist.

The translation of Montale's 'Delta' seems to be particularly significant since, as a poem foreshadowing the lyrics of *Occasioni*, it limits the ability of the self to find a more authentic life and therefore comes closer to Beckett's emerging poetics as revealed in his interpretation of Proust. Finally, then, Beckett's English versions of Franchi, Comisso and Montale not only testify to Beckett's gift as a 'memorable' craftsman of the word, but also document the ongoing, fundamental importance of Italian culture and language in the early stages of Beckett's career, an importance that should invite further consideration of Beckett as a 'trilingual' and 'tricultural' writer.

Notes

1. I am referring to 'Dante. . . Bruno. Vico.. Joyce'.
2. Beckett's admiration for Dante, an admiration that he would describe in a letter to Roger Little of 18 May 1983 as 'the Dante revelation' (James Knowlson, *Damned to Fame*, p. 630, n. 35), not only remained a constant in his life, but gave rise to the sustained commentaries, verbatim quotations and indirect allusions that populate Beckett's essayistic, poetic, narrative and dramatic works. Considering the receptivity of Beckett to Dante, examinations of his debt to the medieval author are very extensive. Representative titles are: Bryden, 'No Stars without Stripes: Beckett and Dante' and 'Beckett and the Three Dantean Smiles'; Ackerley, 'Beckett's "Malacoda"'; Fletcher, 'Beckett's Debt to Dante'; Kennedy, 'Beckett's "Schoolboy Copy" of Dante'; Caselli, '"L'andar su che porta?": Dante nel primo Beckett'; and Carey, 'Stephen Dedalus, Belacqua Shuah, and Dante's Pieta'.
3. The only work on Beckett's translation of Italian literature is an essay by Visconti, 'The Artist and the Artisan'. However, Visconti focuses only on Beckett's translation of Montale's 'Delta'. In light of volumes devoted entirely to Beckett's work as a translator, including Friedman, Rossman and Sherzer (eds), *Beckett Translating/Translating Beckett*, such paucity of critical works on the topic is even more surprising.
4. For additional discussion of Beckett's early years at Trinity, see the section 'The Growth of a Mind 1923–1926' in Knowlson, *Damned to Fame*, pp. 63–80.
5. 'You had to do two languages at the time, so I chose Italian as my second language. It was my good luck to meet Bianca Esposito. She helped me with my literature as well as my Italian language' (interview with Samuel Beckett, 5 July 1989, quoted in Knowlson, *Damned to Fame*, p. 67).
6. Samuel Putnam, 'A Miniature Anthology of Contemporary Italian Literature', p. 566.
7. Ibid. p. 567. Putnam borrows the term *ottocentismo* from Giuseppe Ravegnani, a well-known literary critic and author of *I contemporanei: dal tramonto dell'ottocento all'alba del novecento* (1930). The term, which was widely used in the early decades of twentieth-century Italian literary criticism, refers to belated, even obsolete expressions of Romantic literature. It

generally carries the negative connotations of provincial, melodramatic and decadent art, and corresponds roughly to the terms *fin-de-siècle* aestheticism and late Romanticism in Anglo-American critical parlance.

8. Ibid. p. 568.
9. Putnam, 'I Giovani (Notes on Contemporary Italian Literature)', pp. 687–97.
10. Ibid. p. 689.
11. For additional discussion on Beckett as self-translator, see Anne Beer, 'Beckett's Bilingualism'.
12. For a sample of Beckett's translation from the French poets Alain Bosquet, Paul Eluard, Arthur Rimbaud, Guillaume Apollinaire and Sébastien Chamfort, see Beckett, *Poems 1930–1989*.
13. I am referring to the famed *Anthology of Mexican Poetry*.
14. Cited in Visconti, 'The Artist and the Artisan', from an interview with Paz published in *Leggere*, June 1990, p. 389.
15. See, for example, Giuliano Manacorda, *Storia della letteratura italiana contemporanea*.
16. Comisso was born in 1895, Montale in 1896 and Franchi in 1899.
17. For additional discussion of *Solaria*, see Giuseppe Neri, *Solaria*, and Manacorda, 'Solaria'.
18. Many of the writers championed by the journal *Solaria* were originally described as authors of *decadentismo*. Since this is a term that in Anglo-American critical parlance refers to degenerate expressions of Romantic art, such as those found in works by Fogazzaro, D'Annunzio, Pascoli and other writers of *ottocentismo* (see above, n. 7), it is clearly misleading and, as Paolo Valesio has recently pointed out, reveals how 'in Italian literature the category of "modernism" has never been really at home' ('After *The Conquest of the Stars*', p. ix). Nevertheless, in light of the recent and, to some extent, overdue revisitation of the literary categories of *modernismo* and *decadentismo* in an Italian context, I have chosen to refer to the literature championed by *Solaria* as Italian modernist literature. For additional discussion on the use of these categories in an Italian context, see Mario Moroni and Luca Somigli (eds), *Italian Modernism*.
19. Neri, *Solaria: Una stagione del Novecento italiano*, p. 7: '[d]all'analisi della coscienza allo studio della psiche, perciò dal joycismo al freudismo, dal memorialismo narrativo alla raprresentazione dell'inutilità e dell'alienazione esistenziale' (my translation).
20. Beckett, 'Dante. . . Bruno. Vico.. Joyce', pp. 19–33.
21. 'Assumption' was originally published in *transition*, 16–17, June 1929, but also appeared under the title of 'Alba' in a Dublin magazine. It was reprinted in *transition workshop*. The story deals with the theme of aesthetic creativity and poetic vision but also examines an artist's anguish and turmoil. These feelings centre on the motif of a scream. Borrowed from Munch's expressionistic painting, this motif anticipates the death of the artist himself that occurs at the end of 'Assumption'.
22. 'Whoroscope' was written for a contest, organised by Nancy Cunard and Richard Aldington, for a poem of no more than one hundred lines on the subject of time. Beckett composed the poem, with Descartes narrating it, and won the prize. As Knowlson recalls (pp. 117–18), two days afterwards,

Beckett was named for a possible essay on the topic of time and memory in Proust that was eventually commissioned to him. The text of 'Whoroscope' can be found in Beckett, *Poems 1930–1989*, pp. 3–6.

23. Raffaello Franchi, 'Paesaggio', p. 123.
24. Beckett, 'Landscape', p. 672.
25. Giovanni Comisso, *Giorni di guerra*, p. 175.
26. Beckett, 'The Homecoming', p. 675.
27. Comisso, *Giorni di guerra*, p. 175.
28. Beckett, 'The Homecoming', p. 675.
29. Mario Isneghi, *Il mito della grande guerra*, p. 338.
30. Comisso, *Giorni di guerra*, p. 186.
31. Beckett, 'The Homecoming', p. 682.
32. Ibid. p. 682.
33. Eugenio Montale, 'Delta', *Tutte le poesie*, p. 97.
34. Beckett, 'Delta', p. 630.
35. Ettore Bonora, *Lettura di Montale*, p. 113.
36. Ibid. p. 112.
37. *Occasioni* was published by Einaudi in 1939 and Mondadori in 1949. For the text, see Montale, *Occasioni, Tutte le poesie*, pp. 107–92. For further discussion of *Occasioni* in relation to *Ossi di seppia*, see Gianfranco Contini, *Una lunga fedeltà*, pp. 17–45.
38. Glauco Cambon, *Eugenio Montale's Poetry*, pp. 29–31.
39. As Bonora points out, the verbs 'infebbrare' and 'torbare' do not exist in the Italian language and do not have a recorded literary usage. The first is a neologism on the French 'enfévrier', while 'torbare' is coined from the adjective 'torbida' that in Italian refers to the river waters rendered dark by the detritus and mud that they carry following a rainstorm.
40. I owe this insight to Visconti, 'The Artist and the Artisan'.
41. The line 'fantasma che ti salva' belongs to the opening poem of *Ossi di seppia*, 'In Limine' (*Tutte le poesie*, p. 7). The image of the break in the chain is from 'I limoni', *Ossi di seppia* (*Tutte le poesie*, pp. 11–12).
42. Visconti, 'The Artist and the Artisan', p. 396.
43. See Valentini, *Lettura di Montale*, quoted in Montale (trans. Arrowsmith), *Cuttlefish Bones*, p. 264, but compare also Zampa and Galassi. For Zampa, the addressee is the character of 'Arlette' (p. xxviii), while Arrowsmith considers 'the poem's *tu*, a *donna* [woman] of miraculous, memorial apparition, endowed by the poet with prodigious, indeed almost angelic, power of life' (p. 263). For Galassi, 'It is only when, in "Delta", [M]ontale takes the decisive action of "linking", of fully investing his female interlocutor with "The life that erupts in secret/streams", frontally recognizing and confronting her otherness, that he is able to derive encouragement and succor . . . Thus the blockade of *Ossi di seppia* is broken and the longed-for *varco* opens up' (p. 476).
44. For additional discussion on Beckett's reading of Proust, see Nicholas Zurbrugg, *Beckett and Proust*.
45. Beckett, *Proust*, pp. 4–5.
46. Ibid. p. 20.

Bibliography

Ackerley, C. J., 'Beckett's "Malacoda"', *Journal of Beckett Studies*, 3.1 (autumn 1993), pp. 59–64.

Beckett, Samuel, *Anthology of Mexican Poetry*, ed. Octavio Paz (Bloomington: Indiana University Press, 1958).

Beckett, Samuel, 'Assumption', *transition*, 16–17 (June 1929), pp. 41–4.

Beckett, Samuel, 'Dante. . . Bruno. Vico.. Joyce', in Ruby Cohn (ed.), *Disjecta: Miscellaneous Writings and a Dramatic Fragment* (New York: Grove Press, 1984), pp. 19–33.

Beckett, Samuel, 'Delta', *This Quarter*, 4 (April–June 1930), p. 630.

Beckett, Samuel, 'The Homecoming', *This Quarter*, 4 (April–June 1930), pp. 675–83.

Beckett, Samuel, 'Landscape', *This Quarter*, 4 (April–June 1930), p. 672.

Beckett, Samuel, *Poems 1930–1989* (London: John Calder, 2002).

Beckett, Samuel, *Proust* (New York: Grove Press, 1931).

Beckett, Samuel, 'Whoroscope', in *Poems 1930–1989* (London: John Calder, 2002), pp. 3–6.

Beer, Anne, 'Beckett's Bilingualism', in John Pilling (ed.), *The Cambridge Companion to Beckett* (Cambridge: Cambridge University Press, 1994), pp. 209–21.

Bonora, Ettore, *Lettura di Montale* (Torino: Tirrenia Stampatori, 1980).

Bryden, Mary, 'Beckett and the Three Dantean Smiles', *Journal of Beckett Studies*, 4.2 (spring 1995), pp. 29–33.

Bryden, Mary, 'No Stars without Stripes: Beckett and Dante', *Romanic Review*, 87.4 (November 1996), pp. 541–56.

Cambon, Glauco, *Eugenio Montale's Poetry* (Princeton: Princeton University Press, 1982).

Carey, Phyllis, 'Stephen Dedalus, Belacqua Shuah, and Dante's Pieta', in Phyllis Carey and Ed Jewinski (eds), *Re: Joyce 'n Beckett* (New York: Fordham University Press, 1992), pp. 104–16.

Caselli, Daniela, '"L'andar su che porta?": Dante nel primo Beckett', *The Italianist*, 18 (1998), pp. 130–54.

Comisso, Giovanni, *Giorni di guerra* (Milano: Longanesi, 1960).

Contini, Gianfranco, *Una lunga fedeltà: Scritti su Eugenio Montale* (Torino: Einaudi, 1974).

Fletcher, John, 'Beckett's Debt to Dante', *Nottingham French Studies*, 4.1 (1965), pp. 41–52.

Franchi, Raffaello, 'Paesaggio', in *Piazza natia* (Torino: Fratelli Buratti Editori, 1929), pp. 123–4.

Friedman, Alan Warren, Charles Rossman and Dina Sherzer (eds), *Beckett Translating/Translating Beckett* (University Park: The Pennsylvania State University Press, 1987).

Galassi, Jonathan (trans.), *Eugenio Montale: Selected Poems* (New York: Farrar, 1998).

Isneghi, Mario, *Il mito della grande guerra* (Bologna: Il Mulino, 2002).

Kennedy, Sighle, 'Beckett's "Schoolboy Copy" of Dante', *Dalhousie French Studies*, 19 (1990), pp. 11–19.

Knowlson, James, *Damned to Fame* (New York: Simon and Schuster, 1996).

Manacorda, Giuliano, 'Solaria', in *Storia della letteratura italiana tra le due guerre 1919–1943* (Roma: Editori Riuniti, 1980), pp. 177–210.
Manacorda, Giuliano, *Storia della letteratura italiana contemporanea* (Roma: Editori Riuniti, 2000).
Montale, Eugenio, *Cuttlefish Bones*, trans. William Arrowsmith (New York: Norton, 1948).
Montale, Eugenio, 'Delta', in *Occasioni, Tutte le poesie* (Milano: Mondadori, 1984), p. 97.
Montale, Eugenio, 'I limoni', in *Ossi di seppia, Tutte le poesie* (Milano: Mondadori, 1984), pp. 11–12.
Montale, Eugenio, 'In Limine', in *Ossi di seppia, Tutte le poesie* (Milano: Mondadori, 1984), p. 7.
Moroni, Mario, and Luca Somigli (eds), *Italian Modernism: Italian Culture between Decadentism and Avant-Garde* (Toronto: University of Toronto Press, 2004).
Neri, Giuseppe, *Solaria: Una stagione del Novecento italiano* (Lungro: Marco Editore, 1994).
Putnam, Samuel, 'I Giovani (Notes on Contemporary Italian Literature)', *This Quarter*, 4 (1930), pp. 687–97.
Putnam, Samuel, 'A Miniature Anthology of Contemporary Italian Literature', *This Quarter*, 4 (1930), pp. 566–71.
Ravegnani, Giuseppe, *I contemporanei: dal tramonto dell'ottocento all'alba del novecento* (Torino: Fratelli Bocca, 1930).
Valesio, Paolo, 'After *The Conquest of the Stars*' [Foreword], in Mario Moroni and Luca Somigli (eds), *Italian Modernism: Italian Culture between Decadentism and Avant-Garde* (Toronto: University of Toronto Press, 2004), pp. iv–xxiii.
Visconti, Laura, 'The Artist and the Artisan', *Samuel Beckett Today/Aujourd'hui*, 6 (1997), pp. 387–98.
Zampa, Giorgio, *Eugenio Montale: Tutte le poesie* (Milano: Mondadori, 1984).
Zurbrugg, Nicholas, *Beckett and Proust* (Gerrards Cross: Smythe, 1988).

14.

A Rhetoric of Ill-Saying

Bruno Clément

The validity of the widely held assumption that Samuel Beckett writes 'without style', that is, without resorting to rhetorical figures, while by no means a new idea, is not at all self-evident. Ever since the publication in 1953 of a novel that spoke of the impossibility of naming and that set out to banish rhetorical figures and simply 'to utter. Method or no method'[1] critics have, for the most part, faithfully and uncritically echoed a thesis that is explicitly, though also half-heartedly, supported by the work itself. Maurice Blanchot was the first, aside from the narrator himself, to see *The Unnamable* as a work written 'without resorting to trickery or subterfuge'.[2] Likewise, Gérard Durozoi spoke of Beckett as a writer who 'endlessly impoverishes his material and gradually rejects all of the rhetorical and technical expressive possibilities afforded him by his language'.[3] Others have frequently said of Beckett's style (which has rarely been studied systematically) that it is, rather, a lack of style.

Such comments really only repeat, in a way that suggests a lack of critical distance, the language of the texts that they are supposed to be interpreting. Long before critical discourse arose around it, Beckett's work was already saying that it was 'ill said', that it was poorly written, that it had no method, as though it were a perpetual improvisation. This rather uncommon phenomenon, whereby the language of the work is repeated by the language of the critical discourse that it elicits, will, in this essay, be investigated as attentively as Beckett's texts themselves. The brief list of rhetorical figures that follows does not propose to discredit a critical discourse whose rightness the work necessarily confirms; rather, it offers to the reader a way of understanding what made this discourse not only possible but inevitable.

It is not, to be sure, an exhaustive list of all the figures that appear in Beckett's work. I intend, rather, to indicate those for which he displays a predilection and briefly to explain their function in his work. 'Anadiplosis', 'baroquism', 'epiphonema' or 'expolitio' are not adduced because they are unusual or exotic, but because each contributes in its own way to Beckett's poetics, which is, on the whole, a poetics of duplicity. The continuous self-depreciation of Beckett's texts, the distance that they try repeatedly to establish between what is written and an idealised imaginary text, that is, 'well seen well said', serves as the almost inevitable foundation of a critical discourse that should, in principle, preserve its distance. It seems that one of the sources of this unprecedented congruence is what we could call 'a rhetoric of ill-saying'.

There may well be no one figure, such as Voltairian irony or Proustian metaphor, that characterises Beckett's work, which uses figures not as tools but as raw materials; no figure in whose systematic use we can discern both the author's intention and an essential aspect of his individuality. If there were, the most likely candidate would be 'epanorthosis', broadly understood as a figure of thought, or, as Michel Deguy says, 'the arcanum of thinking'. Indeed, the backwards movement that it generates makes 'compulsive repetition' and 'rethinking', which are derivative figures, possible, and its second phase, which returns to the first not to negate but to weaken it, precludes a third phase which would make them all part of a dialectic or, in any event, a movement. The absence of this third term is precisely what constitutes the 'failure' of Beckett's work.

Ambiguity. It is precisely because it tries to present itself as being what it is not (a work without qualities) that Beckett's work cultivates ambiguity. Some of its key words acquire importance because of their ambiguity: the word 'finish', and the expressions 'to finish' and 'to finish with', for example. Do they indicate the end of the work, of the narrator or of the author? How many critical commentaries are based on this ambiguity! The word 'encore', in *Pour finir encore* (title and first line of one of the 'fizzles'), or in the first sentence of *Mal vu mal dit*, plays on its two meanings in French. Beckett, translating the former as *For to End Yet Again*, inevitably loses the ambiguity. *The Unnamable* is also an ambiguous title (is it a thing or a person?), and the novel surely plays on this ambiguity.

Anacoluthon is 'a breakdown in the syntactical construction of a sentence'[4] and, hence, a grammatical mistake. As one would expect, it occurs frequently in a work claiming to make endless mistakes that confirm the incompetence or the awkwardness of the narrator.

> Up bright and early that day, I was young then, feeling awful, and out, mother hanging out of the window in her nightdress weeping and waving.[5]

> The fact would seem to be, if in my situation one may speak of facts, not only that I shall have to speak of things of which I cannot speak, but also, which is even more interesting, but also that I, which is if possible even more interesting, that I shall have to, I forget, no matter.[6]

Anadiplosis, defined by Dupriez as 'repetition of the last word of one sentence, or line of poetry, as a means of (sometimes emphatic) liaison',[7] appears frequently in a work that explicitly presents itself as an improvisation; anadiplosis 'bounces off' the preceding word, idea or expression in ordinary speech and tries to create, if only superficially, a 'genuinely false' relationship between elements that must continue to appear independent.

> . . . there is nothing but a voice murmuring a trace. A trace, it wants to leave a trace, yes, like air leaves among the leaves, among the grass, among the sand, it's with that it would make a life, but soon it will be the end, it won't be long now, there won't be any life, there won't have been any life, there will be silence, the air quite still that trembled once an instant, the tiny flurry of dust quite settled.[8]

Anastrophe, 'the reversal of the usual order of terms in the same group',[9] is one of the techniques that Beckett uses to spread confusion in the linguistic realm. It throws a wrench into the machinery of language and, in this way, brings literature to an impasse. Watt uses it systematically in a way that makes his sentences difficult to understand, as when he explains how he entered Erskine's locked room: 'Ruse a by, he said, and as he said, Ruse a by, he blushed . . .'[10] Watt also makes use of something like an anastrophe applied to the *dispositio*: 'As Watt told of the beginning of his story, not first, but second, so not fourth, but third, now he told its end. Two, one, four, three, that was the order in which Watt told his story. Heroic quatrains are not otherwise elaborated.'[11]

Antimetabole involves the 'mutual exchange between two sentences or clauses of their constituent words in such a way that each word occurs in the place and with the relationships possessed by the other'.[12] In a work that uses the arbitrary and the accidental as recurrent alibis, the permutations of antimetabole can always be attempted. They impose no responsibilities and are always welcome: 'I say what I hear, I hear what I say, I don't know, one or the other, or both, that makes three possibilities, pick your fancy . . .'[13]

Aposiopesis, 'a sudden interruption, betraying an emotion, a threat, or hesitation',[14] is one of the fundamental figures of Beckett's work. As Fontanier, who calls it 'reluctance', has remarked, it allows the speaker 'to imply through the little that he does say, and with the help of circumstances, something that he pretends not to say, and oftentimes much more'.[15] Aposiopesis can, on a first level of interpretation, be understood as the sign of narrators' inability to express themselves or of a fundamental deficiency of language itself. It is, above all, one of the principal devices that Beckett uses to shift the reader's interest from what is written to what will obviously never be written. More than any other figure, aposiopesis distances the text from itself and succeeds in creating the notion of a 'true text' in relation to which the written text is so meaningless and impoverished that there is no point in wasting time over it: 'I believe him, I know it's my only chance to—my only chance, I believe all I'm told';[16] 'The unthinkable last of all. Unnamable. Last person. I. Quick leave him.'[17] Beckett's work raises this figure to the prominence of a formal principle, especially in novels like *Malone Dies*, in which the last sentence is incomplete, or *The Unnamable*, in which the last sentence imposes the obligation of continuing but stays where it is.

Baroquism: nothing seems further from this technique, defined by Dupriez as 'the search for the rarest, the most surprising, and most curious ideas, figures and words'[18] than Beckett's work, which deliberately pretends to be unpolished so as to appear more natural. In the midst of many pages strewn with trite remarks, however, one discovers – as though it were the sign of an ulterior motive that disclosed the true, secret place of thought – a rare word for which the reader needs a dictionary. Having grown used to the ordinary, the familiar and the everyday, the reader suddenly and unpredictably comes upon a 'diamond in the rough', which he inspects with astonishment, momentarily glimpsing the fact that the terrain that he had been surveying with such calm and confidence was perhaps hiding a secret treasure that shows itself in these rare words.

> Old earth, no more lies, I've seen you, it was me, with my other's ravening eyes [de mes yeux grifanes], too late.[19]

> perhaps I had left my leg behind in the Pacific, yes, no perhaps about it, I had, somewhere off the coast of Java and its jungles red with rafflesia . . .[20]

A comic counterexample is to be found in the narrator's expression of joy when he feels sure that he has found the proper word or expression in a trite or commonplace term: 'it's like shit, there we have it at last, there it is at last, the right word, one has only to seek, seek in vain, to be sure of finding in the end, it's a question of elimination.'[21]

Battology, defined as 'unnecessary, tedious repetition of the same thoughts in the same terms in similar clauses',[22] resembles 'compulsive repetition'. Alluded to in *Watt*, where we are told 'For Watt's sense of chronology was strong, in a way, and his dislike of battology was very strong',[23] it serves to create the impression, so important to the work as a whole, of clumsiness and lack of effort. However, like metabole it also allows the writer to play with words in such a way as to create cracks in language. Between the nearly identical elements of a sentence, a fissure grows little by little until it is a gaping chasm wherein lies the absence of meaning: 'What variety and at the same time what monotony, how varied it is and at the same time how, what's the word, how monotonous.'[24]

Chleuasmos, defined by Dupriez as 'irony turned against oneself. Mockery, persiflage, or sarcasm at one's own expense, but performed with the expectation that others present will protest if only by a gesture',[25] is the usual tactic adopted by narrators who aim to deprecate their text by resorting to self-accusation: 'What rubbish all this stuff about light and dark. And how I have luxuriated in it';[26] 'And when it comes to neglecting fundamentals. I think I have nothing to learn, and indeed I confuse them with accidentals.'[27]

Citation is not as rare as its occasional prohibition might lead one to assume: 'And yet you know our covenant: no communication of dreams on any account. The same holds for quotes. No dreams or quotes at any price.'[28] Its ironic use makes the literature to which it bears witness seem to belong to distant and irrevocably bygone days, as when Winnie tries unsuccessfully to remember her classics in *Happy Days* and Hamm misquotes Baudelaire in *Endgame*.

Comparison, 'the expression of a similarity (or of several similarities) between two entities of the same order, or quality, etc.',[29] is nearly absent from Beckett's work. After being ridiculed or rejected, as, for example, by the narrator of *From an Abandoned Work* when he tells us 'but the rages were the worst, like a great wind suddenly rising in me, no, I can't describe',[30] it is completely abandoned. This absence tells us more about the work than does the presence of many other figures. It corresponds to the desire to deny the work any opening upon another world and to restrict it to a suffocating immanence, as when the narrator of *The Unnamable* says 'Here is my only elsewhere'.[31]

Compulsive repetition creates the impression that the work is turning in circles around a centre that it is incapable of naming, and, having really very little to say, is condemned to repeating that nothing is namable, that nothing is sayable, and that the essential is missing. Such repetition, the possibility of escape from which is never intimated, and which is the object of bitter protests as well as of somewhat tender and friendly exclamations (the tone varies), is what prevents the work from beginning, from ever really ending, or from becoming properly organised. Compulsive repetition is, ultimately, the figure that raises suspicions concerning the plausibility of a statement, the probability of an arrangement, or the value of any verbal flourishes.

> and always muttering the same old mutterings, the same old stories, the same old questions and answers.[32]

> that's why they always repeat the same thing, the same old litany, the one they know by heart, to try and think of something different, of how to say something different from the same old thing, always the same wrong thing said always wrong, they can find nothing, nothing else to say but the thing that prevents them from finding . . .[33]

Concatenation, 'union by chaining or linking together',[34] is one of the least structured tropes. It is used almost continuously in the last pages of *The Unnamable* and in numerous passages in *Texts for Nothing*. The self-generating flow of words that it creates implies the disappearance of any initiative or control on the part of a narrator or an author. In the movement towards the wholesale disintegration of language that is imagined in Beckett's work, concatenation is the stage that immediately follows anadiplosis; one could say of this latter figure that it binds elements without linking them and in this minimal way preserves the unity of the sentence.

> I didn't do anything to me, I didn't do anything to anyone, no one did anything to me, there is no one, I've looked, no one but me, no, not me either, I've looked everywhere, there must be someone, the voice must belong to someone, I've no objection, what it wants I want, I am it, I've said so, it says so, from time to time it says so, then it says not, I've no objection, I want it to go silent, it wants to go silent, it can't, it does for a second . . .[35]

Digression, defined by Dupriez as 'a part in a work which treats matters apparently extraneous to the principal subject, but which nonetheless are essential to the author's goal',[36] is merely apparent in classic texts because it ultimately serves as a means through which the narrator clarifies his principal goal. In Beckett's work, on the contrary, digression, like schematisation, is a flaw that becomes a kind of aesthetic slogan whose function is to devalue the text. In a work that pretends not to have any real subject, it follows either that there cannot be any real digressions or that everything is a digression. The reader's sense that he is forever turning around an absent 'other' corresponds precisely to this use, often foregrounded, of digression. To encourage belief in the digression is one of the work's imperatives because whoever believes in its digressions believes in its subject: 'But instead of saying what I should not have said, and what I shall say no more, if I can, and what I shall say perhaps, if I can, should I not rather say some other thing, even though it be not yet the right thing?'[37]

Dislocation, 'a device for emphasising any part of a sentence by means of agents (personal or demonstrative pronouns) authorising either anticipation or reprise',[38] belongs to the poetics of the fragment and attempts to convey the unpredictable and arbitrary interruptions and resumptions of a voice or of an imaginary discourse over which the narrator, who seems barely able to keep up with his transcription of it, exercises no control. This technique is never completely abandoned after its inaugural appearance in *How It Is*. It corresponds to momentary flashes and fleeting visions that noun clauses, moving in fits and starts, are best able to convey: 'my life last state last version ill-said ill-heard ill-recaptured ill-murmured in the mud brief movements of the lower face losses everywhere';[39] 'All known all white bare white body fixed one yard legs joined like sewn. Light heat white floor one square yard never seen.'[40]

Epanorthosis is 'a return to something already said, either to reinforce or soften it, or to retract it completely'.[41] Beckett's work finds in epanorthosis, which it uses constantly, the figure through which it best represents itself. Epanorthosis does, to be sure, allow movement, but a movement that presupposes a return. It creates a gap between the first assertion and the second, which, while similar to, is also less than the first and, hence, different from it. It is precisely within this gap that the interest of the work finally lies. Epanorthosis is also the source of that impression of bargaining or of making compromises that the work conveys to the reader. Thanks to the quality of 'lessness' introduced by epanorthosis, what is actually written in the text seems always to be there simply for want of anything better. Epanorthosis can affect:

– a word (in which case it is a correction):

> Suddenly, no, at last, long last, I couldn't anymore, I couldn't go on.[42]

– a sentence:

> Not that Watt felt calm and free and glad, for he did not, and had never done so. But he thought that perhaps he felt calm and free and glad, or if not calm and free and glad, at least calm and free, or free and glad, or glad and calm, or if not calm and free, or free and glad, or glad and calm, at least calm, or free, or glad, without knowing it.[43]

– it can also affect an entire work, as evidenced, for example, by the repetition of Act I in the attenuated form of Act II in *Waiting for Godot* and in *Happy Days*. Generally, the tendency of the work to accept, as a final resort and in the absence of anything better, something that it had begun by rejecting as undesirable (questions, imagination, characters, rhetoric, time, space etc.) – a tendency that defines it from beginning to end – corresponds to epanorthosis. Some of the movements of Beckett's characters – especially the crawling that occurs in *Molloy*, in *How It Is* or in *Fizzles* – are an embodied form of epanorthosis.

Epiphonema is defined by Fontanier as 'an exclamation, frequently sententious, made in the course of a narration but that stands on its own because of its generality; it may precede, follow or appear in the midst of the narrative to which it belongs'.[44] Epiphonema is used to discredit, not the form (which systematically calls attention to its inadequacy), but the statement itself, which this figure helps to present as something second rate, ironic or parodic: 'Nothing is funnier than unhappiness, I grant you that';[45] 'What goes by the name of love is banishment, with now and then a postcard from the homeland, such is my considered opinion, this evening'.[46] Remarks such as these constitute a kind of 'philosophy' to whose explication so many commentaries on Beckett's work limit themselves. What Roland Barthes calls 'cultural codes' are an integral part of the work, and such remarks, which would make the reader uneasy if they were only an expression of desperation, are somewhat reassuring precisely because in their very universality they belong more identifiably to a tradition.

Erasure (lexical) occurs when 'instead of using proper names, specific common nouns, or even propositions, the speaker uses demonstratives or indefinite, almost meaningless grammatical and lexical forms (e.g., 'thingamujig', 'what-d'you-call-it').[47] Beckett uses this technique to indicate his lack of interest in identity, as with A and B at the beginning of *Molloy*; to suggest the necessity of vagueness, as when Clov tells Hamm 'Something is taking its course';[48] or to create an ironic statement, as when Mercier alludes dismissively to the human soul: 'Take one [person] for example entirely free from pain all over, both his body and the other yoke.'[49]

Expolitio, also called 'parastasis', is defined by Fontanier as a figure that 'has the same relation to thoughts as the synonym does to words: it repeats the same thought from different angles or through different turns of phrase so as to make it more vivid or interesting'.[50] By making the text lose its balance expolitio causes a periodic yet unpredictable 'breakdown' from which one can never escape except by chance: 'what do I seek now, what it is, it must be that, it can only be that, what it is, what it can be, what what can be, what I seek, no, what I hear, now it comes back to me, all back to me . . .'[51]

While the slightly varied repetitions that constitute expolitio do run the risk of becoming mere *compulsive repetition*, they are nonetheless justified by the possibility that they will lead, against all expectation, to something new.

> With so much life gone from knowledge how know when all began, all the variants of the one that one by one their venom staling follow upon one another, all life long, till you succumb. So in some way even olden things each time are first things, no two breaths the same, all a going over and over and all once and never more.[52]

Extenuation involves 'the substitution, for the real idea under discussion, of an idea of the same kind but weaker'.[53] The difficulty of finding isolated examples of this figure does not change the fact that it serves as the foundation of the greater part of Beckett's work. The actual text often presents itself as a rough, pathetic and crude version of a more finished text that will, of course, never be seen. Several of Beckett's titles explicitly allude to the principle of extenuation: *Roughs*, *Fizzles*, *Catastrophe*, *Texts for Nothing*. Extenuation is one of the duplicitous techniques that Beckett uses to pretend that the text is only a sketch or a leftover: 'Keep going, going on. Call that going, call that on';[54] 'If there may not be no more questions let there at least be no more answers'.[55]

Foregrounding is an operation that can be performed on a figure only if the figure itself is already 'rhetorical' in the pejorative sense of this term. 'Then the author must display with satisfaction the artifice, emphasising that it forms a trick of the trade.'[56] Contemporary literature, with its strongly self-referential quality, uses this figure more frequently than did classical literature. As Roland Barthes once said, in the modern period, literature is a mask that points to itself. Beckett uses foregrounding in order to pass the text off as something transparent, whose readers seem to be witnessing the inner processes of its creation and development. Admitting that one is using a figure, which is itself yet another figure, gives the impression of simplifying and clarifying a text in which it appears while, in fact, making it even more complicated. Hence, it is one of the forms assumed by the ambition of writing without figures. The text thinks that it can compensate for the impossibility of doing without rhetoric by pointing to this necessity of rhetoric or, in other words, by creating even more rhetoric. This attitude of honesty and transparency is more important than the figure itself, which is ultimately unimportant.

Foregrounding appears in its simplest form very early in Beckett's work – for example, 'What stink of artifice'[57] – and all of his figures are, at one time or another, foregrounded:

– *Anacoluthon*: 'If only I could make an effort, an effort of attention, to

try and discover what's happening to me, what then, I don't know, I've forgotten my apodosis' [the main clause of a conditional sentence].[58]
– *Description*: 'Help, help, if I could only describe this place, I who am so good at describing places, walls, ceilings, floors, they are my speciality . . .'[59]
– *Ellipsis*: 'how I manage to hear, if it's I who hear, and how to understand, ellipsis when possible, it saves time . . .'[60]
– *Imagery*: 'in the midst of silence, its great swell rears towards me, I'm streaming with it, it's an image . . .'[61]
Notice, too, the memorable foregroundings of:
– *The Aside*: 'An aside, ape! Did you never hear an aside before!'[62]
– *Baroquism*: 'A few drops mishaphazard. Then strangury.'[63]
– *Linkage*: 'then it will be time enough to institute an inquiry. Moreover, that's right, link, link, you never know, moreover their attitude towards me has not changed.'[64]
– *Litotes*: 'Mrs W: You yourself observed nothing . . . strange! Amy: No, mother, I myself did not, to put it mildly. Mrs W: What do you mean, Amy, to put it mildly, what can you possibly mean, Amy, to put it mildly! Amy: I mean, Mother, that to say I observed nothing . . . strange is indeed to put it mildly. I saw nothing, heard nothing, of any kind. I was not there.'[65]
– *Metaphor*: 'But it's entirely a matter of voices, no other metaphor is appropriate.'[66]
– *Parastasis*: 'if I could remember what I have said I could repeat it, if I could learn something by heart I'd be saved, I have to keep on saying the same thing and each time it's an effort . . .'[67]
– *Reiteration*: 'I don't know if it's big, or if it's small, or if it's closed, or if it's open, that's right, reiterate, that helps you on . . .'[68]

In a general and, no doubt, subversive way, foregrounding is, in Beckett's work, a movement that involves not only writing in such a way as to foreground the act of writing, but, rather, to underline, wherever possible, the gap between what is said and what should be said. Classic examples of this technique reveal a *real* gap between what is to be said and the way in which it is said. Beckett, however, uses an inauthentic form to create, at a point where there is not necessarily any figure to unmask, a *fictive* gap within which the reader must place himself. Statements such as 'I should mention before going any further, any further on, that I say aporia without knowing what it means'[69] are examples, like all the others that seem to foreground a technique, of the duplicitous ends to which Beckett turns this device.

Hypotyposis 'paints things so vividly and with such energy that they become in some way visible; it also turns a narrative or description into an image, a picture, or even a living scene'.[70] Beckett resuscitates hypotyposis (which he calls 'image' and uses as the title of a short work published separately in 1988) by giving it a new status and a new role. It is no longer a more or less successful way of creating a lifelike representation. Rather, it becomes, beginning with *How It Is*, the actual subject of the text. The aesthetic quest involves, at least ostensibly, grasping images (as in earlier works the narrators tried to hear scraps of voices) that, in a sporadic and unpredictable way, pierce through the dark and inert imaginary realm of the narrator. The image is no longer used to create the effect of verisimilitude; rather, it becomes the only reality.

> She is there. Again . . . Without the curtain's being opened. Suddenly open. A flash. The suddenness of all! She still without stopping. On her way without starting. Gone without going. Back without returning. Suddenly it is evening. Or dawn. The eye rivets the bare window. Nothing in the sky will distract it from it more. While she from within looks her fill. Pfft occulted. Nothing having stirred.[71]

Inclusion, 'a device consisting of beginning and ending a poem, story, or play with the same word',[72] is used by Beckett to show that his characters are turning in circles, that they not only are not moving forward but that they cannot move forward, as in Vladimir's song at the beginning of Act II of *Waiting for Godot* (quoted in *The Unnamable*) and in *Texts for Nothing 4*: 'Where would I go, if I could go, who would I be, if I could be, . . . That's where I'd go, if I could go, that's who I'd be, if I could be.'[73] A slightly subversive form of inclusion can also expose the artificiality of the narrative at the same time that it foregrounds itself, as in the famous example of the second part of *Molloy*: 'It is midnight . . .'[74]

Incoherence, or a 'mixed metaphor, that is, one combining two incompatible images',[75] ridicules metaphoricity itself. It is one more opportunity to cast suspicion on the language that contains them and imposes their use: 'Decidedly this eye is hard of hearing';[76] 'The eye breathes again but not for long'.[77]

Irony deprives the text of any hope of neutrality. A distance always separates it from another text, which is absent yet nonetheless potential. Irony compensates for and, in a certain sense, replaces comparison. Thanks to irony, the text, condemned to the here and now by the disappearance of comparison, glimpses the possibility of realms other than its own, even if they seem unlikely or out of reach, and allows that dream of the other text which is so essential to the functioning of Beckett's work.

Isolexism was coined by Dupriez to denote 'the return, within a sentence, of a lexeme already uttered, but in different conditions'.[78] The narrator, who seems to fall into it rather often, shows himself, through his resort to this technique, either careless about the final shape of his work or simply incompetent to rid his work of those elements of repetition that are normally perceived as being a stylistic mistake: 'so many lies, so many times the same lie lying denied' ('le même mensonge et mensongèrement démenti');[79] 'The mind betrays the treacherous eyes and the treacherous word their treacheries'.[80] Beckett's formal procedures are foregrounded by the special use of an isolexism called 'mirroring', which 'consists in subordinating the different lexical parts of an isolexism one to another'.[81] Each element of the narrative is, in turn, drawn into the invisible net of this infernal isolexism. These include: the imaginary ('Imagination Dead Imagine'), questions ('Was it ever over and done with questions!'/'Fut-il jamais un temps où plus question de questions?'), and the self ('Ma voix ni mienne ni voix').

At this point, Beckett's work no longer has anything to do with mere techniques. Even when the proper words cannot be located, the same suicidal procedure can still be carried out: the imaginary imagines the death of the imagination; questioning raises the question of the absence of questions; space tries to locate a space that has no reference points; time tries to suspend chronology, and so on. This figure shows us the one and only constraint that Beckett has been reduced to: that of using up what is until it no longer is. This constraint, which the work cannot acknowledge and which it tries, for this reason, to present as a conscious project, affects, as is only logical, the rhetorical figures themselves. The only way of rescuing them is to find, or to give new meaning to, the fundamental figure of the gap and, in this way, to expose all of them. This is the role reserved for epanorthosis, which is, in the rhetorical sense of the word, a kind of mirror: the figure that 'figures' the figure.

Metabole, defined by Dupriez as 'an accumulation of several synonymous expressions in order to depict with greater force the same thing or idea',[82] plays the same role as expolitio (also called parastasis), with which it has obvious affinities. Celebrated examples occur in *Waiting for Godot* when Vladimir and Estragon reflect on whether their experience is worse than the circus or the pantomime,[83] describe the sound made by 'All the dead voices',[84] hurl at each other a stream of invectives ending with 'Critic!'[85] and explore the synonyms generated by the thought of doing their exercises.[86] Metabole can also be used to give the impression that one is watching the text being written. Expressions that are, one after the other, considered and then rejected as inadequate seem to be in search of the 'mot juste', which, in the best of cases, seems to be found only in the last version of the metabole (see also periphrasis and baroquism).

Metaphor brings irresistibly to mind the poetics of Proust and the correspondences that, thanks to metaphor, the narrator of *Remembrance of Things Past* is able to establish between the external world and the interior self. There is nothing surprising about the absence of this trope in Beckett's work, which claims that it wears itself out trying to establish whether or not this interior self actually exists (see comparison).

Oxymoron, 'the combination of two words whose meanings seem to be mutually contradictory',[87] is used to place in doubt the coherence both of the world and of language. Its existence is, in itself, proof of the arbitrariness of meaning as well as of its relative unimportance. Beckett is certainly being ironic when he implies, not only that an oxymoron is possible, but that it is often the least bad formulation: 'old Geulincx, dead young';[88] 'Of his mortal liveliness little trace remains'.[89]

Paradox, 'an assertion which runs counter to received opinion, and whose very formulation contradicts current ideas',[90] is found everywhere in Beckett's work. Paradox tends to be, on the level of thought, what oxymoron is on the level of meaning. It relegates the quest for truth to a remote and inaccessible realm at the same time that it exposes the futility of the means available to attain it. Hence, Beckettian paradox is one way among others to play with words, to advance without making any progress and to open a little wider the hole out of which the work intends to make a centre.

> It's not true, yes, it's true, it's true and it's not true, there is silence and there is not silence, there is no one and there is someone, nothing prevents anything. And were the voice to cease quite at last, the old ceasing voice, it would not be true, as it is not true that it speaks, it can't speak, it can't cease.[91]

Periphrasis, 'That figure of speech which consists in expressing the meaning of a word, phrase, etc., by many or several words instead of by few or one',[92] can be the occasion for smiling once again at the arbitrariness of words, as when Malone tells us that Macmann pulled up his sleeves in order to 'feel the rain pelting down on his palms, also called the hollows of the hands, or the flats, it all depends'.[93] But more often than not, periphrasis makes going out of one's way worthwhile: it represents a revaluation, as in 'Imagination at wit's end' for the imaginary old woman in *Ill Seen Ill Said*,[94] or a supplementary meaning, even a new meaning, as though it pointed to the desire to overtake language, to surprise it, and to manhandle it until it divulged something that it obviously did not want to: 'The Counter-poison' (for 'the imaginary') and 'Its drivelling scribe' (for 'the narrator').[95]

The futility of this technique, which relates it to all the others, is revealed by its foregrounding: 'In other words, they like other words, no doubt about it . . .'[96]

Questions, not all of which seem to be rhetorical, appear throughout Beckett's work: 'Where now? Who now? When now?'[97] The game that Beckett plays with them helps to define with some precision his attitude towards rhetoric. His narrators try, by using rhetoric, to minimise or neutralise these questions, and in this way to empty the work of anything that seems even remotely to resemble a content, a statement or a concern with knowing something: 'But the mere fact of asking myself such a question gives me to reflect. It is in vain I tell myself that its only purpose is to stimulate the lagging discourse, this excellent explanation does not satisfy me.'[98]

Restart, whereby 'in order to reattach several groups of words to a segment central to the sentence's syntax, the speaker repeats it, at least in part',[99] is required by anyone who uses unusually long sentences, to which he wants to give the appearance of spoken language, where they are common. Dupriez adds that restarts 'give a very natural effect in mimetic reproduction of speech or interior monologue'.[100] The last thirty pages of *The Unnamable*, written in the form of a discourse that is at every moment threatened with extinction, are the setting for a constant restart.

Rewriting. The reader of classic works can read in scholarly editions or see displayed in research collections the different stages through which a text passed on the way to its definitive version. Beckett, who did everything to avoid giving his reader the impression of a finished work, started, after giving his manuscripts to various libraries, publishing different versions of certain of his texts (ten versions of 'Bing' in the *Cahiers de L'Herne*; then, in 1988, 'L'Image', which is the first version of several pages of *How It Is*). The concept of a text begins to lose its meaning since what we read is nothing more than a sketch among others; the real text is, perhaps, nowhere at all. 'L'Image' is, henceforth, as much the text as is *How It Is*, without even talking about the 'second versions', those that are written in 'the other language'. A text such as *How It Is* goes so far as to sketch, in its final pages, a few details of another novel, obviously superior to the one that the reader is about to finish and which would serve as the basis for the actual novel's revision: 'two possible formulations therefore the present and that other beginning where the present ends'.[101] However, imperfection wins out and the idea of a totally finished text evaporates.

Schematisation is defined by Dupriez as a figure in which 'Instead of recounting, describing, or representing an action dramatically, we give a schema or outline of a work'. He then adds:

> In order for schematisation to occur, the text must present itself as a blueprint or diagram of some other text which is the true one and which it is replacing. Its author must also be presented as a commentator of a work already completed or still to be written. The device is part of the movement to dissolve, distort or displace a work in order to destroy its resistance as perfected, totally finished, and to open the imaginary world to a plurality of readings.[102]

Schematisation allows the work to place itself in the realm of the provisional or of the outline, but it also allows deviation (the 'real' work will, of course, never correspond to the outline that is first presented) and, in this way, marks it with the stain of error. Just as principles are established only so that they can be transgressed, outlines are sketched only to underline the distance which separates them from the work itself – if, that is, the work ever does achieve completion: 'Present state, three stories, inventory, there. An occasional interlude is to be feared. A full programme. I shall not deviate from it any further than I must. So much for that. I feel I am making a great mistake. No matter.'[103]

Self-correction is defined by Fontanier as a figure in which 'the speaker appears to retract purposely what he has just said in favor of something stronger, more decisive or appropriate'.[104] Self-correction is the literary equivalent of what, in painting, would be a change that the artist decided to leave visible. It is through the process of self-correction that Beckett's texts search for or invent themselves before our very eyes in that movement of transparence and authenticity which typifies them for so many readers: 'When I think, no, that won't work, when come those who knew me';[105] 'Less than the—more than the empty seat the barred back is piteous'.[106] The eleventh 'Text for Nothing' is, like the work itself, a continuous process of self-correction. Hence, what is important for the writer is not the thing said or to be said (more or less well) but the movement of hesitation, of quest for an object or a shape. The text itself will only rarely acknowledge that, far from attempting hesitantly to choose between two more or less cognate phrases, it has, from the very beginning, made hesitation itself its true subject. Epanorthosis, a characteristically Beckettian figure, is nothing more than an extended self-correction.[107]

Substitution involves 'the replacement within some hackneyed phrase, cliché, fixed syntagma, proverb, quotation, or received idea, of certain lexemes by others opposite in meaning or likely to cause surprise'.[108] Of course, nothing conclusive happens as a result of this technique; however, the reader enjoys a momentary glimpse of how fragile language can be. It implies that, in order to acquit oneself properly, one should perform the same operation on all verbal expressions, as though using them in their everyday form was already to say too much: 'I was on my way to my mother whose charity kept me dying';[109] 'In order to resume. Resume the—what is the word? What is the wrong word?'[110]

Supposition, or 'hypothesis', defined by Dupriez as 'a modality of the assertion consisting in positing something as possible',[111] is equated by Beckett's narrators with questions: 'Questions, hypotheses, call them that.'[112] It is a crude technique used to allow the discourse to continue: 'But let us first suppose, in order to get on a little, then we'll suppose something else, in order to get on a little further.'[113] The use of the conditional mood, of expressions like 'perhaps' and 'doubtlessly', of the verbs 'to have to' ('There has to be a way out'), 'to seem' and 'to appear' – and, more generally, the exposure of everything that is arbitrary or dictated by convention in a work that always treats whatever it undertakes (stories, characters or techniques) as risky – all of this prevents the text from finding a firm grounding upon which to rest while offering it the opportunity of finding refuge or of acting evasively: since there is no real beginning and nothing final has been said, it is always possible to begin again at square one: 'There must be other shifts.'[114] Of course, the abuse of this technique is, like so many others, exposed by a narrator who, in order to promote belief in the precarious, the doubtful and the vague, must from time to time assert his will to certainty: 'No more perhapses either, that old trick is worn to a thread.'[115]

Suspension occurs, according to Fontanier, when 'instead of presenting straight away some expressive trait by which we aim to produce great surprise or a powerful impression, we make the listener wait until the end of the sentence or period to hear it'.[116] When this technique is used on the level not just of a sentence but of a page, a chapter or an entire work, it is called prolongation.[117] The characteristic Beckettian sentence is not naturally suspended. When it is, some form of duplicity is involved: the end does not arrive, in which case we have aposiopesis, or its arrival causes a kind of deflation. Suspension plays with the expectation of the right word, as does the narrator of *Ill Seen Ill Said*: 'Real and—how ill say its contrary? The counter-poison.'[118] Prolongation is, on the contrary, used so systematically that it is possible to refer to Beckett's work as 'prolongated'. The reader is always awaiting the conclusion that will finally lead to the goal that has been talked about and that is imagined as attainable: Godot, the 'namable', the 'something' and so on. Prolongation, rather than suspense, is the formal principle that governs the Beckettian text: 'That's the idea, procrastinate.'[119]

Syllepsis (semantic) is defined by Dupriez as 'a figure by which a word or expression is used simultaneously in its literal and figurative senses'.[120] The multiplicity of a word's meanings produces more confusion than richness. Using this figure has nothing to do with the attempt, whether real or feigned, to fill an empty language and, in this way, give it meaning; rather, it encourages the sombre recognition of the arbitrariness of a language in which a multiplicity of meanings is the same thing as no meaning at all: 'True there was never much talk of the heart, literal or figurative . . .'[121]

Symbol. Even though every effort is made to assure that the work does not slip into symbolism ('No symbols where none intended'), the work does at times undeniably give in to the old temptation of referring to a thing or an idea through recourse to another thing or another idea and, in this way, to make language go beyond itself. Obvious examples include the sucking-stone episode in the first part of *Molloy* and Moran's bees in the second, as well as the mud in *How It Is*. Critics also point to Estragon's boots in *Waiting for Godot*[122] and the centre to which Hamm famously aspires in *Endgame*.[123]

Details such as these help to explain why Beckett has so frequently been viewed as the author of a body of work that speaks to the human condition as well as one in which every scene should be interpreted symbolically. Denials are useless: they are too rare, in any event, and only confuse things further by appearing in the texts themselves. Beckett's work encourages the same attitude towards symbols as it does towards all other narrative or theatrical elements: in aspiring to attain the essential it gets rid of them all. Just as individual identity is presented (in *The Unnamable*, for example) as a way of avoiding or at least of delaying the moment when one will talk about the authentic self, so also the symbol, from the point of view of the work itself, can be thought of as a pointless and cowardly detour. Why not speak openly, without any intermediary whatsoever, about things as they are? The title of *How It Is* points to this desire to bid farewell to symbols and symbolism. The work cannot, however, escape from symbols, no more than it can escape from questions, imaginings, figures, individual identity, or time and space. Beckett's last texts, including *Company*, *Ill Seen Ill Said* and, to a certain extent, *Stirrings Still*, speak unmistakably about the work and the various problems involved in its composition. Through this device of having the work speak about itself, the symbol embraces the mirroring movement associated with isolexism that characterises the way in which Beckett's aesthetic project would define itself and have itself be defined.

It is interesting to note, in conclusion, that what is said about rhetorical figures both by Beckett's narrators and by his critics – that is, that there aren't any – applies equally well to other elements of classical rhetoric. In the case of each, the critic is greatly tempted to follow in the footsteps of the discourse of the work itself, whose fate is, hence, to be regularly repeated on the pretext that it is only used as an illustration. This convergence can be noted, for example, with respect to the *inventio*, or the choice of subject matter. The narrator of *The Unnamable* speaks of the vagueness of the obligation that he speak; Maurice Blanchot then alludes to his predicament by asserting that words in Beckett say nothing. Likewise, with regard to the *dispositio*, or arrangement of the elements of the discourse, Georges Bataille's seminal notion of the 'formless' bears an uncanny resemblance to statements made by Molloy or Malone, or to Hamm's opposing Clov's effort 'to create a little order'.[124] When Robbe-Grillet says that Didi and Gogo are characters without roles, he is merely extending this principle of convergence to the *actio*, which establishes the conditions for the representation of the discourse. The comments of Blanchot and Bataille, who speak of a literature in ruins and of a realm beyond literature, are curiously echoed by *Ill Seen Ill Said*: 'Small slates black too brought from a ruined mansion. What tales had they tongue to tell. Their long tale told.'[125] But who is echoing whom? In this case, it is the *memoria*, which defines the space shared by the work and its readers, which exemplifies the process of imitation.

We can see in Beckett's rhetoric, whose broad outlines have been sketched here, intimations of a somewhat metaphysical discourse that would have nothingness as its centre and subject. This discourse is, to be sure, rarely mentioned explicitly by the work; however, the rhetoric of the work, whose figures are like the tip of the iceberg, does nonetheless provide ample evidence of its existence. It is difficult to escape the temptation of concluding, as Sartre had postulated and Roland Barthes repeated in his own way, that there is really no difference between discussions of technique and of metaphysics.

Translated by Thomas Cousineau

Notes

1. Samuel Beckett, *The Unnamable*, p. 15.
2. Ibid. p. 195.
3. Ibid. p. 141.
4. Bernard Dupriez, *A Dictionary of Literary Devices*, p. 34.
5. Beckett, *From an Abandoned Work*, p. 11.
6. Beckett, *The Unnamable*, p. 4.
7. Dupriez, *A Dictionary of Literary Devices*, p. 36.
8. Beckett, *Texts for Nothing 13*, p. 137.
9. Dupriez, *A Dictionary of Literary Devices*, p. 40.
10. Beckett, *Watt*, p. 128.

11. Ibid. p. 215.
12. Dupriez, *A Dictionary of Literary Devices*, p. 46.
13. Beckett, *The Unnamable*, p. 176.
14. Dupriez, *A Dictionary of Literary Devices*, p. 57.
15. Pierre Fontanier, *Les figures du discours*, p. 135.
16. Beckett, *Molloy*, p. 15.
17. Beckett, *Company*, p. 24.
18. Dupriez, *A Dictionary of Literary Devices*, p. 77.
19. Beckett, *Fizzles*, p. 43.
20. Beckett, *The Unnamable*, p. 41.
21. Ibid. p. 109.
22. See *Littré* and the *Oxford English Dictionary*.
23. Beckett, *Watt*, p. 165.
24. Beckett, *Texts for Nothing 9*, p. 118.
25. Dupriez, *A Dictionary of Literary Devices*, p. 96.
26. Beckett, *The Unnamable*, p. 24.
27. Beckett, *Molloy*, p. 108.
28. Beckett, *Mercier and Camier*, pp. 61–2.
29. Dupriez, *A Dictionary of Literary Devices*, p. 104.
30. Beckett, *From an Abandoned Work*, p. 13.
31. Beckett, *The Unnamable*, p. 162.
32. Beckett, *Texts for Nothing 1*, p. 78.
33. Beckett, *The Unnamable*, p. 121.
34. *OED*.
35. Beckett, *The Unnamable*, pp. 170–1.
36. Dupriez, *A Dictionary of Literary Devices*, p. 135.
37. Beckett, *The Unnamable*, p. 25.
38. Dupriez, *A Dictionary of Literary Devices*, p. 139.
39. Beckett, *How It Is*, p. 7.
40. Beckett, 'Ping', p. 41.
41. Fontanier, *Les figures du discours*, p. 408.
42. Beckett, *Texts for Nothing 1*, p. 75.
43. Beckett, *Watt*, p. 135.
44. Fontanier, *Les figures du discours*, p. 386.
45. Beckett, *Endgame*, p. 18.
46. Beckett, 'First Love', p. 18.
47. Dupriez, *A Dictionary of Literary Devices*, p. 174.
48. Beckett, *Endgame*, p. 13.
49. Beckett, *Mercier and Camier*, p. 58.
50. Fontanier, *Les figures du discours*, p. 420.
51. Beckett, *The Unnamable*, p. 140.
52. Beckett, *From an Abandoned Work*, p. 19.
53. Dupriez, *A Dictionary of Literary Devices*, p. 183.
54. Beckett, *The Unnamable*, p. 3.
55. Beckett, *Ill Seen Ill Said*, p. 43.
56. Dupriez, *A Dictionary of Literary Devices*, p. 193.
57. Beckett, *Mercier and Carnier*, p. 9.
58. Beckett, *The Unnamable*, p. 162.
59. Ibid. p. 157.

60. Ibid. p. 143.
61. Ibid. p. 173.
62. Beckett, *Endgame*, p. 77.
63. Beckett, *Ill Seen Ill Said*, p. 52.
64. Beckett, *The Unnamable*, p. 133.
65. Beckett, 'Footfalls', p. 243.
66. Beckett, *The Unnamable*, p. 52.
67. Ibid. p. 152.
68. Ibid. p. 173.
69. Ibid. p. 4.
70. Fontanier, *Les figures du discours*, p. 390.
71. Beckett, *Ill Seen Ill Said*, pp. 19–20.
72. Dupriez, *A Dictionary of Literary Devices*, p. 229.
73. Beckett, *Texts for Nothing 4*, p. 91; p. 94.
74. Beckett, *Molloy*, p. 7; p. 241.
75. Dupriez, *A Dictionary of Literary Devices*, p. 230.
76. Beckett, *The Unnamable*, p. 103.
77. Beckett, *Ill Seen Ill Said*, p. 22.
78. Dupriez, *A Dictionary of Literary Devices*, p. 245.
79. Beckett, *Texts for Nothing 8*, p. 139.
80. Beckett, *Ill Seen Ill Said*, p. 48.
81. Dupriez, *A Dictionary of Literary Devices*, p. 246.
82. Ibid. p. 274.
83. Beckett, *Waiting for Godot*, p. 23.
84. Ibid. p. 40.
85. Ibid. p. 48.
86. Ibid. p. 49.
87. Dupriez, *A Dictionary of Literary Devices*, p. 312.
88. Beckett, *Molloy*, p. 68.
89. Beckett, *The Unnamable*, p. 5.
90. Dupriez, *A Dictionary of Literary Devices*, p. 314.
91. Beckett, *Texts for Nothing 13*, pp. 139–40.
92. *OED*.
93. Beckett, *Malone Dies*, p. 69.
94. Beckett, *Ill Seen Ill Said*, p. 17.
95. Ibid. p. 40; p. 51.
96. Beckett, *The Unnamable*, p. 110.
97. Ibid. p. 3.
98. Ibid. p. 8.
99. Dupriez, *A Dictionary of Literary Devices*, p. 396.
100. Ibid. p. 396.
101. Beckett, *How It Is*, p. 132.
102. Dupriez, *A Dictionary of Literary Devices*, p. 409.
103. Beckett, *Malone Dies*, pp. 4–5.
104. Fontanier, *Les figures du discours*, p. 366.
105. Beckett, *Texts for Nothing 11*, p. 127.
106. Beckett, *Ill Seen Ill Said*, p. 35.
107. Cf. Dupriez, *A Dictionary of Literary Devices*, p. 88.
108. Ibid. p. 432.

109. Beckett, *Molloy*, p. 28.
110. Beckett, *Ill Seen Ill Said*, p. 17.
111. Dupriez, *A Dictionary of Literary Devices*, p. 435.
112. Beckett, *The Unnamable*, p. 3.
113. Ibid. p. 32.
114. Ibid. p. 34.
115. Ibid. p. 33.
116. Fontanier, *Les figures du discours*, p. 364.
117. Ibid. p. 417.
118. Beckett, *Ill Seen Ill Said*, p. 40.
119. Beckett, 'First Love', p. 30.
120. Dupriez, *A Dictionary of Literary Devices*, p. 440.
121. Beckett, *Texts for Nothing 13*, p. 138.
122. Beckett, *Waiting for Godot*, p. 12.
123. Beckett, *Endgame*, p. 26.
124. Ibid. p. 57.
125. Beckett, *Ill Seen Ill Said*, p. 43.

Bibliography

Bataille, Georges, 'Le Silence de *Molloy*', *Critique*, 7 (May 1951), pp. 387–96.

Beckett, Samuel, *Company* (New York: Grove Press, 1980).

Beckett, Samuel, *Endgame* (New York: Grove Press, 1958).

Beckett, Samuel, 'First Love', in *First Love and Other Shorts* (New York: Grove Press, 1974).

Beckett, Samuel, *Fizzles* (New York: Grove Press, 1976).

Beckett, Samuel, 'Footfalls', in *Ends and Odds* (New York: Grove Press, 1976).

Beckett, Samuel, *From an Abandoned Work*, in *Six Residua* (London: John Calder, 1978).

Beckett, Samuel, *How It Is* (New York: Grove Press, 1964).

Beckett, Samuel, *Ill Seen Ill Said* (New York: Grove Press, 1981).

Beckett, Samuel, *L'Image* (Paris: Éditions de Minuit, 1988).

Beckett, Samuel, *Malone Dies* (New York: Grove Press, 1956).

Beckett, Samuel, *Mercier and Camier* (New York: Grove Press, 1974).

Beckett, Samuel, *Molloy* (New York: Grove Press, 1955).

Beckett, Samuel, 'Ping', in *Six Residua* (London: John Calder, 1978).

Beckett, Samuel, *Stories and Texts for Nothing* (New York: Grove Press, 1967).

Beckett, Samuel, *The Unnamable* (New York: Grove Press, 1958).

Beckett, Samuel, *Waiting for Godot* (New York: Grove Press, 1954).

Beckett, Samuel, *Watt* (New York: Grove Press, 1959).

Blanchot, Maurice, 'Where Now? Who Now?', in *The Sirens' Song* (Bloomington: Indiana University Press, 1982).

Dupriez, Bernard, *A Dictionary* of *Literary Devices* (Toronto: University of Toronto Press, 1991).

Durozoi, Gerard, *Beckett* (Paris: Bordas, 1972).

Fontanier, Pierre, *Les figures du discours* (Paris: Flammarion, 1977).

Robbe-Grillet, Alain, 'Samuel Beckett, or Presence on the Stage', in *For a New Novel* (New York: Grove Press, 1965).

15.

Beckett's Generic Writing

Alain Badiou

The title of this essay refers to Badiou's notion that Beckett's texts express the fundamental categories or 'genres' of human existence in a manner akin to Plato's establishment of such 'axioms' of life as Movement, Rest, the Same, the Other, the Logos. In the lengthy part of the essay that precedes the section translated below, he argues that Beckett's literary career may be divided into two phases. In the first, culminating in Texts for Nothing, *the writing explores the alternation between the solipsistic* cogito *and the 'grey darkness' of being. For Badiou,* How It Is *represents a major breakthrough in that it dismisses a fruitless encounter – between a* cogito *that solicits and a realm of being that maintains its neutrality – and puts in its place the encounter with the figure of the 'Other' that breaks up and dissipates solipsistic enclosure. The first phase alternates between wandering and fixity. This will be progressively replaced by what Badiou calls 'le poème figural des postures du sujet'. The question of identity, so much at work in* The Unnamable, *is likewise replaced by 'occurrences' of the subject, that is, the enumeration of its possible positions. Hence, Badiou sees Beckett as evolving from a project based on the number 'one', governed by an interminable journey or soliloquy, to one based on the creativity of the theme of 'two', which opens upon infinity.*

Beginning with How It Is, *Beckett also creates a form of prose that is subtended by a latent poem. The surface of these texts contains thematic recurrences presented in the form of a slow-motion movement that is itself governed by a hidden poetic structure. Sometimes this structure is very close to the surface, as in* Lessness; *sometimes it is quite distant, as in* Imagination Dead Imagine. *From 1960 onwards, Beckett's texts are the setting for a constant subversion of prose, and its fictional destiny, by the latent poem. They alternate between stories of failure and victorious illuminations. Badiou also sees Beckett as partially curing himself of the 'secret schema of predestination' that runs from* Watt *to* How It

Is *by opening his work to chance encounters and happenings, in which the discovery of the non-coincidence between self and identity becomes possible. This revelation, which deprives being of its totality, frees the human subject from the predestination imposed by its identity.*

The shift from one phase to another may also be described in terms of different attitudes with respect to the events that occur within texts. Beckett begins by classifying these events in relation to a network of significations; he will later replace this initial hermeneutic project with a process of naming which has been freed from the ambition of explaining. In place of interpretation, we have a poetics of naming that tries to preserve in language a trace of the event's separation.

Thomas Cousineau

Beckett's Generic Writing

'The Numericity of Love: One, Two, Infinity'

While the story that Beckett tells is subject to a number of variations, one feature remains unchanged: love begins in a pure encounter, which is neither destined nor predestined except by the chance crossing of two paths. Prior to this meeting, there is only solitude. No 'Two', in particular no sexual duality, exists before this encounter. Sexual difference is inconceivable, except as the encounter unfolds within the process of love; there is no originary difference that conditions or orients the encounter. The encounter is the power from which the Two, and thus love itself, originate. This power, which nothing precedes in the order proper to itself, is practically beyond measure. It is, in particular, incommensurable with the power of feeling and the sexual and desiring power of the body. This boundless excess of the encounter is asserted in the 1930s by Neary in *Murphy*: 'And to meet and part in my sense exceeds the power of feeling, however tender, and of bodily motions, however expert.'[1] Beckett never reduces love to the amalgam of sentimentality and sexuality endorsed by common opinion. Love as a matter of truth (and not merely of opinion) depends upon a pure event: an encounter whose strength radically surpasses both sentimentality and sexuality.

The encounter is a fundamental condition of the Two as such. In the figure of love, as it is encountered by the origin, the Two *occurs*, together with the Two of the sexes or sexualised figures. Love in no way makes a pre-existing Two into One; this is the romantic version of love that Beckett scoffs at. Love is neither fusion nor effusion. It is, rather, the often painstaking condition of Two's existence as Two. An example is provided in *Malone Dies*, by the fictitious encounter engineered by Malone between Macmann and his guardian, Moll. The love that is admirably recounted here, like the love of the aging or the dying, acquires an extraordinary lyrical intensity. Malone comments on the effects of truth issuing from this love: 'But on the long road to this what flutterings, alarms and bashful fumblings, of which only this, that they gave Macmann some insight into the meaning of the expression, Two is company.'[2]

The Two, which is instituted by the encounter and whose truth results from love, does not remain closed upon itself. It is, rather, a passage, a pivotal point, the first numericity. This Two makes way, or authorises passage, between the One of solipsism, which is given initially, and the infinity of beings and experience. The Two of love is a hazardous mediation for alterity in general. It induces a severance, a break, within the One of the *cogito*; but by virtue of this very fact it can hardly be seen as independent, for it provides passage to the limitless multiple without the limitations of Being. One might also state that the Two of love induces the advent of the perceptible. Where there had previously been but the grey darkness of being, a perceptible flexing of the world is carried out by virtue of the truth of the Two. The perceptible and the infinite are identical, for the infinity of the world is, with the One of the *cogito*, the other coherent thesis. Settled between these two positions, the Two of love at once severs and brings together.

It is an axiom of *How It Is* that the One and the Infinite are the two coherent ontological theses. The hero, crawling in the dark, asserts: 'in other words in simple words I quote on either I am alone and no further problem or else we are innumerable and no further problem either'.[3] On the basis of this abstract axiom, which jointly confirms the theses of the One and the Infinite, the Two of love brings about a perceptible version. Love offers beauty, nuance, colour. It presents what one might call the other or second nocturne, not of the grey darkness of being, but of the rustling night – the night of leaves and plants, of stars and water. Under the very strict conditions of the encounter and toil, the Two of love splits darkness into, on the one hand, the grey darkness of being, and, on the other, the infinitely varied darkness of the sensible world.

This is why in Beckett's prose one suddenly discovers poems where, under the sign of the inaugural figure of the Two, something unfolds within the night of presentation, that is, the unfolding of the multiple as such. Love is, above all, an authorisation granted to the multiple, under the never-abolished threat of grey darkness where the original One bears the torture of its own identification. I would like now to quote three of these poems that are latent in his prose so that another Beckett may be heard – one expressive of giving and the happiness of existence. The first is taken from *Krapp's Last Tape* where the hero of the play, a man coming to his end, is catapulted into interminable attempts at anamnesis (he listens to recordings of his voice at different stages of his life), and successfully recalls the crucial moment, that is, when the Two of love had reopened the multiple:

> . . . upper lake, with the punt, bathed off the bank, then pushed out into the stream and drifted. She lay stretched out on the floorboards with her hands under her head and her eyes closed. Sun blazing down, bit of a breeze, water nice and lively. I noticed a scratch on her thigh and asked her how she came by it. Picking gooseberries, she said. I said again I thought it was hopeless and no good going on and she agreed, without opening her eyes. [*Pause.*] I asked her to look at me and after a few moments—[*Pause.*]—after a few moments she did, but the eyes just the slits, because of the glare. I bent over her to get them in the shadow and they opened. [*Pause. Low*] Let me in. [*Pause.*] We drifted in among the flags and stuck. The way they went down, sighing, before the stem! [*Pause.*] I lay down across her with my face in her breasts and my hand on her. We lay there without moving. But under us all moved, and moved us, gently, up and down, and from side to side.
> [*Pause.*]
> Past midnight. Never knew . . .[4]

As one can observe, this is the poem of the opening of waters, the multiple of the absolute moment when love, even were it announcing its own end, proposes the infinity of the sensible world.

The second quotation comes from 'Enough', a short text that is entirely devoted to love. It establishes specific connections between love and infinite knowledge. Two lovers walking, broken in two, in a world of flower-covered hills, are never as close to one another as when they discuss mathematics or astronomy:

> His talk was seldom of geodesy. But we must have covered several times the equivalent of the terrestrial equator. At an average speed of roughly three miles per day and night. We took flight in arithmetic. What mental calculations bent double hand in hand! Whole ternary numbers we raised in this way to the third power sometimes in downpours of rain. Graving themselves in his memory as best they could the ensuing cubes accumulated. In view of the converse operation at a later stage. When time would have done its work.[5]

Another very beautiful passage occurs, again in 'Enough', when the figure of the beloved man becomes this source of knowledge in which the sky is given in its own nature:

> On a gradient of one in one his head swept the ground. To what this taste was due I cannot say. To love of the earth and the flowers' thousand scents and hues. Or to cruder imperatives of an anatomical order. He never raised the question. The crest once reached alas the going down again. In order

> from time to time to enjoy the sky he resorted to a little round mirror. Having misted it with his breath and polished it on his calf he looked in it for the constellations. I have it! he exclaimed referring to the Lyre or the Swan. And often he added that the sky seemed much the same.[6]

Love is when we can say that we have the sky, while the sky has nothing. The multiple of the constellations is thus held in the opening of the Two.

The last poem is taken from *Company*, and it is doubtless the one most related to the metaphor of the division of darkness and of the advent of the second nocturne:

> You are on your back at the foot of an aspen. In its trembling shade. She at right angles propped on her elbows head between her hands. Your eyes opened and closed have looked in hers looking in yours. In your dark you look in them again. Still. You feel on your face the fringe of her long black hair stirring in the still air. Within the tent of hair your faces are hidden from view. She murmurs, Listen to the leaves. Eyes in each other's eyes you listen to the leaves. In their trembling shade.[7]

These are examples of the Two of love as the passage from the One of solipsism to the infinite multiplicity of the world and the nocturnal fissure of the grey darkness of being. One should also mention the web of the Two – an insistence in the form of loyalty. This loyalty organises four functions for Beckett, which are also four figures of the subject within love. It is my conviction (I am unable here to provide a proof) that these functions have a general value, in the sense they are the organising functions of any generic process, whether it be the duration of love, certainly, but also scientific investigation, artistic innovation and political tenacity.

The first of these functions is wandering or travelling, with or without the benefit of a sack – a journey in darkness, which symbolises the infinite risk of the faithful journey of love, the endless crossing that is a world henceforth exposed to the effects of the encounter. This function of wandering, which we observed in its abstract form in *How It Is*, is also the incessant walking of the lovers of 'Enough' among the hills and flowers. It institutes the duration of the two and establishes time as mandated by risk.

The second function is just the opposite, that is, immobility, which holds, maintains, possesses the steady anchor of the first designation, that is, the designation of the event/encounter. We have observed that this function pins the 'incident' to its lack of meaning, and permanently sets within a name that which is beyond numbering. It is the irrational 'I love you', 'We're in love', or what might come in its stead, and which at each occurrence is pronounced for the first time. This immobility is that of the second nocturne, of the small craft caught in the reeds, of gazes penetrating those of the other.

The third function is the imperative: carry on, even through separation – decree that separation itself is a form of continuity. The imperative given by the Two supplants that of the soliloquy ('You must go on . . . I'll go on'), but it removes the pointless torture and imposes the strict law of happiness, whether one be victim or executioner.

The fourth function is the narrative, which delivers, from the standpoint of the Two, the latent infinity of the world, and which recounts its improbable unfolding and inscribes in its wake, in the manner of an archival escort of wandering, all that one may discover in what Beckett calls 'le temps béni du bleu'.

Love (but also any generic process regardless of the specific realm to which it belongs) weaves within its singular duration these four functions: wandering, immobility, imperative and narrative. Beckett formulates the idea of the sexes, of the two sexes, on the assumption of love's occurrence, by combining the four functions. He thus establishes the masculine and feminine polarities of the Two independently of any sexual differentiation, whether empirical or biological.

The functions joined within the masculine polarity are those of immobility and imperative. A 'man' is one who remains motionless in love by retaining the name that founds it and by imposing the law of continuity. Yet, with the absence of the narrative function, this prescriptive immobility is silent. In the case of love, a 'man' is his name's silent sentinel. Given the further absence of the wandering function, to be a man is also not to grant recognition to love, but only to retain of it, motionless in the dark, a powerful but abstract conviction.

The feminine polarity unites wandering and narrative. It concurs not with the rigidity assigned to a name, but with an incessant unfolding in the world, in the narrative of its unending glory. It resists unsupported injunctions and conducts a constant search for the justification of power. In the context of love, to be a 'woman' is to be the protector of meaning, rather than of names. This protective effort implies the wayward fate of inquiries, as well as its perpetual recounting in a narrative.

Love exists as the determination of this polarity, which supports the four functions and sets them out individually. This is why love alone calls for the observation that there truly is 'man' (immobility of the imperative, the guarding of the name) and 'woman' (wandering of a truth, effects of a name within speech). Without love, nothing would bear witness to the Two of the sexes. Instead there would be One, and then another One, but not Two. There would not be man *and* woman.

All this gives rise to an important doctrine concerning all generic processes, which is that of their numericity. Love initially involves the One of solipsism, which is the confrontation or hand-to-hand combat between the *cogito* and the grey darkness of being in an endless, compulsive repetition of words. Next comes the Two, which arises within the event of an encounter and the incalculable poem of its designation by a name. Lastly, there is the Infinity of the sensible world that the Two penetrates and deploys, and where it progressively unravels a truth of the Two itself. This numericity (one, two, infinity) is specific to the process of love. One could demonstrate that the other endeavours of truth, science, art and politics have different numerations, each of which sets apart the given process and illuminates the existence of truths at totally distinct levels.

The numericity of love (one, two, infinity) is the setting of what Beckett quite rightly calls happiness. Happiness also distinguishes the process of love, for happiness can only exist in love. Such is the reward proper to this type of truth. In art there is pleasure, in science joy, in politics enthusiasm, but in love there is happiness. Joy, pleasure, enthusiasm and happiness are relevant to all, gathered together within a subject; they are the advent, within the world, of the emptiness of being. A distinctive aspect of happiness is the intermittence of emptiness, for emptiness is captured within the between-the-Two, in that which constitutes the very character of the Two, and which is its separation, that is, sexual difference as such. Happiness is not in the least associated with the One – a mythic synthesis. It is rather the subjective indicator of a truth of difference, of sexual difference, that love alone brings into existence.

With this observation, as it directly concerns happiness, we naturally turn anew to sexual difference, for it is both the setting and the concern of happiness. In happiness, 'man' is the blind custodian of separation, that is, of the between-the-Two. The heroine of 'Enough' declares: 'We were severed if that is what he desired.'[8] The masculine polarity, indeed, supports a desire for separation. This is not at all a longing to return to solipsism, but rather a yearning for the manifestation of the Two in the severance of the between-the-Two. Two exists only if there is this between-the-Two inhabited by emptiness as the ontological principle of the Two. Man's desire is assigned to or by this emptiness. One might say that man desires the nothingness of the Two, while the feminine polarity desires nothing but the Two, that is, the infinite tenacity where the Two subsists as such. This authority of the 'woman' is magnificently proclaimed at the very end of 'Enough'. It is there that a woman promotes persistence, in opposition to the nothingness of the Two, to the emptiness that internally sways the Two (which takes on symbolic emphasis through a man's departure in order to die), and insists upon the 'nothing but the Two', even if this were a simple memorial path, within the constantly reworked narrative of wandering: 'This notion of calm comes from him. Without him I would not have had it. Now I'll wipe out everything but the flowers. No more rain. No more mounds. Nothing but the two of us dragging through the flowers. Enough my old breasts feel his old hand.'[9]

Happiness is indeterminately 'man' and 'woman'; it is at once a separating emptiness and a disclosing fusion. Both as happiness and the path of happiness, it is the nothingness of the Two and the nothing but the Two, and such is its undifferentiated sexuality, immobile and wandering, imperative and narrative. This happiness is basically what occurs between the beginning and end of *Ill Seen Ill Said*. The entire beginning revolves around the word 'misfortune', while the end leans towards the word 'happiness'. If at the outset we have the reign of the visible and the rigidity of seeing in the grey nocturne (a limbo between life and death), at the end there arises a type of transparent emptiness, which is positioned within the second nocturne. What more is there to do than to listen to what is happening? What follows is the opening passage, in my view one of the most beautiful texts in the French language, one that captures the brilliance of misfortune:

> From where she lies she sees Venus rise. On. From where she lies when the skies are clear she sees Venus rise followed by the sun. Then she rails at the source of all life. On. At evening when the skies are clear she savours its star's revenge. At the other window. Rigid upright on her old chair. It emerges from out the last rays and sinking ever brighter is engulfed in its turn. On. She sits on erect and rigid in the deepening gloom. Such helplessness to move she cannot help. Heading on foot for a particular point often she freezes on the way. Unable till long after to move on not knowing whither or for what purpose. Down on her knees especially she finds it hard not to remain so forever. Hand resting on hand on some convenient support. Such as the foot of her bed. And on them her head. There then she sits as though turned to stone face to the night. Save for the white of her hair and faintly bluish white of face and hands all is black. For an eye having no need of light to see. All this in the present as had she the misfortune to be still of this world.[10]

And now the end, where an instant of happiness is gained in the very brief and trying moment of an encounter with emptiness:

> Decision no sooner reached or rather long after than what is the wrong word? For the last time at last for to end yet again what the wrong word? Than revoked. No but slowly dispelled a little very little like the wisps of day when the curtain closes. Of itself by slow millimetres or drawn by a phantom hand. Farewell to farewell. Then in that perfect dark foreknell darling sound pip for end begun. First last moment. Grant only enough remain to devour all. Moment by glutton moment. Sky earth the whole kit and boodle. Not

another crumb of carrion left. Lick chops and basta. No. One moment more. One last. Grace to breathe that void. Know happiness.[11]

This also illustrates what I would like to call generic writing, which offers an artistic representation of the transition from the misfortune of life and the visible world to the happiness occasioned by an authentic arousal of emptiness. This requires the immeasurable power of the encounter, the wager of a designation by name, the combination of wandering and immobility, of imperative and narrative. If one finds the path traced by all this in the division of the night, then one may repeat with Beckett, in these rare circumstances, 'Stony ground but not entirely'.[12]

Translated by Alban Urbanas

Notes

1. Samuel Beckett, *Murphy*, p. 159.
2. Beckett, *Malone meurt*, p. 144.
3. Beckett, *Comment c'est*, p. 192.
4. Beckett, *La dernière bande*, pp. 24–6.
5. Beckett, 'Assez', pp. 38–9.
6. Ibid. p. 42.
7. Beckett, *Compagnie*, pp. 65–6.
8. Beckett, 'Assez', p. 38.
9. Ibid. p. 47.
10. Beckett, *Mal vu mal dit*, pp. 7–8.
11. Ibid. pp. 75–6.
12. Beckett, 'Assez', p. 35.

Bibliography

Beckett, Samuel, 'Assez', in *Têtes mortes* (Paris: Éditions de Minuit, 1967), pp. 31–47.
Beckett, Samuel, *Comment c'est* (Paris: Éditions de Minuit, 1961).
Beckett, Samuel, *Compagnie* (Paris: Éditions de Minuit, 1980).
Beckett, Samuel, *La dernière bande* (Paris: Éditions de Minuit, 1960).
Beckett, Samuel, *Malone meurt* (Paris: Éditions de Minuit, 2004).
Beckett, Samuel, *Mal vu mal dit* (Paris: Éditions de Minuit, 1981).
Beckett, Samuel, *Murphy* (Paris: Éditions de Minuit, 1965).

16.

This Little Sound Now in Beckett's *From an Abandoned Work*

Justin Beplate

> 'All mingles, times and tenses, at first I only had been here, now I'm here still, soon I won't be here yet, toiling up the slope, or in the bracken by the wood . . .'[1]

Towards the end of his life Beckett voiced his frustration with the failure of age to bring any respite from the elusiveness of words, writing to George Tabori that 'While still "young" I began to seek consolation in the thought that then if ever, i.e. now, the true words at last, from the mind in ruins. To this illusion I continue to cling.'[2] His comment looks back to his disillusionment as a young man, where he had contrasted the 'authenticity of vocation' exhibited by those around him with his own 'absurd' concern with diary-keeping. In an entry dated 2 February 1937, he dismisses his habit as 'the act of an obsessional neurotic':

> An 'open-mindedness' that is mindlessness, the sphincter of the mind limply forever open, the mind past the power of closing itself *to everything but its own content*, or rather its own treatment of a content.
> *I have never thought for myself.*[3]

This chapter explores how Beckett's early contrast of others' authenticity of vocation with his own empty record-keeping informs the narrative voice of *From an Abandoned Work* – a voice that longs to express, beyond the ruinous 'now and then' tense system of articulated time (a time out of mind), an authentic vocalisation of being.

The first-person narrator of *From an Abandoned Work* retraces his steps 'that day then' – a time past when he was young and full of a love for 'all things still and rooted'.[4] The scene is one of pastoral tranquillity, although, being Beckett, the worms of memory are already writhing their way to the surface. And so, after bravely setting forth from his mother's house that fresh morning, the narrator is beaten back by a vague premonition of violence and the rain-darkened sky to come:

> So back with bowed head on the look out for a snail, slug or worm. Great love in my heart too for all things still and rooted . . . Whereas a bird now, or a butterfly, fluttering about and getting in my way, all moving things, getting in my path, a slug now, getting under my feet, no, no mercy. Not that I'd go out of my way to get at them, no, at a distance often they seemed still, then a moment later they were upon me.[5]

The young narrator's about-face *then* ('back with bowed head') mirrors his temporal orientation *now* (the time of his narration) as he turns back to the events of that memorable day. The central confusion of the narrator, as he gropes his way through narrative time, revolves around the judgements he must constantly make concerning his memories: whether, in other words, he has properly fixed them in mind, rooting them in the old landscape of his being, or whether their apparent stillness is only an illusion of distance. As the narrative unfolds, the perplexity of the narrator is matched by the confusion of his language, and the reader is left wondering whether the promise of an authentic memory is being tripped up by his own words or whether, on the contrary, the language is somehow settling around the still centres of an irrevocable self.[6]

This uncertain articulation of language and memory generates one of the central dilemmas of the work, for as the narrator struggles to fix the tense of his unfolding thought there is an 'unstillable' feeling that it is his words that make time for him, that his words are *making up time*. He is unable to make up his own mind on matters of memory, on whether his thought-speech is the empty echo of a 'word overheard' in some half-remembered past, or whether his words point up yet another possibility: the thought that they might be incorporating the fugitive sounds of a moment passing too quickly to mind – 'this little sound perhaps *now* that I don't understand' (my emphasis).[7]

Originally composed as a piece for radio, *From an Abandoned Work* exploits the little sounds of a perplexed narrative language – including the minor variations on 'no', 'know' and 'now' – in order to confound the narrator's attempt to still moments in time and thereby master the effects of unbidden memories upon present-tense thought. His confusion clusters around the fact that there is, so to speak, no knowing now. The narrative consists of the old stories, all *told*; and yet one is left with the uneasy feeling that there is something *telling* in the rhythms and repetitions of the narrator's language, something only half-hinted at through the jerky syntax of the text.

In order to make some sense of this little sound 'now', it is worth briefly comparing the narrator's conception of time with that of St Augustine (a writer whose work Beckett was intimately familiar with). Towards the end of Book XI of his *Confessions*, St Augustine makes it clear that past and future times can have no existence apart from a certain presence of mind, for:

> neither future nor past exist, and it is inexact language to speak of three times—past, present, and future. Perhaps it would be exact to say: there are three times, a present of things past, a present of things present, a present of things to come . . . the present considering the past is the memory, the present considering the present is immediate awareness, the present considering the future is expectation.[8]

The nature of this temporal trinity is developed further in a passage that examines the timing of narrative acts. Suppose, Augustine offers, one is about to recite a psalm which is known by heart. Before commencing, the time of expectation extends over the entire psalm. As it is being recited, however, the verses are taken into the past and thus become memory:

> The life of this act of mine is stretched two ways, into my memory because of the words I have already said and into my expectation because of those which I am about to say. But my attention is on what is present: by that the future is transferred to become the past. As the action advances further and further, the shorter the expectation and the longer the memory, until all expectation is consumed, the entire action is finished, and it has passed into the memory.[9]

This same process holds good not only for each of the elements of the psalm but also longer actions of which the psalm may be only a part; indeed, it holds good for the entire life of a person and even 'the total history of "the sons of men"'.[10]

Beckett's narrator in *From an Abandoned Work*, on the other hand, has little time for Augustine's presence of mind. He lives out a kind of 'syncopated' existence, inhabiting a memory that both anticipates every new expectation that comes to mind and constrains him to lag behind any sense of present-tense being:

> But what is the sense of going on with all this, there is none. Day after unremembered day until my mother's death, then in a new place soon old until my own. And when I come to this night here among the rocks with my two books and the strong starlight it will have passed from me and the day that went before, my two books, the little and the big, all past and gone, or perhaps just moments here and there still, this little sound perhaps now that I don't understand so that I gather up my things and go back into my hole, so bygone they can be told. Over, over, there is a soft place in my heart for all that is over, no, for the being over, I love the word, words have been my only loves, not many.[11]

The narrator is in fact struggling with our common habit of thinking in terms of a succession of presents, a habit also brought to book by Gilles

Deleuze in his early work on the time of memory. 'How', asks Deleuze in *Bergsonism*, 'would any present whatsoever pass, if it were not past *at the same time* as present?'[12] The answer, suggested by his reading of Bergson, leads to 'a fundamental position of time and also the most profound paradox of memory: The past is "contemporaneous" with the present that it *has been*.'[13] The past and the present are not, therefore, two successive moments, but 'two elements which coexist: One is the present, which does not cease to pass, and the other is the past, which does not cease to be but through which all presents pass.'[14]

In effect, Beckett's narrator wrestles with a variation of Bergson's paradox. Reciting moments past as he moves towards making sense of the present ('this night here among the rocks'), he can only ever anticipate his present as a moment that will have already passed; his anticipation of 'this' moment 'here among the rocks' is matched by the knowledge that it will be already old before being told. He inhabits the twilit world of Molloy's 'mythological present';[15] passing from past to past, he denies the sense of going on towards a present that is bound to elude him ('what is the sense of going on with all this, there is none'), towards a 'here and now' that has already dwindled to 'nowhere'.

This apparent confidence in his own logic is, however, countered by the uncertain temporal function of key words in the passage: terms such as 'still', 'now' and 'being'. The phrase 'perhaps just moments here and there still', for example, is unable to resolve the function of 'still' as an adjective (outside time) or an adverb (postpositively prolonging the 'moments here and there'). Still moments here and there might well constitute fixed reference points for an episodic memory that craves 'all things still and rooted'; however, the narrator (and, by extension, the reader) cannot shake the feeling that this quality of stillness may be only an illusion of distance. For, as the narrator remarks of all moving things, 'at a distance often they seemed still, then a moment later they were upon me'.[16]

The key phrase that follows the term 'still' ('this little sound perhaps now that I don't understand') continues to sound out the voice's faint resistance to its own assertion that there is no sense in 'going on with all this'. The vagueness of the demonstrative pronoun in the phrase 'going on with all *this*' is carried over to the demonstrative adjective in '*this* little sound perhaps now that I don't understand', forcing the reader to go back over the line in order to construe whether the little sound has already been designated ('still', perhaps?) or whether it is on the way, about to be mentioned, perhaps even 'now'. The difficulty arises from the way in which Beckett's syntax resists the scanning eye, forcing the reader to attend to the acoustic phrasing in order to make sense of the line. This little sound 'now' lives a fugitive existence at the heart of the sentence; just as the present tense continues to elude the 'I' of the narrative voice, 'now' passes too quickly for the readerly eye to register, echoing instead in the reader's auditory memory.

Similarly, the narrator's admission that 'there is a soft place in my heart for all that is over, no, for the being over, I love the word, words have been my only loves, not many' picks up the memory of his earlier mood when he had set out for a walk with 'Great love in my heart too for all things still and rooted'. The terms 'over' and 'still' are linked by the narrator's profession of love for the word, though whether for the stillness of words in general or the particular word 'over' is not clear. Exactly what, then, is the reader to make of the way in which 'over' migrates across the line 'all that is over, no, for the being over', initially taking 'is' as its verb before modifying 'being'? In fact, this question has already been anticipated by an earlier passage:

> The questions float up as I go along and leave me very confused, breaking up I am. Suddenly they are there, no they float up, out of an old depth, and hover and linger before they die away, questions that when I was in my right mind would not have survived one second, no, but atomized they would have been, before as much as formed, atomized.[17]

The questions assailing the narrator – 'How shall I go on another day? and then, How did I ever go on another day? Or, Did I kill my father? and then, Did I ever kill anyone?' – move from the particular to the general, with his addled mind seemingly confirmed by the addled syntax of his 'breaking up I am'.[18] However, it is the narrator's *being* that the questions are atomising, breaking up 'I am' as his language leads him away from the particularity of the first person singular to 'thoughts, not mine, no matter'.[19]

The narrator gives himself away at this point, alerting the reader to the intimate relations between those questions that atomise his being and the 'thoughts not mine' through a conspicuous repetition of the phrase 'old and weak'. Thus, the narrator laments: 'But these are thoughts, not mine, no matter, shame upon me. Now I am old and weak,'[20] before picking up a couple of pages further on: 'My father, did I kill him too as well as my mother, perhaps in a way I did, but I can't go into that now, much too old and weak. The questions float up as I go along and leave me very confused, breaking up I am.'[21] By attending to the sounds that matter now and then, the repetitions and the little sounds, the reader resists to some degree the relentless atomisation of the narrator's syntax; however, the consonance of sounds migrating across half-remembered episodes can never fully articulate, finally, the staggered times and tenses of voiced memory.

This failure to elude the ongoing equivocations of language – of those questions that relentlessly atomise *being* through the broken, articulated time of 'before', 'after', 'from', 'towards', 'at' – leads the narrator to divine a possible future beyond time:

> But let us get on and leave these old scenes and come to these, and my reward. Then it will not be as now, day after day, out, on, round, back, in, like leaves turning, or torn out and thrown crumpled away, but a long unbroken time without before or after, light or dark, from or towards or at, the old half-knowledge of when and where gone, and of what, but kinds of things still, all at once . . .[22]

He is anticipating a time 'free of the property' at last; he longs for an assumption, in other words, like that of Dante ascending heavenward near the end of *The Divine Comedy* to learn of how time followed the divine act of creation.[23] 'For', as a radiant Beatrice explains, 'no before, nor since, could ever be / Till God moved on the waters in his measure.'[24] Indeed, Beatrice anticipates her lover's queries before they can even be thought:

> 'I tell, not ask, what you would hear,' she spoke thus,
> 'For I have seen it there where every *where*
> And every *when* is brought to that one focus.
> Not for himself to gain any good there
> —Which cannot be—but that his splendour blaze,
> And in reflection its *I am* declare,
> Beyond time . . .'[25]

In a sense, then, the narrator's apprehension of all things 'still, all at once' is a beatified vision of pure spirit, an abstraction that merges the creative act with an intimation of *being outside time*. It is a vision with a long history of literary incarnations. St Augustine, for example, speaks of momentarily touching divine wisdom with his mother – a wisdom in which 'there is no past and future, but only being, since it is eternal' – before returning to 'the noise of our human speech where a sentence has both a beginning and an ending'.[26] In Joyce's *Ulysses*, Stephen Dedalus segues Shelley's image of the mind in creation with a contemporality of past, present and future selves, arguing that 'In the intense instant of imagination, when the mind, Shelley says, is a fading coal, that which I was is that which I am and that which in possibility I may come to be.'[27] A youthful Beckett finds traces of this vision in Proust's art of involuntary memory, where 'Time is not recovered, it is obliterated', while in *Company* the one lying on his back in the dark wonders if the accompanying voice might not be made better, 'Say changing now for some time past though no tense in the dark in that dim mind. All at once over and in train and to come.'[28] And, finally, in *The Unnamable* the narrator's miscreated figments are estranged from their creator by their remoteness from *being in time*: 'Malone revolves,' says the unnamable, 'a stranger forever to my infirmities, one who is not as I can never not be . . . I alone am man and all the rest divine.'[29]

This divine vision begins to be broken up in *From an Abandoned Work*, however, as the narrator is distracted from the full implications of his desire to annihilate 'when' and 'where' by the insistent drone of a voiced dreaming:

> but kinds of things still, all at once, all going, until nothing, there was never anything, never can be, life and death all nothing, that kind of thing, only a voice dreaming and droning on all around, that is something, the voice that once was in your mouth.[30]

This strange oneiric voice recalls Beatrice's lofty dismissal of the pretensions of 'equivocating discourse' (the inevitable condition of imperfect beings), informing her lover that 'Although they're not asleep, they dream indeed / Down there, believing—or not believing—they speak / The truth . . .'[31] Beatrice is in fact disabusing Dante of the misconceived convention that speaks of angels 'understanding' or 'remembering', for their gaze is eternally fixed upon God's own face (from which nothing is hidden): 'Thus, novel things can never come to light / Before their eyes, so they will never need / Abstractions to recall the past from flight.'[32]

While this is the state of temporal grace aspired to by the narrative voice of *From an Abandoned Work*, it is a vital feature of Beckett's aesthetic that such intimations of being beyond time are unsustainable in a world of labouring hearts and equivocating discourse. The 'long unbroken time without before or after' is an otherworldly abstraction belied, finally, by the rhythm of the narrator's body in concert with the bare repetitions of his language:

> Well once out on the road and free of the property what then, I really do not know, the next thing I was up in the bracken lashing about with my stick making drops fly and cursing, filthy language, the same words over and over, I hope nobody heard me.[33]

The narrator remembers himself in his fall to earth. The voiced aspiration of being outside time passes into oblivion, restoring him once more to the urgent repetitions of his thrashing stick and base language ('cursing, filthy language, the same words over and over').

J. D. O'Hara, in his psychoanalytic reading of *From an Abandoned Work*, rightly observes that 'movement in time and space may be the most extended topic of the story'; as O'Hara is principally concerned with the Freudian motifs structuring Beckett's text, however, the movement he traces is described always in relation to the gravitational centre of the mother/home.[34] Thus, the various movements of the narrator – from the rambling recollections of memory to the recurring 'out and return' walks in the countryside – are symptomatic of certain deeper neuroses of hysteria and obsession that the narrator is at pains to repress.[35] Michel Bernard makes a similar claim in his analysis of what he terms the 'hysterico-obsessional' structure of the work, arguing that the narrator's 'discursive journey' is part of a wider questing towards 'the lost object represented by his mother'.[36] In this context, Bernard reads the 'long unbroken time without before or after' as an expression of the narrator's desire to escape the temporal axis that measures the distance between his being *now* and his being *in utero*; in other words, it is the fulfilment of a fantasising desire never to have been separated from his mother.[37]

Although a consideration of general psychoanalytic themes is beyond the scope of this article, which is concerned rather with the question of how Beckett's language betrays a conflict at the heart of narrated memory, the more specific issue of linguistic form and its relation to the unconscious is quite clearly germane to this analysis of the mythological present and 'unbidden' memory in Beckett's text. It is therefore worth asking to what extent, if any, *From an Abandoned Work* might be seen to incorporate Kristeva's notion of 'the semiotic': a concept which draws freely on Freud's theory of the unconscious in order to explain the body's organisation of primary drives in relation to language.

In Kristeva's scheme, developed most fully in her *Revolution in Poetic Language*, the speaking subject is split between unconscious and conscious motivations, with the former taking its lead from physiological processes of the body, and the latter produced primarily through social modes of organisation. In line with this disjunction of the subject, Kristeva's analysis of language proposes two modes of articulation involved in the production of meaning: the semiotic and the symbolic. The semiotic is identified with drives and their articulations: that is, the primary, pre-linguistic charges of the body, which subsequently undergo various stases in response to checks imposed by 'the constraints of biological and social structures'.[38] The material supports susceptible to semiotisation – voice, gesture, colours – are marked by these discontinuities; hence we have discrete phonic, kinetic and chromatic differences as the marks of these bodily stases. The symbolic, on the other hand, refers to the semantic and logical categories that structure language; such categories are assumed by the 'subject of enunciation' in the signifying process. While the biological or genetic code is necessarily semiotic, Kristeva argues that 'the *symbolic*—and therefore syntax and all linguistic categories—is a social effect of the relation to the other, established through the objective constraints of biological (including sexual) differences and concrete, historical family structures.'[39]

At the threshold of enunciation, between the heterogeneous domains of the semiotic and the symbolic, is a break Kristeva denotes as the 'thetic phase': a fundamental disjunction of the subject and the object that opens the way for signification in general.[40] Across this divide – described as the 'deepest structure' conditioning enunciation – passes an arc of 'signifiance', a productive process which exercises the drives 'toward, in, and through language; toward, in, and through the exchange system and its protagonists—the subject and his institutions'.[41] Literature is important within this scheme of signification, as it traces fault lines that mark the 'productive violence' of an encounter between 'the sum of unconscious, subjective, and social relations'.[42]

Unfortunately, this is a confluence which neither linguistics nor literary theory has, in Kristeva's view, been able to accommodate. Taking aim in 'The Ethics of Linguistics' at the prevailing programme of generative grammar, she protests that 'the dramatic notion of language as a risky practice, allowing the speaking animal to sense the rhythm of the body as well as the upheavals of history, seems tied to a notion of signifying process that contemporary theorists do not confront.'[43] Kristeva attacks the 'static thoughts' and inert modelling of contemporary linguistic theorists ('archivists, archaeologists and necrophiliacs') as a misguided exercise in 'listening to the narrative of a sleeping body—a body in repose'.[44]

There are, however, considerable difficulties in Kristeva's account in *Revolution in Poetic Language* of the relations between the pre-verbal, unconscious distributions of the body and the signifiance generated in and through the symbolic order: in particular, her insistence on reading the implications of Freud and Klein at the atomistic level of the pleasurable sounds that run through poetic language. On this reading, word distortions and sound repetitions in texts serve as an unconscious expression of the semiotic economy or *chora*, defined as 'an essentially mobile and extremely provisional articulation constituted by movements and their ephemeral stases'.[45] In fact, Kristeva argues, the rhythms and repetitions so common to avant-garde writing mark a return to 'oralization' – 'a reunion with the mother's body, which is no longer viewed as an engendering, hollow, and vaginated, expelling and rejecting body, but rather as a vocalic one'.[46] In this register, then, the 'oral and glottal pleasure' associated with poetic language is really sounding out those charges and stases that organise the body of the infant:

> Suction or expulsion, fusion with or rejection of the mother's breast seem to be at the root of this erotization of the vocal apparatus and, through it, the introduction into the linguistic order of an excess of pleasure marked by a redistribution of the phonematic order, morphological structure, and even syntax: portmanteau words in Joyce and syntax in Mallarmé, for example.[47]

One difficulty with Kristeva's thesis lies in the timing of her sound/sense relations. Her analysis of phonemic repetition in relation to the semiotic aspect of language situates the instinctual drives of the body as the referents of articulated phonemes. However, by ascribing a pre-linguistic function to isolated phonemes, making them consonant with certain physiological processes of the body, Kristeva risks getting ahead of herself. While it is true that particular sounds may come to be invested with a particular affectiveness, this feeling for sound *follows* the split subject's entry into the symbolic order; the feeling associated with particular combinations of sounds in a signifying practice can never be anticipated ahead of time. In this sense, it is simply illegitimate to assign a particular phoneme as the expression of a certain drive or configuration of desire *prior to its use* in an already constituted symbolic order; the libidinal distributions of the body can never serve as referents for phonemic markers.

Beyond this perplexed issue of phonemic atomisation, however, is the wider question of syntax and its possible relation to the body. In 'The Novel as Polylogue', Kristeva analyses the unpunctuated flow of words in Philippe Sollers' novel *H*, referring to the text as 'a music that is inscribed in language'.[48] The absence of punctuation ensures not only the text's 'semantic and logico-syntactic ambiguities' but also its music.[49] 'By *music*', writes Kristeva, 'I mean intonation and rhythm, which play only a subordinate role in everyday communication but here constitute that essential element of an enunciation and lead us directly to the otherwise silent place of its subject.'[50] This 'instinctual breakthrough' of tone and rhythm is situated 'at the thetic place of an inescapable syntax that abruptly halts the maternal body's vague, autoerotic jubilation', and in so doing 'recognises its reflection in a mirror and shifts instinctual motility into logically structurable signifiers'.[51] Kristeva argues that artistic practices elude this break between 'instinctual motility' and 'logically structurable signifiers', the upshot of which is a certain 'uneasiness' – the inescapable result of 'regressing to a time before the mirror stage'.[52] By the time of *Revolution in Poetic Language*, this uneasiness has developed into a full-scale revolt; 'modern poetic language goes further than any classical mimesis', writes Kristeva, '. . . because it attacks not only denotation (the positing of the object) but meaning (the positing of the enunciating subject) as well.'[53]

To the extent that Kristeva chooses to align Beckett's writing with modern poetic language, however, there is something too hasty in any suggestion that the musicality of Beckett's work issues from the absence of an enunciating subject. While the relations between speaker, hearer and the first person singular may not merge in a perfectly articulated identity, any claim that the flow of poetic language dissolves the speaking subject is in fact belied by Beckett's own writing practice. If Beckett's language does create a certain uneasiness in the reader, it is not, as Kristeva would have it, an effect of infantile regression. Rather, it is an effect of the strange 'self-syncopation' that results when the act of remembering is timed against the accents of language – when, in other words, memory is made to inhabit a time out of mind.

This process is at work in *Company*, for example, where Beckett throws the reader off-centre by matching the narrative perplexity concerning the timing of 'his' language in relation to the contemporal 'no tense' of the dim mind, where the discrete temporal states of past, present and future function as superposed possibilities ('Say changing now for some time past though no tense in the dark in that dim mind. All at once over and in train and to come').[54] The syntactic textures of *Company* both stress and sustain an *other* sense – a blind sense of the body responding to the fugitive sounds of a living memory ('The odd sound. What a mercy to have that to turn to. Now and then. In dark and silence to close as if to light the eyes and hear a sound').[55] Thus, the one on his back in the dark listens as the voice closes in upon him:

> When it ceases long enough vague hope it may have said its last. Mental activity of a low order. Rare flickers of reasoning of no avail. Hope and despair and suchlike barely felt. How current situation arrived at unclear. *No that then to compare to this now* [my emphasis].[56]

Under pressure of Beckett's deformed syntax, words come to be inhabited by the compressed sounds of yet another possibility: the possibility that, despite the narrator's repeated disownment of 'his' vocalised memory, the fugitive sounds of living memory may yet make the voice his own, may yet sustain the 'no' of 'No that then' across the interval to inform the 'now' of 'this now', and thereby undercut the sense of a linguistic tense-system that now breaks, and then articulates, the 'no now and then' time of the mind.

Our habits of syntax tend to be as much a matter of ordering words as they are of word order, of disciplining words to serve some higher reason. And yet, as Deleuze puts it in 'Literature and Life': 'There are no straight lines, neither in things nor in language. Syntax is the set of necessary detours that are created in each case to reveal the life in things.'[57] Beckett's syntax in *From an Abandoned Work* registers the wayward movement of words when 'ordering' buckles under the weight of a loaded memory. It is a deformation that creates folds in the plane of language, narrowing the space between key words and their 'mindless' memories. This folding of syntax tends to occur at the threshold of sound and sense, where the low murmur of the narrative voice verges near to the silence that lies behind its last breath – a 'syntax of weakness', in Beckett's phrase, that responds to the 'authentic weakness of being'.[58]

'The official business of the Beckett sentence', observes Hugh Kenner in his essay 'Shades of Syntax', 'is to affirm a tidy control it cannot quite achieve.'[59] The sentence's claim to be always in control by virtue of its subject-verb-object scheme is always falsified, according to Kenner, 'by some radical incompatibility between syntactic order and human nuance'.[60] This remark surely holds true for *From an Abandoned Work*, where the narrator can never finally master his desire to 'be still' any more than he can silence the equivocating nature of his discourse. 'Being' vocalises both an action and a thing in his language: functioning as a verb, it belies the sense of 'being outside time' by taking on a temporal aspect (as the present participle of 'be'); functioning as a noun, it appropriates 'outside' as a preposition and thus spatialises time. Over and again the narrator returns to the same old words, wavering between their superposed syntactical possibilities without ever resolving them ahead of time. In Beckett's writing the question never stops returning: how to convey, against the grain of grammatical construction (of the preposition's spacing and the temporal succession of tense), against the relentless atomisation of language, the contemporal multiplicity of thought welling into being?

If Beckett's method is, as he suggests, that of boring holes in language,[61] then what comes seeping through the fractured, time-stressed syntax of *From an Abandoned Work* are the old thoughts kept under: 'Now I am old and weak, in pain and weakness murmur why and pause, and the old thoughts well up in me and over into my voice, the old thoughts born with me and grown with me and kept under, there's another.'[62] The narrator wavers between either acknowledging or disowning 'his' thoughts, as he struggles to trace their lineage back to an unremembered origin. And so his disownment of certain 'thoughts, not mine' migrates across a dozen lines of text to echo in 'the sound of my voice all day long muttering the same old things I don't listen to, not even mine it was at the end of the day'.[63] Through the repetitions of his habituated speech are ghosted the barely audible traces of a living memory accompanying him, like the shade of his father in his old tramping rags, in a companionable silence. The wayward movements of a fugitive memory, in hiding from the learned language of his mother and her smothering attentions, register in his voiced narrative as the repetition of old things no longer listened to. These repetitions are, perhaps, the sign of something else – of a voice beside itself with the inarticulate emotion of heart-felt memory, yet perpetually distracted from the pain of this experience through its habit of speech.

Notes

1. Samuel Beckett, *Texts for Nothing*, p. 10.
2. James Knowlson, *Damned to Fame*, p. 684.
3. Ibid. p. 252.
4. Beckett, *From an Abandoned Work*, p. 9.
5. Ibid. pp. 9–10.
6. The term 'irrevocable self' occurs in Beckett's short story 'Yellow', where Belacqua contemplates his pending trial under the surgeon's knife: 'He did not pause to consider himself in this matter, the light that the coming ordeal would shed on his irrevocable self, because he really was tired of that old bastardo' (p. 173).
7. Beckett, *From an Abandoned Work*, p. 20.
8. St Augustine, *Confessions*, p. 235.
9. Ibid. p. 243.
10. Ibid. p. 243.
11. Beckett, *From an Abandoned Work*, p. 20.
12. Gilles Deleuze, *Bergsonism*, p. 58.
13. Ibid. p. 58.
14. Ibid. p. 59.
15. 'I speak in the present tense, it is so easy to speak in the present tense, when speaking of the past. It is the mythological present, don't mind it' (*Three Novels: Molloy*, p. 26).
16. Beckett, *From an Abandoned Work*, pp. 9–10. This doubt concerning the eye's ability to judge movement is reworked in *Company* as doubt over the ear's capacity to judge sound: 'For with what right affirm of a faint sound that it is a less faint made fainter by farness and not a true faint near at hand? Or of a faint fading to fainter that it recedes and not in situ decreases?' (pp. 44–5).
17. Ibid. p. 16.
18. Ibid. p. 16.
19. Ibid. p. 14. Compare Deleuze's late essay on Beckett, 'The Exhausted', where he speaks of *Language I*: 'this atomic language in Beckett—disjunctive, abrupt, jerky, where enumeration replaces propositions, and combinatorial relations replace syntactic relations' (p. 7).
20. Ibid. p. 14.
21. Ibid. p. 16.
22. Ibid. p. 21.
23. Ibid. p. 21.

24. Dante Alighieri, *The Divine Comedy*, III.xxix.20–1.
25. Ibid. III.xxix.10–16.
26. St Augustine, *Confessions*, p. 171.
27. James Joyce, *Ulysses*, p. 160.
28. Beckett, *Proust*, p. 56; *Company*, p. 45.
29. Beckett, *Three Novels*, p. 300.
30. Beckett, *From an Abandoned Work*, p. 21. Ghosted in the 'that is something' phrase is an adaptation of Descartes's affirmation of existence. In his Third Meditation, Descartes argues that 'the mode of being by which a thing exists objectively or representatively in the intellect by way of an idea, imperfect though it may be, is certainly not nothing, and so it cannot come from nothing' (*The Philosophical Writings of Descartes*, p. 29). In effect, Beckett's narrator substitutes 'a voice dreaming and droning' for Descartes's 'idea'.
31. Dante Alighieri, *The Divine Comedy*, III.xxix.82–4.
32. Ibid. III.xxix.79–81.
33. Beckett, *From an Abandoned Work*, p. 21.
34. J. D. O'Hara, *Samuel Beckett's Hidden Drives*, p. 92.
35. Indeed, O'Hara asserts that there is a punning allusion to psychoanalysis in the title itself, whereby 'the work abandoned is the protagonist's imagined therapy' (*Samuel Beckett's Hidden Drives*, p. 90).
36. Michel Bernard, 'The Hysterico-Obsessional Structure', p. 100.
37. Ibid. p. 102.
38. Julia Kristeva, *Revolution in Poetic Language*, p. 28. Her debt to Freud is explicitly acknowledged: 'Our positing of the semiotic is obviously inseparable from a theory of the subject that takes into account the Freudian positing of the unconscious' (p. 30).
39. Ibid. p. 29.
40. Ibid. p. 43.
41. Ibid. p. 44; p. 17.
42. Ibid. p. 16.
43. Kristeva, 'The Ethics of Linguistics', p. 34.
44. Kristeva, *Revolution*, p. 13.
45. Ibid. p. 25. In Plato's 'Timaeus', the *chora* refers to a 'receptacle or nurse of generation', likened to a mother. This 'containing principle', writes Plato, is 'neither earth nor fire nor air nor water, but an invisible and formless being which receives all things, and in an incomprehensible manner partakes of the intelligible' (p. 649).
46. Ibid. p. 153.
47. Ibid. p. 154.
48. Kristeva, 'The Novel as Polylogue', p. 159.
49. Ibid. p. 167.
50. Ibid. p. 167.
51. Ibid. p. 167.
52. Ibid. p. 168. The 'mirror stage' is used by Lacan to denote the transformative self-identification that takes place when the infant comes to 'assume' its own image. Lacan links its function to that of the imago in general: that is, 'to establish a relation between the organism and its reality' ('The Mirror Stage', p. 4).

53. Kristeva, *Revolution*, p. 58.
54. Beckett, *Company*, p. 45.
55. Ibid. p. 24.
56. Ibid. p. 62.
57. Deleuze, 'Literature and Life', p. 2.
58. Lawrence E. Harvey, in his study *Samuel Beckett: Poet and Critic*, reports Beckett using these words in conversation with him in the early 1960s (p. 249).
59. Hugh Kenner, 'Shades of Syntax', p. 28.
60. Ibid. p. 28.
61. In a letter to Axel Kaun in 1937, Beckett writes: 'And more and more my own language appears to me like a veil that must be torn apart in order to get at the things (or the Nothingness) behind it . . . As we cannot eliminate language all at once, we should at least leave nothing undone that might contribute to its falling into disrepute. To bore one hole after another in it, until what lurks behind it—be it something or nothing—begins to seep through; I cannot imagine a higher goal for a writer today' (*Disjecta*, pp. 171–2).
62. Beckett, *From an Abandoned Work*, p. 14.
63. Ibid. p. 14.

Bibliography

Alighieri, Dante, *The Divine Comedy: Hell, Purgatory, Heaven*, trans. Peter Dale (London: Anvil Press Poetry, 1996).

Beckett, Samuel, *Company* (London: John Calder, 1980).

Beckett, Samuel, *Disjecta: Miscellaneous Writings and a Dramatic Fragment*, ed. Ruby Cohn (London: John Calder, 1983).

Beckett, Samuel, *From an Abandoned Work* (London: Faber and Faber, 1958).

Beckett, Samuel, *Proust* (New York: Grove Press, 1957).

Beckett, Samuel, *Texts for Nothing* (London: Calder and Boyars, 1974).

Beckett, Samuel, *Three Novels: Molloy, Malone Dies, The Unnamable* (New York: Grove Press, 1958).

Beckett, Samuel, 'Yellow', in *More Pricks Than Kicks* (London: Calder and Boyars, [1934] 1970), pp. 149–64.

Bernard, Michel, 'The Hysterico-Obsessional Structure of "From an Abandoned Work"', trans. Thomas Cousineau, *Journal of Beckett Studies*, 4.1 (autumn 1994), pp. 93–107.

Deleuze, Gilles, *Bergsonism*, trans. Hugh Tomlinson and Barbara Habberjam (New York: Zone Books, 1988).

Deleuze, Gilles, 'The Exhausted', trans. Anthony Uhlmann, *Substance: A Review of Theory and Literary Criticism*, 24.3 (1995), pp. 3–28.

Deleuze, Gilles, 'Literature and Life', in *Essays Critical and Clinical*, trans. Daniel W. Smith and Michael A. Greco (Minneapolis: University of Minnesota Press, 1997), pp. 1–6.

Descartes, René, *The Philosophical Writings of Descartes*, trans. John Cottingham, Robert Stoothoff and Dugald Murdoch, Vol. 2 (Cambridge: Cambridge University Press, 1985).

Harvey, Lawrence E., *Samuel Beckett: Poet and Critic* (Princeton: Princeton University Press, 1970).

Joyce, James, *Ulysses: The Corrected Text*, ed. Hans Walter Gabler (London: The Bodley Head, 1986).

Kenner, Hugh, 'Shades of Syntax', in Ruby Cohn (ed.), *Samuel Beckett: A Collection of Criticism* (New York: McGraw-Hill, 1975), pp. 21–31.

Knowlson, James, *Damned to Fame: The Life of Samuel Beckett* (London: Bloomsbury, 1996).

Kristeva, Julia, 'The Ethics of Linguistics', in Leon S. Roudiez (ed.), *Desire in Language: A Semiotic Approach to Literature and Art*, trans. Thomas Gora, Alice Jardine and Leon S. Roudiez (Oxford: Basil Blackwell, 1980), pp. 23–35.

Kristeva, Julia, 'The Novel as Polylogue', in Leon S. Roudiez (ed.), *Desire in Language: A Semiotic Approach to Literature and Art*, trans. Thomas Gora, Alice Jardine and Leon S. Roudiez (Oxford: Basil Blackwell, 1980), pp. 159–209.

Kristeva, Julia, *Revolution in Poetic Language*, trans. Margaret Waller (New York: Columbia University Press, 1984).

Lacan, Jacques, 'The Mirror Stage as Formative of the Function of the I as Revealed in Psychoanalytic Experience', in *Écrits: A Selection*, trans. Alan Sheridan (New York: Norton, 1977), pp. 1–7.

O'Hara, J. D., *Samuel Beckett's Hidden Drives: Structural Uses of Depth Psychology* (Gainesville: University Press of Florida, 1997).

Plato, 'Timaeus', in *The Dialogues of Plato*, trans. B. Jowett, 4th edn, Vol. 3 (Oxford: Clarendon Press, 1953), pp. 339–516.

St Augustine, *Confessions*, trans. Henry Chadwick (Oxford: Oxford University Press, 1991).

17.

Endgame in the Subjunctive

Paul Lawley

'What are Clov's visions?' Alan Schneider asked Beckett in the twelfth of twenty questions he listed in a letter of 8 November 1957 from New York as he prepared to direct the first production of the English version of *Fin de partie*[1]. Beckett replied in this way:

> I only know the one alluded to—his light dying. This if you like is an ironical allusion to Acts 2.17. They endure their 'thing' by projection away from it, Clov outwards towards going, Hamm inwards towards abiding. When Clov admits to having his visions less it means that his escape mechanism is breaking down. Dramatically this element allows his perception of life (boy) at the end and of course of the rat to be construed as hallucinations.[2]

The key moment upon which the point bears is Clov's claim, near the end of the play, to have sighted a small boy outside the refuge, and Hamm's decision, following from it, to end the game. The playwright gives his director guidance about the parameters within which the audience should be invited to make sense of the action at that moment: 'Dramatically,' he says, 'this element *allows* [Clov's] perception[s] . . . *to be construed as* hallucinations.' Schneider's fifteenth question registers his mock (or maybe not so mock) desperation in capitals: 'ANYTHING YOU WANT TO TELL ME ABOUT HAMM'S STORY WILL BE WELCOME!'[3] Beckett's response again focuses on an audience's reading of the action, and again points to Clov's sighting of the boy:

> What more can I say about Hamm's story? Technically it is the most difficult thing in the play because of the number of vocal levels. Dramatically it may be regarded as evoking events leading up to Clov's arrival, alone presumably, the father having fallen by the way, and to the beginning of the particular horror to which this play is confined. It also allows Clov's 'perception' of boy at end to be interpreted as vision of himself on last lap to 'shelter'.[4]

The terms are the same: 'Dramatically *it may be regarded* . . . *It also allows* Clov's 'perception' . . . *to be interpreted as* . . .' The phrasing is judicious – and I don't mean to speak ironically. He doesn't hedge; he doesn't decline to commit himself. He explains his intention.

Nor is that intention to trick the audience. The often-quoted letter of 29 December in which Beckett told Schneider, '[i]f people want to have headaches among the overtones, let them. And provide their own aspirin', plainly constitutes a gesture of reassurance and solidarity with a director hard-pressed by 'these bastards of journalists' and 'those bastards of critics' rather than a neutral statement of intention.[5] (The letter of Schneider's which prompted this one is missing.) The earlier, equally well-known letter of 21 June 1956 which describes *Fin de partie* as '[r]ather difficult and elliptic, mostly depending on the power of the text to claw' fits better with the later advice about staging, in which Beckett explains exactly *how* the text should claw, where and at what.[6] Clawing does not sound friendly (this play is, Beckett famously comments, 'more inhuman than *Godot*') but nor is it merely misleading.

If, as it is customary to note, 'Das Stück ist voller Echos, alle antworten einander', then right reading is a matter of listening for those echoes and assessing their conversation.[7] The echo of the small boy of Hamm's chronicle in the small boy of Clov's terminal observation is arguably the most important of such effects, having as it does potentially decisive implications for meaning. The more sensitive of Beckett's early critics got the point. Having just written a paragraph in which the word 'perhaps' appears five times, Ruby Cohn wrote (in 1962): 'Clov may have invented the small boy who will serve as Clov, even as Clov may have been the small boy in Hamm's literary invention.'[8]

However, the accuracy of one critic's perceptions should not distract us from the particular significance of those responses of Beckett to Schneider with which I began. Beckett's remarks presuppose a spectator who is extraordinarily sophisticated. It may be retorted, of course, that most spectators are engaged, more or less unawares, in reading-manoeuvres which, when examined, turn out to be extraordinarily sophisticated, even though they are quite commonplace. However, it is not my impression that many critics, and certainly not many of the early ones, show the agility in reading the action which the playwright supposes he might expect in his advice to Alan Schneider. Of course the indeterminacy of *Endgame* (or what since the advent of theory we refer to as indeterminacy) has been fully appreciated. But that this indeterminacy may qualify particular reading strategies – or make spectators aware of commonplace operations of understanding which might not hitherto have risen above the horizon of perception – has been less often considered.

By the time Clov sights the small boy an alert audience would be inclined to be sceptical. 'Why do you lie to me?' asks Hamm – and that is before the episode with the dog, where we *see* that Clov is lying.[9] Nonetheless, when he reports sighting the boy we do require grounds for not believing him. Both of Beckett's comments to Schneider presuppose this and point out how the play has provided these, even if Clov as visionary is different from Clov as liar. For Beckett as dramaturg, Clov as visionary allows a particular reading which can be expressed thus: if Clov were to have (had) visions, then the boy may not exist. Further: if Hamm's chronicle were to have given us 'events leading up to Clov's arrival', then Clov's 'perception' of the boy may be a vision of 'himself on last lap to "shelter"'. We are not expected to resolve the alternatives (the boy exists; the boy does not exist); rather we are expected to hold them simultaneously in our minds. We read, so to speak, subjunctively. That is, what grammarians refer to as the past (or *were*-) subjunctive[10] operating within the context of a conditional statement (if this were, then that would) gives us the model for understanding the moment.

Beckett's word 'allows' (this *allows* that to be interpreted thus; that *allows* this to be construed thus) could be thought of as disingenuous: the audience should be *allowed* to fall into the trap of believing they know what the thing means. This view is I think implicit in Gabriele Schwab's position. Schwab argues as follows:

> In the reception process we have to follow the play's strategy to let us shift between invitations to closure and required reopenings. Thus we may experience the extent to which our need for meaning induces us to close the gaps of the play by projecting our imaginations into them. This offers us some insight into our need for projective closures, as well as into the defensive qualities of our own communicative behaviour.[11]

The reader Beckett presupposes in his letter to Schneider is perhaps cannier than the one implicit in Schwab's formulation. For Beckett we entertain hypotheses; for Schwab we continually re-experience (and here I use a selection of her words) frustration, rejection, impediment or exclusion, and gain insight thereby. If Beckett's readers maintain themselves in a state of continuous suspension in respect of meaning, Schwab's repeatedly commit themselves and are repeatedly thwarted.

Schwab's Iseresque[12] idea of 'projective closures' resonates interestingly with this of all plays. Beckett speaks about the characters' 'projections', towards either going or abiding, and he speaks of Clov's arrival as 'the beginning of the particular horror to which this play is *confined*'. They have, we might say, too much confinement and not enough closure. In this sense, our interpretative situation has similarities to theirs, for in coping imaginatively with this 'thing' we too are expected to project in the way that the subjunctive mood provides for. This alignment of characters and spectator is one way in which the play educates its audience in this mode of perception: we repeatedly witness Hamm and Clov operating in the subjunctive mood until we recognise the possibility of a vitally subjunctive reading at the moment when Clov sights the boy.

An obvious first example of Hamm in the subjunctive is the episode of the 'rational being'. Hamm wonders hesitantly if they are not beginning to 'mean something'. Clov dismisses this with a brief laugh but Hamm continues:

> I wonder. [*Pause.*] Imagine if a rational being came back to earth, wouldn't he be liable to get ideas into his head if he observed us long enough. [*Voice of rational being.*] Ah, good, now I see what it is, yes, now I understand what they're at![13]

At this point Clov starts scratching himself – a flea, he supposes. The passage is quoted by Schwab to illustrate how 'the characters deride this meaning as a conventional projection of preconceived ideas'.[14] But she cuts it off at this point. In fact Hamm continues, with '[*n*]*ormal voice*':

> And without going so far as that, we ourselves . . . [*with emotion*] . . . we ourselves . . . at certain moments . . . [*Vehemently.*] To think perhaps it won't all have been for nothing![15]

Clov may deride; the playwright may deride; but Hamm does not. His emotion and vehemence are signs of a residual desire for meaning – or, if we want to state it more cautiously, it is not clear that they are not. And that desire takes the form of subjunctive projections: 'Imagine if . . . To think perhaps . . .'

Hamm's fantasies of escape are framed subjunctively (we read 'if I could' as 'if I were able to'): 'If I could sleep I might make love. I'd go into the woods. My eyes would see . . . the sky, the earth. I'd run, run, they wouldn't catch me.'[16] And later: 'If I could drag myself down to the sea! I'd make a pillow of sand for my head and the tide would come.'[17] Here the projections beyond confinement are projections beyond the refuge. But in his monologue Hamm anticipates the end as the real escape from confinement. The anticipation follows from a subjunctive gesture:

> Perhaps I could throw myself out on the floor. [. . .] . . . It will be the end and there I'll be, wondering what can have brought it on and wondering what can have . . . [*he hesitates*] . . . why it was so long coming. [*Pause.*] . . . If I can hold my peace, and sit quiet, it will be all over with sound, and motion, all over and done with.[18]

The subjunction, as conditional clause, manifests a fantasy of personal control: *if* I were to do that, *then* it would be the end.

Hamm's self-location is similarly subjunctive, and no less fantastical. 'Did you ever think of one thing?' he exclaims, '[t]hat here we're down in a hole. [*Pause.*] But beyond the hills? Eh? Perhaps it's still green. Eh? [*Pause.*] Flora! Pomona! [*Ecstatically.*] Ceres!'[19] It's a little imaginative experiment: if this were the case, then perhaps that . . . ? The same structure is perceptible behind Clov's anticipation of his end, in his exit-speech: 'I say to myself that the earth is extinguished, though I never saw it lit.'[20] If the earth were to be thought of as once illuminated, then now it could be thought of as extinguished. The subjunctive formulation within an implied conditional clause acknowledges its own subjunctivity by virtue of the self-awareness of the proposition: 'I say to myself . . .'

And then there are the jokes. Hamm and Clov: 'Why don't you kill me?' / 'I don't know the combination of the larder.'[21] (*If* I knew the combination of the larder, *then* I'd kill you.) Clov on Hamm: 'If I could kill him I'd die happy.'[22] Hamm and Nagg: 'Scoundrel! Why did you engender me?' / 'I didn't know.' / 'What? What didn't you know?' / 'That it'd be you.'[23] (*If* I'd known it would be you, *then* I wouldn't have engendered you.) Hamm on God: 'The bastard! He doesn't exist!'[24] (*If* He were to exist, He *would* be a bastard.) They are all jokes involving the conditional, that is, jokes with a relational logic. It would be straining a point to say that these are all funny *because* of their subjunctivity (or even to claim that they are all strictly subjunctive in grammar), but just as their humour is distinctive of this play, their mood (in more than just the grammatical sense) is distinctly subjunctive.

I return to the moment from which I started by way of something which is no longer in the play – and indeed never was in *Endgame*, though it is there in the first edition of *Fin de partie*. This is the original version of the moment when the boy is sighted, which Beckett cut extensively for *Endgame*. Schneider enquired about this, and Beckett replied (17 March 1958):

> We cut most of the boy scene during rehearsals here [for the premiere of *Fin de partie*] because we found it dragged and also because [Roger] Blin couldn't bring it into line with his interpretation of the role. It's not important and I think the play is better without it. It seemed to break the tension.[25]

Thus the reasons for the cut were practical theatrical ones. However, at least one early critic made, as I am doing, the subjunctive gesture: it's not there; but if it were there, then this is what would follow (an odd echo, of course, of Hamm's final response to the sighting *inside* the play). For Martin Esslin the original French text 'clearly reveals the religious or quasi-religious symbolism of the little boy', but 'Beckett seems to have felt that he had been too explicit'.[26] This latter judgement, at least, is very plausible, though Beckett's explanation to Schneider is along different lines.

The original French Hamm at first seems to assume the reality of the boy; then he asks for more information – about distance, proxemics, sex and activity. When Clov tells him what the boy is doing, Hamm's sarcasm implies firm scepticism, yet simultaneously he provides an arbitrary elaboration of the significance which he clearly feels he is being invited to read into the event. Clov reports: 'Il a l'air assis par terre, adossé à quelque chose'; Hamm responds: 'La pierre levée. (*Un temps.*) Ta vue s'améliore. (*Un temps.*) Il regarde la maison sans doute, avec les yeux de Moïse mourant.'[27] Clov does not take the ironic bait, and Hamm continues to request information, perhaps testing Clov out, before telling him not to bother going out to kill the boy.

If Blin could not accommodate this Hamm in his reading, we can speculate on the qualities which might have prevented him from doing so. This Hamm seems both more susceptible to what he identifies as offered meanings and more sceptical of them. The degree of irony contained in his rejection communicates a bitterness which suggests the opposite drive: this Hamm really wants meaning, and is savage when offered something he considers fake. This Hamm, we may say, is a little more psychologically penetrable than the one we are left with. And the uncut episode has the effect of alerting us – perhaps too emphatically for the playwright – to the extent of Hamm's similarity to the spectator as a reader of potential meaning. But then at the very moment it invites identification, such an episode also alerts us to, or reminds us of, the game the play is playing with us. Or rather, it would, if it were there. And if the passage is 'not important', it is only because it does explicitly what the play has been doing all along.

'They endure their "thing"', Beckett explained to Schneider, 'by projection away from it' – their 'thing' being 'the particular horror to which this play is confined'. It is this dialectic of projection and confinement which is manifested in the subjunctive mood of *Endgame*. Its subjunctivity typifies this play's way of imagining that provisionality of being which is a central element of Beckett's work. The 'crooked' thinking of Hamm and Clov finds its shape through subjunctivity and ultimately, as Beckett's notes to Schneider indicate, the audience is invited (for dramaturgically I think this is what 'allows' amounts to) to read subjunctively.[28] Furthermore the subjunctive mood provides a suggestive echo of the fundamentally relational being of Hamm and Clov. When the subjunctive operates within a conditional clause, it facilitates the joined-togetherness of interdependent clauses: if this were, then that would. Protasis and apodosis: without the second clause the first is not necessary, and without the first clause the second is not possible. Hamm and Clov.

One of the uses of the subjunctive is of course to anticipate by forming hypotheses. Hamm is keen throughout the play to anticipate the end of the game. When he finally signals that end, as a consequence of the episode of the boy, this does not end the anticipation but rather renews its vigour and power. (As always in Beckett, there is nothing like the prospect of death to put life in them.) As Clov prepares for his exit, Hamm requests '[a] few words . . . to ponder . . . in my heart' and procedes to narrate, in the past tense, an absurdly literary anticipation of that exit, projecting it as a moment of epiphany, climactic resolution and heroic reconciliation:

> Yes. [*Pause. Forcibly.*] Yes! [*Pause.*] With the rest, in the end, the shadows, the murmurs, all the trouble, to end up with. [*Pause.*] Clov . . . He never spoke to me. Then, in the end, before he went, without my having asked him, he spoke to me. He said . . .[29]

This is simultaneously an extravagant anticipation and an attempt to dictate Clov's behaviour to him. In the revised text[30] Hamm's interjections ('Articulate!' and 'Enough!') are cut, largely one imagines because it is clear that Clov's speech escapes Hamm's attempt substantially to script it.[31] Hamm orders something 'from your heart', but gets a speech delivered with '[*f*]*ixed gaze, tonelessly, towards auditorium*'.[32] Hamm's is a failed hypothesis.

Then Clov delivers his own hypothesis. His projected imminent departure is envisioned in the present tense:

> I open the door of the cell and go. I am so bowed I only see my feet, if I open my eyes, and between my legs a little trail of black dust. I say to myself that the earth is extinguished, though I never saw it lit. [*Pause.*] It's easy going. [*Pause.*] When I drop I'll weep for happiness.[33]

If '[o]utside of here it's death', and if he were to go, this would be likely to happen. Clov describes himself as issuing forth out of their confinement into the '[c]orpsed' world.[34] It is, perhaps, another version of that familiar Beckettian figure, the birth into death (which never properly happens). Insofar as the outside is the place where the small boy was supposed (or not supposed) to be, and insofar as the small boy can be perceived, in Beckett's words, 'as vision of himself on last lap to "shelter"', Clov's is an imaginative move by which he associates himself once again with the boy. That is, he associates himself (again) with what may be a fictional construct, a subjunctive element ('If he exists . . .').[35] '[I]f I open my eyes', in echoing 'I open the door', hints at the operation of imagination here: 'opening' in Beckett is often a figure for the initiation of fictional invention.[36] Opening the door is not merely an action in the real, spatial world. It is an imaginative act which has the effect of proposing an hypothesis. What the door opens on, in *Endgame*, may be death, but is certainly an imaginative projection, a world with a virtual existence. If and when Clov exits, he will exit into subjunctivity. Their revels now are ended, and their little life is rounded with an hypothesis.

But of course Clov never does go out, perhaps never will go out. His imagining of dissolution and fall is the imagining of an end which, as ever in Beckett, only renders increasingly unimaginable the end of imagination itself. Anticipation distances us from the thing itself even as it allows us to approach it. The tormented pyrrhonism of *Endgame* commits Hamm and Clov to hypothesis as a necessary activity. As they are performers, their hypothesis is a form of rehearsal. The thing itself, the end, never happens. Indeed, rehearsal ensures that it never happens. They are stuck in a world of continuous rehearsal, their grey room a green room. The tragedy, the meaning, the grand gestures, can only happen offstage, in a world elsewhere, subjunctively.

Notes

1. Maurice Harmon, *No Author Better Served*, p. 20.
2. Ibid. p. 22.
3. Ibid. p. 20.
4. Ibid. pp. 22–3.
5. Ibid. p. 24.
6. Ibid. p. 11.
7. Beckett speaking as director of *Endspiel* in 1967, reported by his assistant Michael Haerdter and quoted in Ruby Cohn, *Just Play: Beckett's Theater*, p. 107. A translation of Haerdter's 'Rehearsal Diary' is to be found in Dougald McMillan and Martha Fehsenfeld, *Beckett in the Theatre*, pp. 204–38. The statement about echoes is on p. 208.
8. Ruby Cohn, *Samuel Beckett*, p. 242.
9. Samuel Beckett, *Endgame*, p. 104; pp. 111–12.
10. See Randolph Quirk, Sidney Greenbaum, Geoffrey Leech and Jan Svartvik, *A Comprehensive Grammar of the English Language*, p. 158. Of the three major categories of the subjunctive mood, the mandative, formulaic and past (were-), I have focused almost exclusively upon the last. I am aware that most of my instances are not, strictly speaking, examples of the

grammatical subjunctive, but I have chosen to persevere with the word in its wider sense (*Oxford English Dictionary* definition c): 'Characteristic of what is expressed by the subjunctive mood; contingent, hypothetical.' If (as the authors of the *Comprehensive Grammar* put it) '[t]he were-subjunctive may be regarded as a fossilised inflection', it would seem an apt one for the consideration of Beckett's abodes of stone. And insofar as the were-subjunctive 'refers to circumstances contrary to fact', it presents itself as a useful category for the discussion of a play in which facts are perhaps not what they were. For in *Endgame* that which is contrary to fact can be thought of as at least as important to the game as that which is in agreement with it. We need, in other words, a language that will enable us to describe how indeterminacy works in *Endgame*. This is what I am calling the language of subjunctivity.

11. Gabriele Schwab, 'On the Dialectic', p. 93.
12. Wolfgang Iser's own account of *Endgame* is to be found in 'The Art of Failure: The Stifled Laugh in Beckett's Theater'.
13. Beckett, *Endgame*, p. 108.
14. Schwab, 'On the Dialectic', p. 91.
15. Beckett, *Endgame*, p. 108.
16. Ibid. p. 100.
17. Ibid. p. 122.
18. Ibid. p. 126.
19. Ibid. p. 111.
20. Ibid. p. 132.
21. Ibid. p. 96.
22. Ibid. p. 105.
23. Ibid. p. 116.
24. Ibid. p. 119.
25. Harmon, *No Author Better Served*, p. 41.
26. Martin Esslin, *The Theatre of the Absurd*, p. 72; p. 70.
27. Beckett, *Fin de partie*, p. 104.
28. Beckett, *Endgame*, p. 97.
29. Ibid. p. 131.
30. In S. E. Gontarski (ed.), *The Theatrical Notebooks of Samuel Beckett, Volume II: Endgame*, p. 40 (line 1435); p. 41 (line 1440). The revised text of the play, with numbered lines, is on pp. 1–42.
31. Beckett, *Endgame*, p. 131; p. 132.
32. Ibid. p. 131.
33. Ibid. p. 132. Here I adopt the reading of the revised text, where 'drop' replaces 'fall'; see Gontarski, p. 41 (line 1451).
34. Beckett, *Endgame*, p. 96; p. 106.
35. Ibid. p. 131.
36. See for example the Opener in *Cascando* (1963) with his 'outings' (*The Complete Dramatic Works*, p. 303); '[h]ave yourself opened . . . opened up' (*The Complete Dramatic Works*, p. 279) in *Rough for Radio II* (early 1960s); and the spotlight in *Play* (1963), '[m]ere eye . . . Opening and shutting on me' (*The Complete Dramatic Works*, p. 317).

Bibliography

Beckett, Samuel, *Cascando* (pp. 295–304), *Endgame* (pp. 89–134), *Play* (pp. 305–20) and *Rough for Radio II* (pp. 273–84), in *The Complete Dramatic Works* (London: Faber and Faber, 1986).

Beckett, Samuel, *Fin de partie* (Paris: Éditions de Minuit, 1957).

Cohn, Ruby, *Just Play: Beckett's Theater* (Princeton: Princeton University Press, 1980).

Cohn, Ruby, *Samuel Beckett: The Comic Gamut* (New Brunswick, NJ: Rutgers University Press, 1962).

Esslin, Martin, *The Theatre of the Absurd*, revised and enlarged ed. (Harmondsworth: Penguin, 1968).

Gontarski, S. E. (ed.), *The Theatrical Notebooks of Samuel Beckett, Volume II: Endgame* (London: Faber and Faber, 1992).

Harmon, Maurice (ed.), *No Author Better Served: The Correspondence of Samuel Beckett and Alan Schneider* (Cambridge, MA: Harvard University Press, 1998).

Iser, Wolfgang, 'The Art of Failure: The Stifled Laugh in Beckett's Theater', in *Prospecting: From Reader Response to Literary Anthropology* (Baltimore: Johns Hopkins University Press, 1989), pp. 176–93.

McMillan, Dougald, and Martha Fehsenfeld, *Beckett in the Theatre: The Author as Practical Playwright and Director, Vol. 1: From 'Waiting for Godot' to 'Krapp's Last Tape'* (London: John Calder, 1988).

Quirk, Randolph, Sidney Greenbaum, Geoffrey Leech and Jan Svartvik, *A Comprehensive Grammar of the English Language* (London: Longman, 1985).

Schwab, Gabriele, 'On the Dialectic of Closing and Opening in *Endgame*', in Steven Connor (ed.), Waiting for Godot *and* Endgame*: Contemporary Critical Essays* (London: Macmillan, 1992), pp. 87–99.

18.

'All the Dead Voices': Beckett and the Ethics of Elegy

Shane Weller

The Murderous Art of Mourning

For a writer whose *oeuvre* might well be described as an almost uninterrupted *memento mori*, those works by Samuel Beckett that fall squarely within the category of the elegiac in the stricter modern sense of the term are decidedly uncommon – and this despite the fact that, according to both of his major biographers, Beckett's poetry contains his most clearly personal, autobiographical writing.[1] Among the poems that come closest to being elegies proper are 'Malacoda' and 'Da tagte es' – both written shortly after the death of Beckett's father on 26 June 1933, and both included in *Echo's Bones and Other Precipitates* (1935)[2] – and 'Mort de A. D.', written in 1949 in memory of Dr Arthur Darley, a colleague of Beckett's at the Irish Red Cross Hospital at Saint-Lô in northwestern France, where Beckett served as quartermaster and interpreter from August 1945 until early 1946.[3] That each of these poems should take a male figure as its object of commemoration is far from being a mere coincidence. Indeed, Beckett tends to reserve the more conventionally elegiac mode for the male dead.

Other poems that reflect explicitly upon memorialisation include 'ne manquer pas à Tanger' and 'plus loin un autre commémore', in the 1978 collection *Mirlitonnades*. An indication of the complication facing any analysis of elegy in Beckett, and in particular his treatment of the feminine in relation to elegy, is to be found in the fate of the second of these two French poems when he came to rewrite it in (rather than translate it into) English. The French text refers to the 'philosophie' of the Irish-born Caroline Hay Taylor (deceased in August 1932) as being simply 'espoir tant qu'il y a vie'.[4] Where there's life there's hope: this is, of course, a cliché whose very inscription in epitaph marks the exhaustion of hope's possibility; indeed, as an epitaph this 'philosophie' lives on only in the form of its own negation. In Beckett's English version, however, this irony is itself subjected to a second-order negation, since the dead woman is now elegised as one who 'held we fall to rise, are baffled to fight better, sleep to wake'.[5] The English version challenges the original cliché not through irony, then, but rather by intimating that death is not the obliteration of hope but its very precondition. In short, were it not for death, there would be no hope. Beckett's own practice as an elegist is often governed by just such a principle of negating repetition, the ethics of which are considerably less easy to determine than has often been assumed.

Beyond the above-mentioned works of elegy, Beckett's *oeuvre* may of course be described as essentially elegiac not simply because it commemorates the dead in general, but more radically and more problematically because Beckett comes to see art itself as, by definition, forever in mourning for its object ('en deuil de l'objet'), as he puts it in the 1948 essay 'Peintres de l'empêchement', and because the voices that find expression in literature are increasingly, for Beckett, in a certain sense the voices of the dead.[6] As Beckett's own reading of Proust helps to bring out, for both Proust and Beckett (and arguably for Joyce too) art is predicated on a certain separation or death, and more precisely the death, or even the active negation, of the feminine in the form of both the mother and the (female) lover. Considerably complicating, without simply contradicting, this notion of art as in mourning for its own unattainable object or as serving as the medium for 'All the dead voices' – as they are described in *Godot* – there is another strain in Beckett's *oeuvre*, namely the sense that art depends upon the non-appearance, resistance or death of its object, and even that art is the enactment of a veritable death drive that has for its aim not only the self but also the other.[7] That this other often takes the form of the feminine, and that the elegising of the masculine and the feminine should take very different forms in Beckett, certainly suggests that Beckett remains tied for much of his writing life to a thinking of the feminine that is decidedly Schopenhauerian in nature. If, however, in his later works he seeks to free himself from such a vision of the feminine, then this is nowhere more apparent than in his movement towards a new form of elegy, a form that is neither ethical nor unethical but what might be termed 'anethical'. It is the movement towards this anethical form of elegy that I will attempt to trace here.

Despite the many claims for the essential ethicality of Beckett's art or, more recently, the claim that his art is grounded in an ethics of alterity, any reflection upon the ethics of elegy in Beckett is faced, from the outset, with a distinction between male and female dead, and with a highly problematical interweaving of mourning and murderousness, an interweaving that is at its most explicit in those works that take a female figure as the object of elegy. This is perhaps most obviously the case in the 1948 poem 'Je voudrais que mon amour meure', which may be read as a response to, or even a radical translation of, Yeats's 'He wishes his Beloved were Dead'.[8] Whereas Yeats's poem is addressed to the 'beloved', apostrophising and thereby granting her the possibility of a voice, Beckett's poem turns Yeats's 'you' into a 'celle'.[9] And whereas in Yeats's poem it is a desire for the consoling presence of the 'beloved' that lies behind the wish for her death,[10] in Beckett's poem it is a desire for mourning as such that lies behind that wish, and with it a desire for the work of elegy:

> Je voudrais que mon amour meure
> qu'il pleuve sur le cimetière
> et les ruelles où je vais
> pleurant celle qui crut m'aimer
>
> I would like my love to die
> and the rain to be raining on the graveyard
> and on me walking the streets
> mourning her who thought she loved me[11]

As so often with Beckett's works, commentators on this poem have sought to ethicalise it – or, more precisely, to coordinate an ethics with an aesthetics. Lawrence E. Harvey, one of the few critics to have devoted concentrated attention to Beckett's poetry, argues that the speaker's wishing for the death of his beloved is not contradictory in the least, since in Beckett's world death is quite simply a blessing.[12] Here, then, death would be a gift, and all the more of a gift for its entailing suffering in the giver.[13] What such an analysis leaves out of account, however, is not only the possibility that mourning is itself a pleasure in Beckett, or that in Beckettian mourning pain and pleasure are bound to each other in a highly paradoxical manner that suggests a proximity to Sade, but also that the work of art itself is tied to a negativity that takes the other – the female other – as its object.

Ruby Cohn avoids the co-implication of mourning and murderousness in this poem in a slightly different manner from Harvey, arguing that the poem's 'delicate phrasing' and 'gentle rhythm' counters the 'seeming cruelty of the death wish'; in other words, the death drive that targets the feminine here would be countered by the aesthetic.[14] Again, such a reading surely underestimates not only the violence that arguably characterises all of Beckett's works (a violence that in the early works is directed principally towards the feminine), not only the 'metaphysical ecstasy' to which he confesses on reading Sade in 1938,[15] but the almost systematic implication of the aesthetic within the dream of a nihilation that is effected both in this poem and, in different ways, throughout his *oeuvre*.

This implication of the aesthetic within the death drive, without the aesthetic ever being simply an unqualified expression of that drive, is Beckett's response to Schopenhauer's notion of art as 'einstweilen ein Trost' ('occasional consolation').[16] Rather than constituting a liberation from the savage economy of the will that, in its ignorance, turns back upon itself (as enacted so graphically in part two of *Comment c'est/How It Is*), the aesthetic, and more particularly the aesthetic as essentially elegiac, tends to function in Beckett as a paradoxical consolation-exacerbation, which it would be problematical to describe as either ethical or unethical. It is not that Beckett's works testify to the value of the other or to the 'primacy of love' (as it has recently been termed), but rather that the perceived valuelessness of the other repeatedly fails to be ratified through an act of consummating negation, not least because the work of elegiac art depends upon the very misrecognition of that valuelessness (that '*ibi nihil velis*', as Beckett, quoting Geulincx, puts it in *Murphy*).[17] Now, this failure of the negative is the very experience of the anethical.

Neither ethical nor unethical, the anethical might seem to be easily recuperable within recent deconstructive readings of the work of mourning in Beckett, so efficiently summarised by Angela Moorjani when she observes:

> many commentators have bound Beckett's writing to figurations of mourning and melancholy, especially in Freud, Klein, and Abraham and Torok. For these psychoanalytic thinkers, phantasms of lost ones live on buried in the mind, pinioned in an enclave in the ego, banished to a place of exile within a subject divided from itself. This memorial space encloses a lost one both living and dead, hated and loved, as mourning is unremittingly deferred. Abraham and Torok call this site of unfinished mourning a crypt whose cryptonyms are fetish signs that hide the encrypted name and body and keep the subject exterior to itself.[18]

One such commentator is Leslie Hill. Applying Nicolas Abraham and Maria Torok's founding distinction between incorporation and introjection, Hill argues that the work of mourning in Beckett is essentially incorporative rather than introjective, with mourning becoming an interminable process, a 'constant movement of inscription and effacement, embodiment and disembodiment'.[19] As for the ethics of this process, Hill observes, 'the fantasy of incorporation, by guarding the other as though the other were still alive, in the manner of a ghost, is a more faithful way of mourning the loss of the other than if that loss were to be introjected . . . But,' Hill continues, 'as Derrida suggests in his commentary on the work of Abraham and Torok, one can of course also argue the reverse.'[20] In other words, that introjection is in fact the least faithful way of mourning the loss of the other.

Derrida's deconstructive reading of the introjection–incorporation distinction, and his later thinking of an 'ethic of hospitality', is governed, however, less by a principle of simple reversibility than by an aporetic logic that implicates all possible hospitality in hostility, all possible love in a certain irreducible violence: thus Derrida's coinage 'hostipitalité' ('hostipitality'), which incorporates the aporetic relation between hospitality and hostility characterising any possible relation to the other.[21] Only an impossible, absolutely unconditional hospitality to the other would escape hostility. Crucially, then, Derrida's thinking of 'hostipitality' is underwritten by an unconditional ethical commitment to the other, an *il faut* ('you must') grounded in the value of the other in its absolute alterity, and a fundamental distinction between what he terms the 'good violence of the Other' and that 'bad violence' which would constitute the negation of the other, a violence that is 'mechanical' and 'repetitive'.[22]

If there is such a 'hostipitality' in the relation to the dead in Beckett's works of elegy, however, it is anethical in that it works against the very distinction between good and bad violence, between the ethical and the unethical, a distinction that would humanise that which is not necessarily either human or humane. Furthermore, if there is a commitment to the impossible in Beckett's work of mourning, a commitment that finds perhaps its clearest expression in the *il faut* of *L'Innommable*, then this commitment is anethical in that it remains ungrounded, even in the kind of impossible unconditionality underlying Derrida's deconstructive ethics.

Elegising the Father

According to Julia Kristeva, Beckett's entire *oeuvre* is to be read as a work of interminable mourning for a father whose putrescent corpse remains visible throughout: a corpse that in Beckett is immeasurable, uncoverable and uncoffinable.[23] Although there are undoubtedly a number of problems with such a reading, not least the damage that Beckett does to the male–female distinction in certain works, it nonetheless helps to remind us that the question of gender is no less important than the question of genre in any analysis of both the work of mourning and the writing of elegy. Certainly, for the most part in Beckett, this work of mourning is performed by a male figure. Furthermore, as already mentioned, those poems that come closest to being elegies in the strict sense also take as their object a male figure: the father in 'Malacoda' and 'Da tagte es', and a male friend in 'Mort de A. D.'.

As is well known, 'Malacoda' draws its demonic cast from canto XXI of Dante's *Inferno*, in which Malacoda (literally 'bad end') is a deceitful demon who, thwarted by Virgil, 'avea del cul fatto trombetta' ('had made a trumpet of his arse').[24] Although Harvey describes both this poem and 'Da tagte es' as 'tributes of a son to his cherished father', 'Malacoda' is no tribute in the ordinary sense of the word.[25] Recounting the three acts of measuring, coffining and covering the paternal corpse, the poem focuses upon what an unnamed 'she' (the widow) must hear and see, building in three parts to the articulation of an anethical compulsion: 'hear she must see she must'.[26] The poem's last word, isolated from the rest of the text, is not 'must', however, but 'nay'.[27] This 'nay' is the poem's own *mala coda* or 'bad end', having caused its readers considerable difficulty. It has been read, on the one hand, as an act of resistance to the 'obscenity of death',[28] a 'refusal to let the father go',[29] and, on the other hand, as an acceptance of death as a liberation, a negation that 'negates not only the preceding line but the whole poem', there being no reason to lower the flag to half-mast in sign of mourning, since death here 'is not a penalty but a welcome release from the cruelty of life'.[30] A third reading has this final 'nay' denying 'the hope of everlasting life after death'.[31]

However, the syntactical and spatial isolation of that final 'nay', that bad end of a negation, renders its object far from easy to pin down, and indeed opens up the very space in which such seemingly irreconcilable readings may congregate, often in unacknowledged war with one another. And readings of the 'nay' are far from being limited to those given above. In addition to being read as a resistance to death's obscenity or as an acceptance of death as release, this final 'nay' might also be read as a refusal to accept the departure heralded by the 'aye aye' that precedes it, and thus as a negating commitment to remembrance, and even as an authoritative rather than desperate denial of departure; in other words, a countering affirmation that, for all the measuring (including poetic measuring), coffining (including poetic coffining) and covering (including poetic covering), the dead remain unmeasured, uncoffined, uncovered and alone, in or even as the work itself.[32] The isolation of the 'nay' here is, then, both its strength and its weakness, at once enriching and impoverishing it. And 'nay' is, of course, not just any old word in Beckett. For, in his attentiveness to the paradoxicalities of negation, and not least the paradoxicalities at work in the memorialisation of negation, Beckett has few equals. To follow John Pilling in dismissing this particular 'nay' as far less effective than the 'It is not' that terminates the 1932 short story 'Dante and the Lobster' is to exhibit a decided preference for precisely the kind of judgemental authority that is opened to question by the bad end of 'Malacoda', a bad end that is nothing less than the most highly compacted form of elegy as such.

Elegising the (Male) Friend

When we turn from 'Malacoda' to a poem on the death of a male friend, we find that it is not just the precise object of negation in Beckettian elegy but also the ethical nature of elegy that proves far from easy to determine. As already mentioned, the poem 'Mort de A. D.' was written in 1949 in memory of Arthur Darley, a Catholic colleague of Beckett's at the Irish Red Cross Hospital at Saint-Lô. The poem's title is, of course, playfully self-translating, while also encrypting not only the name of Arthur Darley but also that of Christ (Anno Domini). The poem certainly prompts a reading in ethical terms, counterpointing the elegist and elegised throughout. The idea of sin – less the sin of being born (so often invoked by Beckett) than the sin of being alive when others are dead – is certainly present in this poem, not least in the reference to the elegised other as 'mort hier pendant que je vivais'.[33] Such a sense of guilt at surviving the other is, of course, at the very heart of many testimonies produced by survivors of the Holocaust shortly after the war: one finds it in the work of Paul Celan, and it is also in Celan that one finds a concern with the very possibility of witnessing; the poem 'Aschenglorie' ends with the assertion that 'Niemand / zeugt für den / Zeugen' ('No one / witnesses for the / witness').[34] Beckett's 'Mort de A. D.' ends with the elegist himself having become a witness not just to the death of the other but also to that haunting which will increasingly dominate Beckett's *oeuvre* in his later years: the elegist is now a 'témoin des départs / témoin des retours'.[35]

If the implication of the elegist-witness in the death of the other is much less apparent in 'Mort de A. D.' than it is (as a desire) in 'Je voudrais que mon amour meure', it is nonetheless present. And yet, just as was the case with 'Malacoda', so too with 'Mort de A. D.' most commentators have sought to present the Beckett elegy as essentially ethical in nature. According to Harvey, for instance, the poem expresses 'the narrator's hopeless anguish before the suffering and death of A. D.', but also enacts an heroic movement on the part of the would-be elegist, a progress from horizontality to verticality, from passivity to activity, from waiting to writing.[36] Pilling even goes so far as to claim that the poem 'proves conclusively that [Beckett's] work is not entirely solipsistic and self-regarding'.[37] For both Harvey and Pilling, then, although in rather different ways, this elegy is properly ethical. For Harvey, its ethicality lies in an heroic resistance to death and in a passage towards the act of writing (that is, the act of elegising as bearing witness to the effect of the other's death on the self). For Pilling, on the other hand, the poem's ethicality lies in its openness to the other, its break with a narcissism that, he suggests, mars much of Beckett's earlier poetry. Neither reading takes account, however, of the ways in which such versions of the ethical are opened to question in the poem. For instance, the movement of the elegist from being 'pressé contre' to being 'agrippé à' is one that follows upon a 'being there' ('être là') that is unaffected by attempts either to persist in or to desist from it: 'à être là à ne pas fuir et fuir et être là'.[38] And if there is indeed a break with narcissism that is occasioned by the trauma of the other's death, then this break produces a witness ('témoin') of departures and returns in which the very distinction between self and other no longer quite holds. In other words, the poem moves not in the direction of an unambiguous openness to the other, but rather in the direction of an anethical conflation or imbrication of self and other.

Sero te amavi: Elegising the Female Beloved (Again)

The poem 'Je voudrais que mon amour meure' suggests that the anethical relation in Beckett's elegiac art between love and hate, grief and murderousness, openness to and nullification of the other, is perhaps nowhere more evident than in his treatment of the death of the (female) lover. The television play *Eh Joe* might serve as another example of just such an economy, not least through the very different endings (one with a smile and one without) to the two versions that Beckett directed for Süddeutscher Rundfunk. In Beckett's later works, however, it is less the ambivalence of love and hate in the elegist's relation to the dead woman than the ironies of the elegiac art itself that come to the fore. In other words, Beckett shifts his attention more directly towards the writing of what might be termed the elegisation of elegy.

In the radio play *Words and Music* (1962), we witness the production of a poem in which a dead female beloved returns as a 'face in the ashes', and from as early as *Dream of Fair to Middling Women* (written 1931–2) the female beloved's face is to be radically distinguished from the grotesque materiality of the rest of the Beckettian female body: the Smeraldina, for instance, is presented as a being who is split not, like the Geulincxian Murphy, between mind and body, but between a monstrous corporeality (the sex-body) and another form of corporeality that might be described as the image-body, the love-body or even a certain kind of art-body.[39] On the one hand, she exhibits a corporeality that is 'wobbly, mammose, slobbery-blubbery'; on the other hand, her face is 'the loveliest little pale firm cameo of a birdface'.[40] In *Words and Music*, it is precisely this radiant face that returns 'in the ashes', the irony here being not simply that the elegiac art is predicated on the death of the female beloved, but also that this art proves to be fatal rather than consoling in its effect upon the male elegist: the poet (Croak) is not only stripped of all mastery (his club falls) but he shuffles off into the silence.

The ironies characterising the elegiac art in Beckett's later works are perhaps nowhere more effectively brought out, however, than in the late television play *. . . but the clouds . . .* (1976). Whilst the poem 'Je voudrais que mon amour meure' is a relatively early response to Yeatsian elegy, *. . . but the clouds . . .*, which takes its title from the final stanza of Yeats's poem 'The Tower', is a later, and ostensibly very different, response. Yeats's long poem concludes with a resolution to reduce the significance of death, if not to degree zero then at least to a kind of natural insignificance. In other words, the poem would submit the negativity of death to a countering negation in the interests of life, and more precisely the life of the soul rather than that of the heart:

> Now shall I make my soul,
> Compelling it to study
> In a learned school
> Till the wreck of body,
> Slow decay of blood,
> Testy delirium
> Or dull decrepitude,
> Or what worse evil come—
> The death of friends, or death
> Of every brilliant eye
> That made a catch in the breath—
> Seem but the clouds in the sky
> When the horizon fades;
> Or a bird's sleepy cry
> Among the deepening shades.[41]

Here, then, the naturalisation of death is a means of negating its significance to the imperishable (because super-natural) soul; in other words, this naturalisation of death is a second-order negation, or a negation of a negation in the interests of life (as the life of the soul).

What becomes of this commitment to a productive negation in Beckett, who distances himself very early in his career from the very notion of the imperishable soul, mocking it in *Murphy* (1938), for instance, where, as

C. J. Ackerley observes, a Democritean materialism operates with comic force against the rigorous Cartesian distinction between mind or soul (*esprit*, *âme*; *mens*, *anima*) and body (*corps*; *corpus*)?[42] First and foremost, Beckett does not rewrite Yeats's poem, as he had earlier rewritten 'He wishes his Beloved were Dead'. Rather, the words and images of Yeats's poem are preserved, but also ripped from their original context, to be repeated in fragmented form. The 'I' (or Voice) of Beckett's play is, like so many other figures (both male and female) in his *oeuvre*, unable to have done with the dead; he will beg again and again for the image of the dead woman to return to him, and this 'begging of the mind' constitutes the principal activity of that mind.[43] In radical contrast to Yeats's poem, there is in Beckett's play no resolution to negate death's power through its naturalisation; rather, the dead woman becomes the only hope of consolation for the living male – aside, that is, from mathematics (the calculation of cube roots) and the nothing – 'that MINE'.[44]

Seeking consolation in the return of the dead woman, Beckett's male figure is subject to a principle of irony that lies at the very heart of elegy in Beckett's hands, and that functions by way of an intertextual space that connects him above all to Dante (in whom he finds the very archetype of the female beloved's return) and Yeats. Arguably, late Beckett makes of Dante's *Commedia* perhaps the most remarkable work of male elegy ever written, but in doing so it asserts the anethical nature of that elegy. The Dantean elegiac is perhaps slightly easier to detect in *Ohio Impromptu* (1981) and *Nacht und Träume* than in *. . . but the clouds . . .*, since in those works it is less obscured by Beckett's response to Yeats. In *. . . but the clouds . . .*, Yeats's words, mouthed by a dead woman but ventriloquised by a man who cannot live without the dead, speak in their new context not of a resolution to negate death through its naturalisation (with the soul being immortal and thus immune to nature) but rather of elegy as both the affirmation and the negation of that resolution – in other words, the affirmation *and* the negation of elegy itself.

Elegising the Art of Elegy

In Beckett, then, we find the art of elegy taking a very strange, and almost fatal, turn. The work of memorialisation may still take place – indeed, arguably nothing else takes place – but at certain moments it does so within an anethical economy, and this despite the many obvious changes of attitude. Certainly the murderousness exhibited in *Eh Joe*, or the torment prompted by the work of elegy in a play such as *Words and Music*, gives way in late plays such as *Ghost Trio*, . . . *but the clouds* . . . and *Nacht und Träume* to a need for the dead other (in each case a woman), a need that appears to be far less compromised by a countering need to reduce that other to nothing. And yet, a doubleness certainly remains, as in the late poem 'one dead of night', written in Stuttgart on 26 June 1977 and anticipating *Nacht und Träume* but insisting upon an anethicality much harder to detect in the television play:

> a hand on his
> faintly closed
> for good or ill
> for good and ill[45]

In . . . *but the clouds* . . ., Beckett explores, by way of Yeats, both with and against Yeats, some of the most telling ironies of the elegiac art by grafting Yeats's words onto a woman's lips that counter what they mutely mouth through the very act of mouthing. The male elegist in Beckett is caught, then, within at least three basic ironies, which mark the history of Beckett's practice of elegy: that which elegy commemorates is that which it would kill in order that the art of commemoration might take place; that which is commemorated returns in elegy only as that which was never quite there; and the consolation promised by elegy proves to be 'for good and ill'. If there is a commitment to the impossible, an *il faut*, behind the art of elegy in Beckett, then that commitment, or rather that compulsion, is itself neither the foundation of an ethics (be it a Geulincxian ethics of humility or an ethics of failure) nor the undoing of all possible ethics. Rather, it is the experience of the anethical as that which does not ratify any affirmation – not even a Derridean unconditional affirmation – beyond all possible negation. In short, the 'on' in Beckettian elegy is not privileged ethically over the 'no'. Beckett's works of elegy, then, not only challenge the distinctions between the elegist and the elegised, between love and hate of both self and other, between commemoration and negation, they make of elegy an anethical art that finds itself compelled, paradoxically, to elegise itself. If Hölderlin can be said to be the poet's poet, then Beckett, through and against both Dante and Yeats, might be said to be the anethical elegist not only of the father, the mother and the female beloved, but also of the elegist and indeed of elegy itself.

This leaves us, of course, with the question of whether Beckettian elegy is, even in its anethicality, ultimately limited by a gendering of the elegist. There is no easy answer to this question. That Beckett only very rarely figures the elegist as a woman, and arguably never does so in the stricter (that is, conventional) form of elegy, cannot be said to be owing simply to the fact (or at least the contention) – and here we are returned to our point of departure – that his poetry is his most autobiographical writing and that it is therefore natural and only reasonable for him to figure the elegist as male, and indeed as heterosexually male. Rather, it is precisely Beckett's movement towards an anethical treatment of gender that is one of the preconditions for his being in a position to achieve an anethical elegisation of elegy.[46] That such anethical elegisation is not characteristic of all his works, or indeed of every part of a given work, is indisputable. It is to be detected, however, there where the work of mourning, as an art of mourning, is shown to occur not prior to any ethical framing but in that space where the very distinction between the ethical and the unethical fails to hold. It is precisely this failure to hold that an ethicalising reading of the elegiac in Beckett would negate, the irony of this gesture being that it is in Beckettian elegy that such negations *in the name of the ethical* are submitted to a scrutiny that one might think would cause us to hesitate before deploying them.

Notes

1. Deirdre Bair, Beckett's first biographer, claims that each of the poems in *Echo's Bones* is 'intensely personal' (p. 187); James Knowlson describes them as 'personal and highly autobiographical' (p. 222); and Martin Esslin argues that Beckett's poetry 'contains his most directly autobiographical utterance . . . we briefly hear the voice of Samuel Beckett himself' (p. 55).
2. 'Malacoda' was subject to repeated revision prior to its publication in *Echo's Bones*; its autobiographical nature is suggested by Beckett's own inscription of the word 'father' at the top of the manuscript.
3. Darley died of tuberculosis on 30 December 1948. His death is also memorialised in *Stirrings Still* (1988): 'The same place and table as when Darly [*sic*] for example died and left him' (*The Complete Short Prose*, p. 260). 'Mort de A. D.' was first published in *Les Cahiers des saisons*, p. 2 (October 1955).
4. Beckett, *Poems*, p. 90.
5. Ibid. p. 45.
6. Beckett, 'Peintres de l'empêchement', p. 135.
7. Beckett, *The Complete Dramatic Works*, p. 58.
8. From *The Wind Among the Reeds*, 1899.
9. Beckett, *Poems*, p. 70.
10. 'Were you but lying cold and dead, / And lights were paling out of the West, / You would come hither, and bend your head, / And I would lay my head on your breast; / And you would murmur tender words, / Forgiving me, because you were dead: / Nor would you rise and hasten away, / Though you have the will of the wild birds, / But know your hair was bound and wound / About the stars and moon and sun: / O would, beloved, that you

lay / Under the dock-leaves in the ground, / While lights were paling one by one' ('He wishes his Beloved were Dead', in *The Collected Works of W. B. Yeats*, pp. 72–3).

11. Beckett, *Poems*, pp. 70–1. Beckett's translation.
12. 'In the light of other Beckett poems, we immediately understand that he could wish her no greater good' (Harvey, *Samuel Beckett*, p. 230).
13. 'What is so affecting in the lover's words is that her death, the disappearance of the origin of his only experience of another's love, will be an enduring source of suffering for him. The gift he would give her, then, is the only gift love knows, the sacrifice of self to the good of the other' (Harvey, *Samuel Beckett*, p. 230).
14. Ruby Cohn, *A Beckett Canon*, p. 157.
15. In a letter of 21 February 1938 to Thomas MacGreevy, Beckett declares of Sade's *Les 120 journées de Sodome*: 'The obscenity of surface is indescribable. Nothing could be less pornographical. It fills me with a kind of metaphysical ecstasy' (quoted in Knowlson, *Damned to Fame*, p. 293).
16. Arthur Schopenhauer, *The World as Will*, p. 267.
17. Beckett, *Murphy*, p. 178.
18. Angela Moorjani, 'Beckett and Psychoanalysis', p. 185.
19. Leslie Hill, 'Late Texts', p. 21.
20. Ibid. p. 18.
21. Jacques Derrida, 'Hostipitality', p. 419.
22. Derrida, 'Hostipitality', p. 364; 'I Have a Taste', p. 92.
23. Julia Kristeva, 'The Father', pp. 150–1.
24. Dante Alighiere, *Inferno*, XXI.139.
25. Harvey, *Samuel Beckett*, p. 111.
26. Beckett, 'Malacoda', line 26.
27. Ibid. line 27.
28. Cohn, *A Beckett Canon*, p. 61.
29. John Pilling, *Beckett before Godot*, p. 89.
30. Harvey, *Samuel Beckett*, p. 112.
31. Esslin, 'Samuel Beckett's Poems', p. 57.
32. Beckett, 'Malacoda', line 29.
33. Beckett, *Poems*, p. 64.
34. Paul Celan, *Gesammelte Werke*, p. 72. 'Aschenglorie' appears in the 1967 collection *Atemwende/Breathturn*.
35. Beckett, *Poems*, p. 64.
36. Harvey, *Samuel Beckett*, pp. 230–1; p. 233.
37. Pilling, *Samuel Beckett*, p. 180.
38. Beckett, *Poems*, p. 64.
39. Beckett, *The Complete Dramatic Works*, p. 291.
40. Beckett, *Dream of Fair to Middling Women*, p. 15.
41. W. B. Yeats, *The Collected Works*, p. 199.
42. See Ackerley, *Demented Particulars*, pp. 211–12.
43. Beckett, *The Complete Dramatic Works*, p. 420.
44. Ibid. p. 421.
45. Beckett, *Poems*, p. 44.
46. For an analysis of Beckett's anethical treatment of gender, see Weller, *Beckett, Literature, and the Ethics of Alterity*, Chapter 6.

Bibliography

Ackerley, C. J., *Demented Particulars: The Annotated* Murphy, 2nd edn (Tallahassee: *Journal of Beckett Studies* Books, 2004).
Alighieri, Dante, *The Divine Comedy: Inferno*, trans. Charles S. Singleton (Princeton: Princeton University Press, 1980).
Bair, Deirdre, *Samuel Beckett: A Biography* (London: Jonathan Cape, 1978).
Beckett, Samuel, *The Complete Dramatic Works* (London: John Calder, 1990).
Beckett, Samuel, *The Complete Short Prose, 1929–1989*, ed. S. E. Gontarski (New York: Grove Press, 1995).
Beckett, Samuel, *Dream of Fair to Middling Women*, ed. Eoin O'Brien and Edith Fournier (Dublin: Black Cat, 1992).
Beckett, Samuel, *Murphy* (London: George Routledge & Sons, 1938).
Beckett, Samuel, 'Peintres de l'empêchement', in Ruby Cohn (ed.), *Disjecta: Miscellaneous Writings and a Dramatic Fragment* (London: John Calder, 1983), p. 135.
Beckett, Samuel, *Poems 1930–1989* (London: John Calder, 2002).
Beckett, Samuel, *Proust and Three Dialogues with Georges Duthuit* (London: Calder and Boyars, 1970).
Celan, Paul, *Gesammelte Werke in fünf Bänden*, ed. Beda Allemann and Stefan Reichert, Vol. 2 (Frankfurt am Main: Suhrkamp, 1983).
Cohn, Ruby, *A Beckett Canon* (Ann Arbor: University of Michigan Press, 2001).
Derrida, Jacques, 'Hostipitality', in Gil Anidjar (ed. and trans.), *Acts of Religion* (New York: Routledge, 2002), pp. 358–420.
Derrida, Jacques, 'I Have a Taste for the Secret', in Derrida and Maurizio Ferraris, *A Taste for the Secret*, ed. Giacomo Donis and David Webb, trans. Giacomo Donis (Cambridge: Polity, 2001), pp. 3–92.
Esslin, Martin, 'Samuel Beckett's Poems', in *Beckett at 60: A Festschrift* (London: Calder and Boyars, 1967), pp. 55–60.
Harvey, Lawrence E., *Samuel Beckett: Poet and Critic* (Princeton: Princeton University Press, 1970).
Hill, Leslie, 'Late Texts: Writing the Work of Mourning', *Samuel Beckett Today/Aujourd'hui*, 1: *Samuel Beckett 1970–1989* (1992), pp. 10–25.
Knowlson, James, *Damned to Fame: The Life of Samuel Beckett* (London: Bloomsbury, 1996).
Kristeva, Julia. 'The Father, Love, and Banishment', in Leon S. Roudiez (ed.), *Desire in Language: A Semiotic Approach to Art and Literature*, trans. Thomas Gora, Alice Jardine and Leon S. Roudiez (Oxford: Blackwell, 1980), pp. 148–58.
Mercier, Vivian, *Beckett/Beckett* (New York: Oxford University Press, 1977).
Moorjani, Angela, 'Beckett and Psychoanalysis', in Lois Oppenheim (ed.), *Palgrave Advances in Samuel Beckett Studies* (Basingstoke: Palgrave, 2004), pp. 172–93.
Pilling, John, *Beckett before Godot* (Cambridge: Cambridge University Press, 1997).
Pilling, John, *Samuel Beckett* (London: Routledge and Kegan Paul, 1976).
Schopenhauer, Arthur, *The World as Will and Representation*, trans. E. F. J. Payne, 2 vols (New York: Dover, 1967).

Weller, Shane, *Beckett, Literature, and the Ethics of Alterity* (Basingstoke: Palgrave, 2006).

Yeats, W. B., *The Collected Works, Vol. 1: The Poems*, ed. Richard J. Finneran (New York: Macmillan, 1989).

Contributors

C. J. Ackerley is Professor and former Head of English at the University of Otago, Dunedin, New Zealand. He is, with S. E. Gontarski, author of the Grove Press and Faber *Companion to Samuel Beckett*. His annotations of *Murphy* and *Watt* have recently been republished by Edinburgh University Press (2010). He is currently working on a study of *Samuel Beckett and Science*, and is annotating a recently rediscovered novel by Malcolm Lowry.

Alain Badiou, agrégé de philosophie, teaches at the Université de Paris VIII (Saint Denis). His publications include two novels, *Almagestes* (1964) and *Portulans* (1967), a book on mathematical theory, *Le Concept de modèle* (1969), a play, *L'Echarpe rouge* (1979), which was directed at the Théâtre de Chaillot by Antoine Vitez, two books on political theory, *Théorie de la contradiction* (1965) and *Peut-on penser la politique?* (1985), and numerous philosophical works, including *Théorie de sujet* (1982), translated as *Theory of the Subject* (Continuum, 2009), *L'Etre et l'evénement* (1988), translated as *Being and Event* (Continuum, 2006), *Conditions* (1992), *Ethics: An Essay on the Understanding of Evil* (Verso, 2002) and *The Adventure of French Philosophy* (Verso, 2012), among many others.

Phil Baker's book *Beckett and the Mythology of Psychoanalysis* (Macmillan, 1997) was described by *The Cambridge Introduction to Samuel Beckett* as an 'important book . . . a breakthrough in this field because it merged a psychoanalytical approach with a consciousness of historical location'. His other books include *Absinthe* (2001), *William S. Burroughs* (2010) and a study of the artist *Austin Osman Spare* (2011). He reviews regularly for the *Times Literary Supplement*.

Justin Beplate is a Lecturer in English at the Université Panthéon-Assas in Paris. He has published articles on James Joyce and Samuel Beckett in various journals, including the *Modern Language Review*, *Journal of Beckett Studies* and *Journal of Modern Literature*. He is also a regular contributor to the *Times Literary Supplement*.

Norma Bouchard is a professor at the University of Connecticut, Storrs. Among her book-length publications are *The Politics of Culture and the Ambiguities of Interpretation: Umberto Eco's Alternative* (1998); *Céline, Gadda, Beckett: Experimental Writers of the 1930s* (2000); *Risorgimento in Modern Italian Culture: Revisiting the 19th Century Past in History, Narrative, and Cinema* (2005); *Reading and Writing the Mediterranean: Essays by Consolo* (2006); *Italian Cultural Studies: Negotiating Regional, National and Global Identities, Annali d'Italianistica*, 24 (2006); and *Southern Thought and Other Essays on the Mediterranean* (2011), as well as critical essays and translations. She has recently edited a journal issue on the 150th anniversary of Italian unification, *Italy @ 150: National Discourse at the Sesquicentennial 1861–2011*, and is completing two monographs, *Writing, Screening, and Sounding Beyond the Nation: Italy and the Mediterranean after the Cold War and into the Twenty-First Century* and *Cultural Interventions: Umberto Eco's Historic Imaginary*.

Mary Bryden is Professor of French at the University of Reading, and Co-Director of the Beckett International Foundation. She is a past President of the International Samuel Beckett Society. Many of her publications bring Beckett's work into an interdisciplinary perspective, including theology, philosophy (especially Deleuze and Guattari), music and the arts. She has published analyses of Beckett's work in relation to questions of translation, and in relation to other French novelists and dramatists, including Jean-Jacques Bernard, Giono, Cixous, Proust, Malraux and Balzac. Her books include *Women in Samuel Beckett's Prose and Drama* (1993); *Samuel Beckett and Music* (ed.) (1998); *Samuel Beckett and the Idea of God* (1998); *Gilles Deleuze: Travels in Literature* (2007) (contains chapter on Beckett); and *Beckett's Proust/Deleuze's Proust*, co-edited with Margaret Topping (2009). Her forthcoming collection *Beckett and Animals* will be published by Cambridge University Press in 2012/13.

Daniela Caselli teaches English at the University of Manchester. She is the author of *Beckett's Dantes: Intertextuality in the Fiction and Criticism* (2005) and *Improper Modernism: Djuna Barnes's Bewildering*

Corpus (2009). She has edited *Beckett and Nothing* (2010), and co-edited (with Steven Connor and Laura Salisbury) *Other Becketts* (2001) and (with Daniela La Penna) *Twentieth-century Poetic Translations: Literary Cultures in Italian and English* (2008).

Bruno Clément is Professor at Paris VIII University, former President of the International College of Philosophy (2004–7) and currently a member of the Institut universitaire de France (IUF). Originally a specialist in rhetoric, he studies the links between literature and philosophy and especially the style of the philosophers, but also matters related to hermeneutics (the act of reading, the commentary and the question of misunderstanding). He is also a specialist of Samuel Beckett's work. He has published, among other works, *L'oeuvre sans qualités, rhétorique de Samuel Beckett (1994)*, *Le lecteur et son modèle: Voltaire, Pascal – Hugo, Shakespeare – Sartre, Flaubert* (1999), *L'invention du commentaire: Augustin, Jacques Derrida* (2000), *Le récit de la méthode* (2005), *La voix verticale* (2012) and, with Danielle Cohen-Levinas, *Emmanuel Levinas et les territoires de la pensée* (2007).

Thomas Cousineau is Professor of English (emeritus) at Washington College and the author of four books: *Waiting for Godot: Form in Movement*; *After the Final No: Samuel Beckett's Trilogy*; *Ritual Unbound: Reading Sacrifice in Modernist Fiction*; and *Three-Part Inventions: The Novels of Thomas Bernhard*. Along with guest-editing the 'Beckett in France' issue of the *Journal of Beckett Studies*, he served for several years as the editor of the newsletter of the Samuel Beckett Society and was co-director of the 'Présence de Samuel Beckett' conference held at Cerisy la Salle in the summer of 2005. He is currently completing a book for the Dalkey Archive Press on Fernando Pessoa's modernist epic *The Book of Disquiet* and beginning one on the 'Daedalus Complex' in modernist writing.

Francis Doherty was Emeritus Professor of English at the University of Keele, where he divided his interests between the eighteenth and twentieth centuries. His *Samuel Beckett* appeared in 1971.

S. E. Gontarski is Robert O. Lawton Distinguished Professor of English at Florida State University. His most recent books are: (with C. J. Ackerley) *The Faber Companion to Samuel Beckett: A Reader's Guide to His Works, Life, and Thought* (London: Faber and Faber, 2006); (with Anthony Uhlmann, eds) *Beckett after Beckett* (University Press of Florida, 2006); *Krapp's Last Tape and Other Short Plays*, ed. and with a Preface and notes on the texts by S. E. Gontarski (London: Faber and Faber, 2009); *A Companion to Samuel Beckett*, ed. and with an Introduction by S. E. Gontarski (Oxford: Wiley-Blackwell, 2010); (with Paul Ardoin and Laci Mattison, eds) *Understanding Bergson, Understanding Modernism* (London and New York: Continuum Books, 2012); and *The Edinburgh Companion to Samuel Beckett and the Arts*, ed. and with an Introduction by S. E. Gontarski (Edinburgh: Edinburgh University Press, forthcoming in 2013).

James Knowlson is Emeritus Professor of French at the University of Reading, where he founded the Beckett Archive (now the Beckett International Foundation). Earlier, he was Lecturer in French at the University of Glasgow, where he lectured mainly on eighteenth-century French literature and thought. Among his publications in this area was *Universal Language Schemes in England and France (1600–1800)* with the University of Toronto Press. He was the co-founder (with John Calder) of the *Journal of Beckett Studies* in 1976 and its first editor. He was also general editor of the four-volume series of *The Theatrical Notebooks of Samuel Beckett* with Faber and Faber, and editor of the *Waiting for Godot* and *Krapp's Last Tape* volumes. He was a friend of Samuel Beckett for almost twenty years and his authorised biographer, publishing *Damned to Fame: The Life of Samuel Beckett* with Bloomsbury in 1996. This was short-listed in Britain for the Whitbread Biography of the Year and the James Tait Black Memorial Prize and won the Southern Arts Non-Fiction Prize in 1996. It won the George Freedley Memorial Award for an Outstanding Contribution to the Literature of the Theater in the USA and has been translated into most European languages, as well as into Japanese. He has written or edited many other books and essays on Beckett and modern drama, including, most recently, *Images of Beckett* (Cambridge University Press, 2003) with the British theatre photographer John Haynes and *Beckett Remembering, Remembering Beckett* (Bloomsbury, 2006) with his wife Elizabeth Knowlson. In 2006 he was awarded an Honorary D. Litt of the University of Reading and in 2011 he became an Officier dans l'Ordre des Palmes Académiques.

Paul Lawley is Lecturer in English at the University of Plymouth. Over many years he has published widely, in books and scholarly journals, on the drama and fiction of Samuel Beckett. His book *Waiting for Godot: Character Studies* appeared from Continuum in 2008.

Mark Nixon is Reader in Modern Literature at the University of Reading, where he is also Director of the Beckett International Foundation. He is an editor of *Samuel Beckett Today/Aujourd'hui*, a member of the editorial board of the *Journal of Beckett Studies*, and the Co-Director of the Beckett Digital Manuscript Project. He has published widely on Beckett's work; recent books include the monograph *Samuel Beckett's German Diaries 1936–37* (Continuum, 2011) and the edited collection *Publishing Samuel Beckett* (British Library, 2011). He is currently working on *Samuel Beckett's Library* (Cambridge University Press, 2013) with Dirk Van Hulle, and is also preparing critical editions of Beckett's unpublished short story 'Echo's Bones' (Faber and Faber, 2013) and Beckett's 'German Diaries' (Suhrkamp, 2015).

J. D. O'Hara is Emeritus Professor of English at the University of Connecticut, Storrs. He has edited *Twentieth Century Interpretations of Molloy, Malone Dies, The Unnamable: A Collection of Critical Essays* and is the author of *Samuel Beckett's Hidden Drives: Structural Uses of Depth Psychology* (University Press of Florida, 1997).

John Pilling is Emeritus Professor of English and European Literature at the University of Reading, where he was Director of the Beckett International Foundation. Among his many and distinguished writings on Beckett are: *Samuel Beckett* (1976); (with James Knowlson) *Frescoes of the Skull* (1979); (with Mary Bryden) *Ideal Core of the Onion: Reading Beckett Archives* (1992); *Beckett before Godot* (1997); an annotated edition of *Beckett's 'Dream' Notebook* (1999); *A Companion to 'Dream of Fair to Middling Women'* (2004); *A Samuel Beckett Chronology* (2006); and *Samuel Beckett's 'More Pricks Than Kicks': In a Stream of Two Wills* (2011).

Alban W. Urbanas is Professor of Philosophy and French at Wesley College. He is the author of *La notion d'accident chez Aristote* (Paris/Montréal: Les Belles Lettres) and has served on the selection committee of the Laurence Wylie Prize in French Cultural Studies.

Shane Weller is Professor of Comparative Literature and Co-Director of the Centre for Modern European Literature at the University of Kent. His publications include the monographs *A Taste for the Negative: Beckett and Nihilism* (2005); *Beckett, Literature, and the Ethics of Alterity* (2006); *Literature, Philosophy, Nihilism: The Uncanniest of Guests* (2008); and *Modernism and Nihilism* (2011). Edited volumes include *The Flesh in the Text*, co-edited with Thomas Baldwin and James Fowler (2007), the Faber edition of Samuel Beckett's *Molloy* (2009), a special issue of the journal *Comparative Critical Studies* on the theme 'Archive', co-edited with Ben Hutchinson (2011), and *Modernist Eroticisms: European Literature after Sexology*, co-edited with Anna Katharina Schaffner (2012). He is also a General Editor of the book series Palgrave Studies in Modern European Literature.

David Wheatley is Senior Lecturer in English at the University of Hull. He is the author of four collections of poetry with Gallery Press, most recently *A Nest on the Waves* (2010), and features in *The Penguin Book of Irish Poetry*. He has edited Beckett's *Selected Poems 1930–1989* (Faber and Faber, 2009); other work on Beckett has appeared in *The Oxford Handbook of Irish Poetry* (Oxford University Press, 2012), *Beckett and Animals* (Cambridge University Press, 2012), the *Journal of Beckett Studies* and *Irish Studies Review*.

Index

'ns' indicates that there is more than one note on a particular subject on the page cited.

EU Authorised Representative:
Easy Access System Europe Mustamäe tee 50, 10621 Tallinn, Estonia
gpsr.requests@easproject.com

Printed and bound by CPI Group (UK) Ltd, Croydon, CR0 4YY
03/08/2026
02185328-0004